PENGUIN CLASSICS

EMILY BRONTË:
THE COMPLETE POEMS

EMILY JANE BRONTË was born at Thornton in Yorkshire on 30 July 1818, the fifth of six children of Patrick and Maria Brontë (neé Branwell). Two years later, her father was appointed perpetual curate of Haworth, a small, isolated hill village surrounded by moors. Her mother died shortly after her third birthday and she and her sisters and brother were brought up by their aunt, Elizabeth Branwell. Apart from a few short periods, she remained in Haworth. Her only close friendships were those with her brother Branwell and her sisters Charlotte and Anne; only three perfunctory letters by her survive.

From accounts by those who knew Emily Jane Brontë, there emerges a consistent portrait of a reserved, courageous woman with a commanding will and manner. In the biographical notice to the 1850 edition of *Wuthering Heights*, Charlotte Brontë attributes to her sister 'a secret power and fire that might have informed the brain and kindled the veins of a hero'. Monsieur Heger, who taught her in Brussels, was impressed by her 'powerful reason'.

Emily Jane Brontë began writing poems at an early age and published twenty-one of them, together with poems by Anne and Charlotte, in 1846 in a slim volume titled *Poems by Currer, Ellis, and Acton Bell*. At an even earlier age, she collaborated with Charlotte, Branwell and Anne on the 'plays' and tales that developed into the Glass Town saga. By 1834, Emily and Anne were thoroughly engaged in writing their own saga involving two imaginary islands in the north and south Pacific, Gondal and Gaaldine. No early prose narratives survive, but several poems by Emily and Anne refer to Gondal places and characters. Emily Jane Brontë is best known for her only novel, *Wuthering Heights*, published under her pseudonym of Ellis Bell in 1847, almost exactly a year before her death on 19 December 1848. She became ill after attending Branwell's funeral, and died of tuberculosis after an illness of about three months.

JANET GEZARI is Professor of English at Connecticut College. She has published several articles and is the author of a critical book on Charlotte Brontë.

EMILY BRONTË

The Complete Poems

Edited and with an Introduction by
JANET GEZARI

PENGUIN BOOKS

PENGUIN CLASSICS

UK | USA | Canada | Ireland | Australia
India | New Zealand | South Africa

Penguin Books is part of the Penguin Random House group of companies
whose addresses can be found at global.penguinrandomhouse.com.

Penguin
Random House
UK

This edition first published 1992

039

Introduction and notes copyright © Janet Gezari, 1992
All rights reserved

Printed in England by Clays Ltd, Elcograf S.p.A
Set in 10/11.5 pt Monophoto Ehrhardt

ISBN-13: 978-0-140-42352-5

www.greenpenguin.co.uk

Contents

THE COMPLETE POEMS

II. Dated Poems

III. Undated Poems

IV. Poems of Doubtful Authorship

Introduction

Historical Survey

Emily Jane Brontë – the name she preferred on the title page of her *Gondal Poems* notebook – published only twenty-one poems during her lifetime in a book undertaken jointly with her sisters, *Poems by Currer, Ellis, and Acton Bell* (1846). The book, which also included nineteen poems by Charlotte Brontë and twenty-one poems by Anne Brontë, was published at the authors' own expense. It was encouragingly reviewed, but only two copies had been sold a year after the publication date. Emily Brontë selected her twenty-one poems for publication from two notebooks into which she had begun transcribing poems in 1844, choosing fifteen from the notebook now known as the Honresfeld manuscript and six from the notebook titled *Gondal Poems*. The Honresfeld manuscript, last located in the collection of Sir Alfred Law (at Honresfeld in Lancashire), is now missing, but a reproduction in facsimile was published in the Shakespeare Head edition of the poems of Emily Jane and Anne Brontë in 1934. It has twenty-nine pages and contains thirty-one poems. None makes any reference to Gondal, the mythic country Emily and Anne Brontë invented as young adolescents and about which Emily continued to write for the rest of her life. The descendants of George Smith, Charlotte Brontë's publisher, presented the *Gondal Poems* notebook to the British Museum in 1933. It has sixty-eight pages and contains forty-four poems. In preparing her Gondal poems for publication in 1846, Emily Brontë consistently removed any references to Gondal places and characters from them.

The history of Emily Brontë's poems since 1846 has been complicated, first by Charlotte Brontë's editing of seventeen poems to accompany a new edition of *Agnes Grey* and *Wuthering Heights* in 1850, then by the publication of poems incorrectly attributed to Emily Brontë or correctly attributed to her but

inaccurately transcribed. Holograph manuscripts indicate that
Charlotte Brontë substantially revised as well as retitled most of
the poems she printed in 1850; no manuscript of one poem,
'Often rebuked, yet always back returning', survives, and its
authorship has been disputed. Sixty-seven poems were printed in
a limited edition in 1902, but Clement Shorter attempted the first
complete edition of the poems in 1910 (*The Complete Works of
Emily Brontë*, 2 vols., London: Hodder & Stoughton). It con-
tained 177 poems, seventy-one of them printed for the first time;
twenty-five of these poems were later attributed to one of the
other Brontës by C. W. Hatfield, who had access to more accurate
transcriptions of some of the poems and to the manuscripts of
some sixty poems by Emily Brontë in the important collection of
Mr H. H. Bonnell.

Hatfield's findings were the basis for a new edition published
in 1923: *The Complete Poems of Emily Jane Brontë*, edited by
Clement Shorter but arranged and collated, with bibliography
and notes, by C. W. Hatfield (London: Hodder & Stoughton).
This edition attempted the first chronological arrangement of the
poems by printing the poems published posthumously in three
categories: Selections from *Poems by Ellis Bell*, Dated Manuscripts
Arranged in Chronological Order, and Undated Manuscripts. *The
Poems of Emily Jane Brontë and Anne Brontë* (in the Shakespeare
Head series, published in 1934) added no new poems to those
already attributed to Emily Brontë in 1923. Its editors, Thomas J.
Wise and John A. Symington, had access to the Honresfeld
manuscript but not the *Gondal Poems* notebook. Six poems from
this notebook were printed in full for the first time in 1938 in a
slim addition to the Shakespeare Head series, *Gondal Poems by
Emily Jane Brontë*, edited by Helen Brown and Joan Mott.

The landmark event in this history of the publication of Emily
Brontë's poems is C. W. Hatfield's edition of *The Complete Poems
of Emily Jane Brontë* (New York: Columbia University Press,
1941). Any editor of Emily Brontë's poems will be deeply indebted
to Hatfield, whose edition established what has, in all but a few
instances, become the accepted canon, and whose formidable
talent for deciphering difficult lines provided new and consider-
ably more accurate readings of many poems. Hatfield derived his
text for all but fourteen of the poems from the holograph manu-

scripts. In the case of these fourteen, he relied on Shorter's transcriptions, as printed in 1910, because the manuscripts from which the transcriptions had been made were no longer available. The manuscripts of all of these poems have since reappeared in the Robert H. Taylor Collection of the Princeton University Libraries. One poem, 'I've been wandering in the greenwoods', is signed by Charlotte Brontë and has therefore been attributed to her. Hatfield printed 'Often rebuked, yet always back returning' in an appendix, believing that it 'savors more strongly of Charlotte than Emily, seeming to express Charlotte's thoughts about her sister, rather than Emily's own thoughts' and that Charlotte Brontë's motive in preparing the 1850 edition, together with the 'editorial liberties' she took with the other poems, could explain her offering 'an interpretation of her sister in the guise of Emily's own words' (p. 255). Other Brontë scholars have questioned this judgement, but I find it persuasive and therefore print 'Often rebuked, yet always back returning' in a special section of this edition, 'Poems of Doubtful Authorship'.

Apart from Philip Henderson's *The Complete Poems of Emily Brontë* (London: The Folio Society, 1951), no complete edition of the poems has been published since 1941, although such an edition is in press in the Oxford English Texts series. Henderson's edition is based on 'a re-examination of the manuscripts' and claims to differ from Hatfield's in preserving Emily Brontë's original punctuation. Nevertheless, some forty fragments are excluded from Henderson's index and are punctuated as in Hatfield, not as in the manuscripts; other poems I have examined follow the manuscripts imperfectly, sometimes rejecting Hatfield's punctuation, sometimes not. Juliet R. V. Barker's *The Brontës: Selected Poems* (London: Dent, 1985) uses Hatfield's text of the poems, except where it prefers 1846 or 1850. The helpful notes provide information not only about the text but also about Gondal, biographical elements in the poems, and the relation of the poems to other works by the Brontës. According to the introduction to *Selected Brontë Poems* (London: Basil Blackwell, 1985), the editors, Edward Chitham and Tom Winnifrith, have taken their texts from 'the latest manuscript', while taking 'into account the published text' of poems printed during the lifetime of the poet. The result is a text which not only silently corrects punctuation, spelling, and capitalization, but silently conflates manuscript and 1846 readings. The commentary in the notes is at once uninformative, noncommittal, and leadenly literal, and the suggested relations to other poets lack the support of demonstrated linguistic parallels.

Despite its genuine virtues, Hatfield's 1941 edition of the poems is unsatisfactory. He takes as his copy-text the latest manuscript version of the poems, but his decision to represent the poems Emily Brontë published in 1846 as if they were variants on the poems in manuscript, with the same status as Charlotte Brontë's revisions for 1850 and earlier manuscript versions, is, at the least, misleading. Many elements of the text, including conjectural datings, doubtful readings, and changes in punctuation, are undescribed. One of the innovations of the edition of 1923 was Hatfield's chronological presentation of the poems, but in 1923, he had ordered the poems dated by Emily Brontë and printed the undated ones in a section at the end. In 1941, he ordered all the poems according to a date of composition, sometimes dating an undated poem by means of a date elsewhere on the same manuscript page and sometimes, silently, by other means. A good example is no. 85 ('I am the only being whose doom'), which was dated 17 May 1839 in 1910 and 17 May 1837 in 1941. The manuscript was not available to Hatfield, and his new date for the poem is presumably based on the poem's reference to the age of its speaker as eighteen, Emily Brontë's age in 1837. The manuscript has since reappeared, and the year of composition Emily Brontë recorded on it is clearly 1839.

Because Hatfield notes as doubtful only a few readings, he implies that other readings are more certain than they are. For instance, he does not acknowledge that some characters at the ends of lines of poems in the Ashley Library manuscript are actually missing as a consequence of the method of binding, and he does not always acknowledge questionable readings that result from Emily Brontë's revisions or from the difficulty of reading her handwriting. He does not explain his punctuation of the poems, which occasionally follows the punctuation in the manuscripts but more regularly approximates (without following) that of 1846 or 1850. The poems as printed are marred by asterisks at the ends of lines that mark Hatfield's new readings and by letters and figures at their heads that code the manuscript source from which the text has been derived. Hatfield provides a list of words which have been altered to agree with ordinary spelling but also preserves obsolete spellings in his text. And apart from a brief account of the Gondal story and a chronological arrangement of the poems as an epic of Gondal by Fannie E. Ratchford, he provides no contextual commentary on the poems.

This Edition

1. *Copy-text and Order.* I have taken the published text of the poems printed in 1846 as my copy-text for these poems and, reversing Hatfield's procedure, presented the manuscript readings as variants in my notes. An exception has been made for the poem titled 'The Prisoner (A Fragment)' in the 1846 volume. It appears in three different versions in the present edition: the 1846 version together with the other 1846 poems; the very much longer manuscript version, 'Julian M. and A.G. Rochelle', together with the rest of the dated, posthumously published poems; and the 1850 version, 'The Visionary', together with the other poems Charlotte Brontë published at that time.

The poems Emily Brontë published in 1846 are given first, in their order of appearance in that volume, where they were interspersed with poems by Charlotte and Anne Brontë. Their arrangement in 1846 suggests several ordering principles, no one of which is followed consistently. With a few exceptions, each sister's poems are separated from each other by the poems of the other two; in some cases, poems that are contiguous have a common subject (e.g., hope, memory, or despair); in at least one case, poems by Charlotte and Emily ('Life' and 'Hope') seem to respond to one of Anne's poems, 'If This Be All'. There is no evidence that Charlotte Brontë revised or edited Anne's or Emily's poems for the 1846 volume. Although we lack information about how much of the punctuation or the division into stanzas is to be attributed to the authors and how much to the printer, the Brontës accepted the poems as printed and saw fit to send presentation copies to writers they admired. All that stands against our giving full value to the 1846 text of Emily Brontë's poems as the text she wished to have presented to the public is the long tradition of viewing publication as alien or irrelevant to her genius. This tradition relies on a conception of Emily Brontë's relation to her work that is necessarily speculative and certainly more influenced by Charlotte Brontë's account of her sister's acute distress over the discovery of her poems than by Emily Brontë's clear decision to join her sisters' project to publish them. That decision follows reasonably enough from the decision, eighteen months earlier, to revise and copy her poems into the two transcript volumes, whether with a view to publication or not.

I have taken the latest manuscript version as my copy-text for the poems not published in 1846. All variant readings in earlier manuscripts, excluding variations in punctuation, are presented in the notes, together with cancelled readings where these are legible. In the case of all but the poems in the Honresfeld manuscript and two poems in the Harry Ransom Humanities Research Center of the University of Texas at Austin – no. 24 ('The organ swells the trumpets sound') and no. 176 ('But the hearts that once adored me') – which I have examined in photocopies, I have re-examined the holograph manuscripts, profiting always from Hatfield's transcription of them but differing from him in some cases. I have presented all the posthumously published poems in their order of composition where this can be determined, or where a conjecture about compositional date is probable. Titles of the poems printed in 1846 are inserted at the appropriate point within the chronological ordering. Undated poems for which no conjectural date is probable are printed together in a separate section, as in 1923.

In instances where Brontë recorded more than one date of composition on different manuscript versions of the same poem or on a single fair copy manuscript, I have given both dates of composition in the note to the poem, but I have ordered the poems according to the latest date of composition. In instances where a poem is undated but a conjectural date is likely, I have explained my dating of it in the notes. My conjectures about compositional date are of three kinds:

(a) Some manuscript leaves contain several poems not all of which are dated. Other manuscripts indicate that some single leaves contain poems with dates spanning almost two years. The absence of dates on some poems may suggest that the undated poems bear a date close to that of a dated poem above or below it on the same manuscript leaf, or it may not. I follow Hatfield in assuming that the former is the case.

(b) Some poems which were printed as dated in 1923 now survive only in manuscripts that bear no compositional dates. They are no. 13 ('Sleep not dream not this bright day'), no. 85 ('I am the only being whose doom'), no. 98 ('It is not pride it is not shame'), and no. 108 ('Come, walk with me'). In one case, that of no. 85, the manuscript, which was unavailable to Hatfield, has since reappeared (see above), and the date printed in 1910 and 1923 can be confirmed. In the other cases, no dated manuscripts have reappeared, but the decision in 1923 to print a poem as dated, the specificity of the date provided (year, month, and day), and in one case the presence of an additional stanza, strongly suggest the existence at that time of another manuscript with a compositional date. In her census of Brontë manuscripts in the United States (1947), Mildred G. Christian cites the sales record for several autograph manuscripts which were, at that time, known but untraceable.

(c) In three cases, no. 64 ('The evening sun was sinking down'), no. 95 ('Mild the mist upon the hill'), and no. 101 ('Alcona in its changing mood'), the last digit of the date on the manuscript is obscure. The notes for these poems give my reasons for choosing one year instead of another.

The poems published by Charlotte Brontë in 1850 have historical interest, especially in cases where poems were for a long time known only in their 1850 versions, and I have gathered them in an appendix, where they are printed in the order of their appearance in the 1850 volume. For obvious reasons, no 1850 readings appear as variants in my notes to the poems.

2. *Poems and Poetical Fragments.* None of Emily Brontë's editors has acknowledged the difficulty of determining where poems begin and end. In the case of no. 162 ('Heavy hangs the raindrop'), there are two traditions. In 1850, Charlotte Brontë printed this poem together with 'Child of Delight! with sunbright hair' under the title 'The Two Children'. 1938 also treats this poem as a single poem in two parts and records Emily Brontë's title, 'A. E. and R. C.'. But in 1941, Hatfield prints 'Heavy hangs the raindrop'

and 'Child of Delight! with sunbright hair' as separate poems. This edition follows 1850 and 1938 in printing the poem as a single poem in two parts.

In three other related cases, no. 11 ('The night of storms has passed'), no. 31 ('The night is darkening round me') and no. 41 ('O evening why is thy light so sad'), I have incorporated poems which appear on the same manuscript leaf, and which previous editors have printed as separate items, as distinct parts of larger poetic projects. My notes to these poems explain my reasoning in each case. Although the evidence of the manuscripts is ambiguous, treatment of these poems as separate items obscures Brontë's distinctive way of formulating poetic occasions and her habitual representation of internal conflicts dramatically as colloquies.

In two other cases, nos. 15 and 38, this edition differs from Hatfield's and from all other editions of the poems in amalgamating poems previously printed as discrete fragments. Once again, the evidence of the manuscripts cannot be conclusive. In her rough draft manuscripts, Brontë usually divides poems or poetical fragments from other poems or poetical fragments by means of short, horizontal marks; in some manuscripts, she also uses crosses or both horizontal marks and crosses as dividers. A strong case for treating no. 15 (amalgamating 'The battle had passed from the height', 'How golden bright from earth and heaven', 'Not a vapour had stained the breezeless blue', and 'Only some spires of bright green grass') as a single poem can be made from the manuscript: the lines composing what have previously been printed as separate items are separated by rows of crosses, but a horizontal mark appears after thirty lines of verse and, on the same manuscript leaf, below two other poems or poetical fragments. Although I have treated these thirty lines as composing a single poem, the crosses that divide this poem into sections appear in the text. The manuscript of no. 38 (amalgamating 'Deep deep down in the silent grave', 'Here with my knee upon thy stone', 'O come again what chains withhold', and 'Was it with the fields of green') makes a less strong case for reading these formerly separate items as composing a single poem, but I have been persuaded to treat them as parts of a single poem by their form and content, and by the model presented by no. 8 ('Redbreast early in the morning'), a poem all of Brontë's previous editors have printed as a single poem of twenty-one lines, even though there are short, horizontal marks in the manuscript dividing it into four parts. In this edition, the marks that divide both these poems into parts appear in the text.

Hatfield printed 'Redbreast early in the morning' from Shorter's transcription, so that it is impossible to know whether, had he seen the manuscript, he would have been consistent with his own practice in treating the poem as four poetical fragments, divided in the manuscript by free-hand marks after lines 4, 13, and 17. The claim that 'Redbreast early in the morning' is the first line of a twenty-one-line poem, not the first line of a four-line fragment, followed in the manuscript by three other fragments, rests primarily on the poem's content. In line 3, the poet refers to 'wildly tender . . . music', and in line 21, she refers to 'That wild, wild music', at once a 'shriek of misery' and a wailing. And the pronoun *it* in lines 14 and 18 has no antecedent without the preceding verses. The poem's prosody and rhyme scheme exhibit some variation from stanza to stanza, but such variations also occur in other poems.

'Redbreast early in the morning' conveys some important information about Brontë's usual process of composition: she begins with an occasion, the song of the redbreast, moves from it to an investigation of her own state of mind, and asks a question, as if uncertain about the direction in which the poem is tending. The question produces new images, interesting in themselves and pointing to a second listener whose very different hearing of the redbreast's song helps make the speaker's perceptions more distinct. In the draft manuscripts of this poem, of 'The battle had passed from the height', and of 'Deep deep down in the silent grave', we can watch the poet in the quick of invention. They register her uncertainty about where her poem begins and ends and how it takes its direction. Since she destroyed most of the rough drafts of poems she copied into her transcript volumes, no examples of how she might have made these decisions survive.

3. *Titles.* Emily Brontë assigned titles to all the poems she published in 1846, but most of the poems in her manuscripts lack them. The names or initials of speakers appear above some titled and many untitled poems in the manuscripts, usually at the right-

or left-hand margin. I have noted the presence of such names or initials and identified speakers wherever possible in my notes to the poems, but I have not ordinarily treated names or initials as titles, except where a manuscript names both the speaker and the person being addressed (for example, no. 23, 'A. G. A. to A. E.'). The table of contents identifies poems by titles (where these exist) and by first lines.

4. *Spelling and Capitalization.* In keeping with the usual practice for the Penguin English Poets series, the spelling in this edition has been modernized. Both where spelling appears a matter of indifference to the author, as in *today* and *tomorrow* (each of which is regularly spelt as a single word, as a hyphenated word, and as two words), and where it appears a matter of preference, as in an incorrect spelling that is habitual (*divine, despair, grief*, and *watch* are in most cases spelt *devine, dispair, greif*, and *whach*), Brontë's spelling has been made correct and consistent. In cases where a deviant spelling is correct but obsolete (e.g., *dongeon* for *dungeon*, a spelling Brontë occasionally but by no means consistently prefers) or makes a difference to the sense or the sound of a line, the notes refer to the spelling in the manuscript. I have not revised Brontë's spelling to assist the regularity of her metres, as Hatfield does, when he substitutes *wintry* for the manuscript reading *wintery* in line 14 of no. 78, 'How still, how happy! those are words': ''Tis wintery light o'er flowerless moors –'. The likelihood of a difference in meaning attaching to a decision about capitalization has seemed to me to justify retaining the author's capitalizations, despite the difficulty of discriminating between an intended and a careless use of a capital letter in a rough draft manuscript and the different difficulty of distinguishing between capital and lower-case letters like *F* and *W*.

5. *Punctuation.* Decisions about punctuation have proved complicated, and I have tried to weigh the advantages and disadvantages of the two main options.

(a) Punctuating the poems as they are punctuated in the manuscripts. To treat this as a single option is to obscure the differences among the manuscripts. Some of these differences can be explained as those between rough drafts and fair copies. The

Honresfeld manuscript and *Gondal Poems* notebook present the poems at the latest stage of composition and in general present them with more punctuation than the other manuscripts, but even within these manuscripts, the punctuation of individual items varies considerably, and does not correspond to the punctuation for publication in 1846. Poems within other manuscripts, including not only some rough copy manuscripts but the fair copy Ashley Library manuscript, are entirely without punctuation. Presenting the unpunctuated Ashley Library manuscript poems as they appear in the manuscript makes them look less finished than they are and more resistant to punctuation than Brontë herself would have thought them, judging from her practice in both the transcript volumes and 1846. A decision not to add punctuation abrogates an editorial responsibility that has been an accepted feature of this series: it risks not showing the poems at their best and, in Pat Rogers's formulation, fails to give a modern reader 'the kind of signals he or she would have received' as the poet's contemporary (*The Complete Poems of Jonathan Swift*, p. 20).

(b) Punctuating the poems as if for publication at the time, with reference to principles of punctuation established by the 1846 edition. Although Hatfield articulates no principles governing his punctuation of the poems, his punctuation of them does not differ sharply from that of 1846. In both cases, punctuation is provided at the ends of all lines that are end-stopped. In addition, Hatfield provides punctuation within a line where it helps to clarify its sense, sometimes limiting sense by doing so. Occasionally, he removes punctuation.

The idea of presenting the poems as Emily Brontë would have been likely to present them, had she published them in her lifetime, is appealing, but even if we acknowledge Emily Brontë's responsibility for the punctuation of 1846, there is much to be said against this plan. First, it imposes an appearance of readiness for publication on poems that exist only in rough draft versions, often as fragments. Second, it collapses the difference between an author's intentions towards her manuscript and her intentions towards her published text. Third, the particular adjustments required to make the poems look familiar in 1846 are not required by readers of modern and contemporary verse, and may stand in

the way of what such readers most want to recover about Emily
Brontë's poems, what Frank Bidart calls 'the pauses, emphases,
urgencies and languors in the voice'. The losses attributable to
excessive punctuation are clear in Hatfield's edition and involve
the sense of the poems as well as their sound. The movement of
the line, its momentum, and the play of the line as a unit of sense
against larger units of sense – groups of lines or stanzas – are all
altered by punctuation.

The received intelligence about Emily Brontë and punctuation
has been briefly put by Chitham and Winnifrith: 'The Brontës
were not greatly interested in punctuation, and their manuscripts
exhibit many anomalies or omissions' (*Selected Brontë Poems*, pp.
vii–viii). But on 24 September 1847 Charlotte Brontë confirms
her interest in punctuation by writing to Smith, Elder to thank
them for punctuating *Jane Eyre* (*The Brontës: Their Lives, Friend-
ships and Correspondence*, II, 142), and in a letter of 21 December
1847 she notes that the 'orthography and punctuation of [*Wuther-
ing Heights* and *Agnes Grey*] are mortifying to a degree: almost all
the errors that were corrected in the proof-sheets appear intact in
what should have been the fair copies' (II, 165). The evidence of
Emily Brontë's poetical manuscripts also contradicts the assump-
tion that she was 'not greatly interested in punctuation', despite
the many anomalies and omissions.

If we put aside the poems Brontë deliberately left unpunctuated
and attend to those she did punctuate, what can her practice tell
us about her interest in punctuation? For one thing, she is more
consistent than has usually been acknowledged. She regularly
uses a single comma where more conventional punctuation would
require two:

> Their dark, their deadly ray would more than madden me
> (no. 71)

The comma Hatfield adds after *ray* changes the rhythm of the
line. Hatfield also regularly inserts a comma between pairs of
adjectives, as in the following instances:

> Wave their brown, branching arms above (no. 92)
> In the moonless, midnight dome (no. 66)

In the first instance, the effect of the comma after *brown* is to alter, subtly, the movement of the line. In the second, the effect is this plus the assignment of the modifier *moonless* to *dome* rather than to *midnight*. Nor do we lack examples of Brontë's use of commas to separate modifiers:

> Dost think fond, dreaming wretch, that *I* shall grant thy prayer?
> (no. 165)

In 1846, she has:

> Dost think, fond, dreaming wretch, that *I* shall grant thy prayer?
> (no. viii)

Hatfield repunctuates the line as follows:

> Dost think, fond dreaming wretch, that *I* shall grant thy prayer?

The omission or addition of punctuation also alters the sense of several lines. In no. 112, for example, Hatfield omits the comma that is clearly present in the manuscript after the first word in line 73, producing 'Well thou hast paid me back my love!' instead of 'Well, thou hast paid me back my love!' In line 142 of no. 165, he adds a comma, producing these lines:

> And I, who am so quick to answer sneer with sneer;
> So ready to condemn, to scorn, a coward's fear,

from these:

> And I, who am so quick to answer sneer with sneer;
> So ready to condemn to scorn a coward's fear

Brontë would have been more likely to insert a comma after *condemn*, omitting the comma after *scorn*, if she had wanted to insist on Hatfield's interpretation of the line. Reproducing the punctuation of the manuscript permits a reading that subordinates the phrase 'to scorn' to 'to condemn' rather than putting it in apposition.

The case for Brontë's intelligence in punctuating her poems asks that we look at whole stanzas and whole poems. Take, for example, no. 62 ('For him who struck thy foreign string'), punctuated as it is in the *Gondal Poems* notebook. Brontë's careful use of the dash at the end of stanza two brings out the parallelism of stanzas two and three and her equally careful choice of the colon at the end of stanza three announces the logic of the concluding stanza, less an answer to the question posed in the first stanza than a restatement of it that has been given new meaning by what has intervened. These effects are lost when Hatfield substitutes periods for both the dash and the colon.

We need not make the case that Brontë's punctuation is, in every case, productive of an altered or improved reading to allow that she paid some attention to punctuation. And in many cases, for example no. 168 ('Why ask to know the date – the clime'), her punctuation is more meaningful in its emphasis and its rhythm than Hatfield's. Hatfield prints the following:

> Four score shot down – all veterans strong;
> One prisoner spared – their leader – young,
> And he within his house was laid
> Wounded and weak and nearly dead.

Brontë's manuscript has this:

> Four score shot down – all veterans strong –
> One prisoner spared, their leader young –
> And he within his house was laid,
> Wounded, and weak and nearly dead.

A poem like no. 5 ('High waving heather 'neath stormy blasts bending'), which is entirely without punctuation in the manuscript, will sound pedestrian when commas and semi-colons are inserted at the ends of lines, interrupting the powerful momentum of the poem's feminine endings.

On balance, then, the disadvantages of punctuating the poems as if for publication seem to me to outweigh the disadvantages of printing them as they appear in the manuscripts. On the manuscript page, the poems are more than usually resistant to punctuation because they are more than usually resistant both to the standard of rational syntactic construction that punctuation conventionally signals and to the rhythms of colloquial prose. At their best, Emily Brontë's poems insist on their difference from such prose, a difference twentieth-century readers may better hear in the absence of punctuation. Although I have silently added apostrophes for possessives, for contractions, and for elisions, my principle throughout has been to add little and to add nothing substantive silently. On the few occasions where spaces between words in the manuscripts suggest pauses, I have added commas and indicated these additions in the notes.

6. *Gondal. Wuthering Heights* is the only prose fiction by Emily Brontë that survives. The evidence that Emily, in collaboration with Anne, wrote a connected group of prose narratives about an imaginary country called Gondal consists primarily of references to Gondal fiction in six surviving diary papers. Emily and Anne wrote the first two of these together. The one for 24 November 1834 includes the information that 'The Gondals are discovering the interior of Gaaldine'; the one for 26 June 1837 refers to Emily's writing 'Agustus-Almedas life 1st v. $1-4^{th}$ page from the last' and notes a coronation in Gondal corresponding to the one anticipated in England (Victoria succeeded to the throne on 20 June 1837). In 1841 and 1845, in honour of Emily's twenty-third and twenty-seventh birthdays, Emily and Anne wrote separate diary papers to be exchanged after a four-year interval; these suggest their different attitudes towards Gondal. In the first, Emily notes that the 'Gondalians are at present in a threatening state', and Anne wonders 'whether the Gondaliand will still be flourishing, and what will be their condition'. In the second, Emily seems optimistic: 'The Gondals still flourish bright as ever. I am at present writing a work on the First Wars.' Anne notes that 'Emily is engaged in writing the Emperor Julius's life' and provides a more tentative summary of their joint enterprise:

We have not yet finished our Gondal Chronicles that we began three years and a half ago. When will they be done? The Gondals are at present in a sad state. The Republicans are uppermost, but the Royalists are not quite overcome. The young sovereigns, with their brothers and sisters, are still at the Palace of Instruction. The Unique Society, above half a year ago, were wrecked on a desert island as they were returning from Gaul [or Gaaldine]. They are still there, but we have not played at them much yet. The Gondals in general are not in first-rate playing condition. Will they improve?

Two more items deserve mention. One, a barely legible list of Gondal characters and their attributes on a manuscript leaf that contains three poems and a part of a fourth by Emily, has been analysed by David R. Isenberg (*Brontë Society Transactions*, 14 [1962]). The characters are minor, and only one of them, Flora, is mentioned in any of the poems (no. 118). The other, a list of place names inscribed by Anne in the family's copy of *A Grammar of General Geography for the Use of Schools and Young Persons*, provides the most reliable information we have about Gondal geography. It identifies Gondal as 'a large island in the North Pacific' with Regina as its capital and Gaaldine as 'a large island newly discovered in the South Pacific' and including six kingdoms or provinces, Alexandia [sic], Almedore, Esleraden, Ula, Zelona, and Zedora.

Fannie Ratchford's *Gondal's Queen: A Novel in Verse* (1955) is the first and still the most comprehensive attempt to reconstruct a narrative of Gondal on the basis of this information, inferences drawn from the poems, and the model provided by Charlotte's and Branwell's narratives of Glass Town and Angria. Because Ratchford does not distinguish between events narrated in the poems and her own 'narrative prose links in the reconstruction', later commentators on the poems have regularly failed to separate what can be known about the Gondal narrative from what Ratchford has conjectured.

Ratchford's thesis is in three parts: (1) 'Gondal was a compact and well-integrated whole' (p. 23); (2) 'the life story of A.G.A., from dramatic birth, through tempestuous life, to tragic death' is 'the great body' of this 'epic' (p. 27); and (3) all of Emily Brontë's verse 'falls within the Gondal context' (p. 32). Ratchford's ability to assign less than half the poems a place in the Gondal narrative weakens the third hypothesis, and Emily Brontë's own distinction between Gondal and non-Gondal poems when she copied her poems into her two transcript notebooks contradicts it. A reading of the poems themselves does not easily sustain Ratchford's first hypothesis. Since its persuasiveness depends largely on the second hypothesis – that the Gondal epic tells the life story of A.G.A. – it is necessary, briefly, to consider this claim.

The idea that Gondal tells the story of A.G.A.'s life requires the conflation of three important female characters mentioned in the poems – A.G.A., Geraldine or G.S., and Rosina of Alcona. Ratchford's identification of A.G.A. and Geraldine relies on a guess at the name for which A.G.A.'s middle initial stands and is

probably required by the relation of Julius Brenzaida to a charac-
ter identified as both G.S. and Geraldine S. in several poems.
Geraldine is Julius's lover and almost certainly his wife; in no.
125, 'Geraldine', we learn that they have a child. At the same
time, no. 148, 'The Death of A.G.A.', presents A.G.A. as
Julius's lover and probably his wife. Both A.G.A. and G.S. have
black hair and eyes.

The identification of A.G.A. as Rosina, for whom no physical
description is provided, is far less plausible. It relies entirely on
the similarity between the account of Fernando De Samara's
relation to A.G.A. in two poems (nos. 71 and 111) and the
account in poem 101 of the relation between an unidentified man
who is associated with Areon Hall and is probably Fernando De
Samara and a woman referred to as Alcona.

It is plain, therefore, that A.G.A. is Alcona. But Rosina is Alcona. It
follows then that A.G.A. and Rosina are one, unless, as Miss Dodds
guessed, A.G.A. is the daughter of Rosina and Julius, inheriting her
mother's territorial designation. (*GQ*, p. 27)

But there is another possibility. The wars in Gondal allow for the
redistribution of territories, and both Rosina and A.G.A. may, at
different times, have the same territorial designation, especially
if both are married to Julius. In no. 154 Julius addresses Rosina
as his queen and accuses her of being responsible for his
imprisonment.

Ratchford's idea that Julius Brenzaida is involved with only
one woman makes his love-life very different from that of the
other Gondal characters. Besides, Julius speaks of a heart 'slighted'
by G.S. and of other 'bosoms bound to mine/With links both
tried and strong' in no. 67, 'Song by J. Brenzaida to G.S.'.
A.G.A./G.S. does not mourn for Julius. Rosina, on the other
hand, responds to his death in two important poems. One (no.
126, 'Rosina') describes her first reaction after 'weeks of wild
delirium'; the other (no. iv, 'Remembrance') recounts her feelings
fifteen years later.

Even if a prose narrative of Gondal, oral or written, provided
the scaffolding that enabled Brontë to construct some of her
poems, the literary interest Gondal has for us nevertheless depends
on the poems that have survived, not on the lost Gondal stories.

But the assumption that the lost pieces of a prose narrative told a coherent story, and that the poems emerged out of it, is anyway open to serious question. The poems may instead explore possible, even contradictory and mutually exclusive, narrative outcomes. *They* may provide the scaffolding that enabled Emily and Anne to write the prose pieces. In this edition, I have made no effort to reconstruct a coherent Gondal narrative in my notes to the poems, or to enlarge on a Gondal context for the stories they tell. Instead, I identify Gondal characters and places wherever possible and cross-reference other poems in which these characters and places appear, both to avoid repetition of information and to make whatever narrative connections the poems permit.

Chronology

1812   *29 December* Marriage of Patrick Brontë and Maria
        Branwell.

1814   *23 April* Maria Brontë christened.

1815   *8 February* Elizabeth Brontë born.

1816   *21 April* Charlotte Brontë born.

1817   *26 June* Patrick Branwell Brontë born.

1818   *30 July* Emily Jane Brontë born.

1820   *17 January* Anne Brontë born.
        25 February Patrick Brontë licensed to Haworth.
        29 April The Brontës move to Haworth.

1821   *May* Elizabeth Branwell, Maria Branwell Brontë's
        sister, arrives in Haworth.
        15 September Maria Branwell Brontë dies.

1824   *21 July* Maria and Elizabeth enter Cowan Bridge School.
        10 August Charlotte enters Cowan Bridge School.
        25 November Emily enters Cowan Bridge School.

1825   *14 February* Maria leaves Cowan Bridge in ill-health.
        6 May Maria dies.
        31 May Elizabeth leaves Cowan Bridge in ill-health.
        1 June Charlotte and Emily leave Cowan Bridge.
        15 June Elizabeth dies.

1826   *5 June* Patrick Brontë returns from a clerical conference
        in Leeds with a set of ninepins for Charlotte, a toy
        village for Emily, a dancing doll for Anne, and a box of
        toy soldiers for Branwell; for the next six years, the
        children are engaged in writing stories about the 'Young
        Men', as they call the soldiers.

1831   *17 January* Charlotte leaves home to attend Roe Head
        School.

1832   *May* Charlotte returns from Roe Head.

1834   *24 November* Emily and Anne write their first (extant)
        diary paper, including the earliest mention of Gondal:
        'The Gondals are discovering the interior of Gaaldine'.

1835   *29 July* Charlotte and Emily leave Haworth for Roe Head
        School, where Charlotte is to be a teacher, Emily a pupil.
        October Emily, her health 'quickly broken', returns to
        Haworth, and Anne joins Charlotte at Roe Head.
        October (?) Branwell, who had travelled to London
        intending to study painting at the Royal Academy, also
        returns to Haworth, not having enrolled as a pupil and
        having spent his cash.
        7 December Branwell writes to *Blackwood's*, applying
        for a position on the magazine's staff.

1836   *12 July* Emily writes her first (extant) dated poem,
        'Will the day be bright or cloudy'.
        29 December Charlotte writes to Robert Southey, asking
        for his opinion of her poems.

1837   *19 January* Branwell writes to Wordsworth, asking for
        his opinion of Branwell's poems.
        26 June Emily and Anne write their second (extant)
        diary paper, in which Emily says she is writing
        'Agustus-Almedas life 1st v. $1-4^{th}$ page from the
        last' and speaks of a coronation in Gondal as well as a
        coronation in England (Victoria succeeded to the throne
        on 20 June 1837).

1838   *September* Emily assumes a position as a teacher at Law
        Hill, a school in Halifax.

1839   *March* Emily returns to Haworth from Law Hill.
        April Anne assumes a post as governess to the Ingham
        family at Blake Hall, near Roe Head.
        May Charlotte assumes a post as governess to the
        Sidgwick family at Stonegappe, near Skipton.

Branwell gives up his studies at Bradford and returns home; at this time, Branwell took to opium.

July Charlotte ends her engagement as governess at Stonegappe and returns to Haworth.

August William Weightman assumes his position as Patrick Brontë's curate.

December Anne, dismissed from her post at Blake Hall, returns to Haworth.

1840   *1 October* Branwell leaves home to take a post as Assistant Clerk for the Manchester–Leeds railway.

2 March Charlotte leaves home to take a post as governess to the White family at Upperwood House in Rawdon.

March Anne leaves home to take a post as governess to the Robinsons at Thorp Green, near York.

1841   *30 July* Emily and Anne write diary papers in honour of Emily's birthday; Emily's speaks of 'a scheme at present in agitation for setting us up in A School of our own as yet nothing is determined but I hope and trust it may go on and prosper and answer our highest expectations'.

29 September Charlotte proposes that she and Emily go abroad to perfect their languages in preparation for opening a school.

December Charlotte parts from the Whites, on good terms.

1842   *8 February* Charlotte and Emily set out with their father for Brussels, arriving at the Pensionnat Héger a week later.

March Branwell dismissed from his post with the railway as the result of a default in his accounts for which he is held responsible.

15 May Emily writes her first (extant) French devoir, *Le Chat*.

June Another devoir, *Portrait: Le Roi Harold avant la Bataille de Hastings*.

16 July Two more devoirs, *Lettre: Madame* and *Réponse*.

26 July Another devoir, *Lettre: Ma chère Maman*.

5 August Two more devoirs, *L'Amour Filial* and *Lettre d'un Frère à un Frère*.

11 August Another devoir, *Le Papillon*.

6 September Death of William Weightman, Patrick Brontë's curate, aged twenty-eight, of cholera.

12 October Death of Martha Taylor, Charlotte's close friend Mary Taylor's sister, aged twenty-three, at school in Brussels.

18 October Another devoir, *Le Palais de la Mort*.

29 October Death of Elizabeth Branwell; Charlotte and Emily receive the news on 3 November and leave Brussels on 6 November.

28 December Elizabeth Branwell's will provides her nieces with an inheritance of £350 each.

1843   *January* Anne returns to Thorp Green, taking Branwell with her as tutor to the Robinsons' son Edmund; Charlotte returns to Brussels without Emily.

1844   *1 January* Charlotte returns from Brussels.

February Emily begins to transcribe her poems into two notebooks, one untitled and the other titled *Gondal Poems*.

July and August The scheme to open a boarding school at Haworth is revived, Charlotte writes to her friends by way of advertising it, and prospectuses are printed, but without response.

1845   *11 June* Anne returns to Haworth from Thorp Green.

30 June Anne and Emily go on their 'first long journey' by themselves, reaching York and returning to Haworth after two days.

July Branwell is dismissed from his post as tutor at Thorp Green and returns to Haworth in disgrace.

30 July Emily and Anne write diary papers; Emily's includes the information that 'The Gondals still flourish bright as ever   I am at present writing a work on the First Wars'; Anne writes that 'The Gondals in general are not in first-rate playing condition. Will they improve?'

Autumn Charlotte discovers a ms. volume of verse in Emily's handwriting, probably the *Gondal Poems* transcript notebook

1846   *28 January* Charlotte writes to Aylott & Jones asking whether they would undertake the publication of a one-volume collection of short poems at their own risk, or 'on the Author's account'.

31 January Charlotte acknowledges a favourable reply and discusses details of format, type, and cost.

7 February Charlotte dispatches the completed ms. of the poems.

11 March Charlotte sends Aylott & Jones the corrected first proof sheets of *Poems by Currer, Ellis, and Acton Bell*.

6 April Charlotte writes to Aylott & Jones, announcing that 'C. E. & A. Bell are now preparing for the Press a work of fiction, consisting of three distinct and unconnected tales'.

End of May Poems by Currer, Ellis, and Acton Bell published.

4 July The Brontës offer three tales to Henry Colburn in hopes of their publication as a work of fiction in three volumes; the offer is refused.

1847   *July Wuthering Heights* and *Agnes Grey* accepted for publication by Thomas Newby.

September Jane Eyre accepted for publication by Smith, Elder & Co.

19 October Six copies of *Jane Eyre* arrive in Haworth, for the author.

14 December Six copies of *Wuthering Heights* and *Agnes Grey* arrive in Haworth, for the authors.

1848   *January* Reviews of *Wuthering Heights* begin to appear; Emily saves the five from the *Examiner*, *Britannia*, *Douglas Jerrold's Weekly Newspaper*, *Atlas*, and an unidentified journal.

July Anne and Charlotte prove that there are at least two Bells by travelling to London and introducing themselves to George Smith, Charlotte's publisher.

31 July Charlotte writes to W.S. Williams at Smith, Elder regretting her admission that there were 'three sisters' and citing Emily's opposition to this revelation.
24 September Branwell dies.
19 December Emily dies.
22 December Emily's funeral.

1849   *28 May* Anne dies.

The Complete Poems

I. Poems Published in 1846

i [153]. *Faith and Despondency*

'The winter wind is loud and wild,
Come close to me, my darling child;
Forsake thy books, and mateless play;
And, while the night is gathering grey,
We'll talk its pensive hours away; –

'Iernë, round our sheltered hall
November's gusts unheeded call;
Not one faint breath can enter here
Enough to wave my daughter's hair,
10 And I am glad to watch the blaze
Glance from her eyes, with mimic rays;
To feel her cheek so softly pressed,
In happy quiet on my breast.

'But, yet, even this tranquillity
Brings bitter, restless thoughts to me;
And, in the red fire's cheerful glow,
I think of deep glens, blocked with snow;
I dream of moor, and misty hill,
Where evening closes dark and chill;
20 For, lone, among the mountains cold,
Lie those that I have loved of old.
And my heart aches, in hopeless pain
Exhausted with repinings vain,
That I shall greet them ne'er again!'

'Father, in early infancy,
When you were far beyond the sea,
Such thoughts were tyrants over me!

I often sat, for hours together,
Through the long nights of angry weather,
30 Raised on my pillow, to descry
The dim moon struggling in the sky;
Or, with strained ear, to catch the shock,
Of rock with wave, and wave with rock;
So would I fearful vigil keep,
And, all for listening, never sleep.
But this world's life has much to dread,
Not so, my Father, with the dead.

'Oh! not for them, should we despair,
The grave is drear, but they are not there;
40 Their dust is mingled with the sod,
Their happy souls are gone to God!
You told me this, and yet you sigh,
And murmur that your friends must die.
Ah! my dear father, tell me why?
For, if your former words were true,
How useless would such sorrow be;
As wise, to mourn the seed which grew
Unnoticed on its parent tree,
Because it fell in fertile earth,
50 And sprang up to a glorious birth –
Struck deep its root, and lifted high
Its green boughs, in the breezy sky.

'But, I'll not fear, I will not weep
For those whose bodies rest in sleep, –
I know there is a blessed shore,
    Opening its ports for me, and mine;
And, gazing Time's wide waters o'er,
    I weary for that land divine,
Where we were born, where you and I
60 Shall meet our Dearest, when we die;
From suffering and corruption free,
Restored into the Deity.'

'Well hast thou spoken, sweet, trustful child!
    And wiser than thy sire;
And worldly tempests, raging wild,
    Shall strengthen thy desire –
Thy fervent hope, through storm and foam,
    Through wind and ocean's roar,
To reach, at last, the eternal home,
70   The steadfast, changeless, shore!'

ii [160]. *Stars*

Ah! why, because the dazzling sun
    Restored our Earth to joy,
Have you departed, every one,
    And left a desert sky?

All through the night, your glorious eyes
    Were gazing down in mine,
And with a full heart's thankful sighs,
    I blessed that watch divine.

I was at peace, and drank your beams
10   As they were life to me;
And revelled in my changeful dreams,
    Like petrel on the sea.

Thought followed thought, star followed star,
    Through boundless regions, on;
While one sweet influence, near and far,
    Thrilled through, and proved us one!

Why did the morning dawn to break
    So great, so pure, a spell;
And scorch with fire, the tranquil cheek,
20   Where your cool radiance fell?

Blood-red, he rose, and, arrow-straight,
    His fierce beams struck my brow;
The soul of nature, sprang, elate,
    But *mine* sank sad and low!

My lids closed down, yet through their veil,
    I saw him, blazing, still,
And steep in gold the misty dale,
    And flash upon the hill.

I turned me to the pillow, then,
30   To call back night, and see
Your worlds of solemn light, again,
    Throb with my heart, and me!

It would not do – the pillow glowed,
    And glowed both roof and floor;
And birds sang loudly in the wood,
    And fresh winds shook the door;

The curtains waved, the wakened flies
    Were murmuring round my room,
Imprisoned there, till I should rise,
40   And give them leave to roam.

Oh, stars, and dreams, and gentle night;
    Oh, night and stars return!
And hide me from the hostile light,
    That does not warm, but burn;

That drains the blood of suffering men;
    Drinks tears, instead of dew;
Let me sleep through his blinding reign,
    And only wake with you!

iii [157]. *The Philosopher*

'Enough of thought, philosopher!
  Too long hast thou been dreaming
Unenlightened, in this chamber drear,
  While summer's sun is beaming!
Space-sweeping soul, what sad refrain
Concludes thy musings once again?

  '"Oh, for the time when I shall sleep
    Without identity,
  And never care how rain may steep,
10   Or snow may cover me!
  No promised heaven, these wild desires,
    Could all, or half fulfil;
  No threatened hell, with quenchless fires,
    Subdue this quenchless will!"'

'So said I, and still say the same;
  Still, to my death, will say –
Three gods, within this little frame,
  Are warring night and day;
Heaven could not hold them all, and yet
20   They all are held in me;
And must be mine till I forget
  My present entity!
Oh, for the time, when in my breast
  Their struggles will be o'er!
Oh, for the day, when I shall rest,
  And never suffer more!'

'I saw a spirit, standing, man,
  Where thou doth stand – an hour ago,
And round his feet three rivers ran,
30   Of equal depth, and equal flow –
A golden stream – and one like blood;
  And one like sapphire seemed to be;
But, where they joined their triple flood
  It tumbled in an inky sea.

ent his dazzling gaze
rough that ocean's gloomy night
ing all, with sudden blaze,
deep sparkled wide and bright –
e sun, far, far more fair
40 Than its divided sources were!'

'And even for that spirit, seer,
    I've watched and sought my life-time long;
Sought him in heaven, hell, earth, and air –
    An endless search, and always wrong!
Had I but seen his glorious eye
    Once light the clouds that wilder me,
I ne'er had raised this coward cry
    To cease to think, and cease to be;
I ne'er had called oblivion blest,
50   Nor, stretching eager hands to death,
Implored to change for senseless rest
    This sentient soul, this living breath –
Oh, let me die – that power and will
    Their cruel strife may close;
And conquered good, and conquering ill
    Be lost in one repose!'

iv [158]. *Remembrance*

Cold in the earth – and the deep snow piled above thee,
Far, far, removed, cold in the dreary grave!
Have I forgot, my only Love, to love thee,
Severed at last by Time's all-severing wave?

Now, when alone, do my thoughts no longer hover
Over the mountains, on that northern shore,
Resting their wings where heath and fern-leaves cover
Thy noble heart for ever, ever more?

Cold in the earth – and fifteen wild Decembers,
10   From those brown hills, have melted into spring:
Faithful, indeed, is the spirit that remembers
After such years of change and suffering!

Sweet Love of youth, forgive, if I forget thee,
While the world's tide is bearing me along;
Other desires and other hopes beset me,
Hopes which obscure, but cannot do thee wrong!

No later light has lightened up my heaven,
No second morn has ever shone for me;
All my life's bliss from thy dear life was given,
20   All my life's bliss is in the grave with thee.

But, when the days of golden dreams had perished,
And even Despair was powerless to destroy;
Then did I learn how existence could be cherished,
Strengthened, and fed without the aid of joy.

Then did I check the tears of useless passion –
Weaned my young soul from yearning after thine;
Sternly denied its burning wish to hasten
Down to that tomb already more than mine.

And, even yet, I dare not let it languish,
30   Dare not indulge in memory's rapturous pain;
Once drinking deep of that divinest anguish,
How could I seek the empty world again?

v [156]. *A Death-Scene*

'O Day! he cannot die
When thou so fair art shining!
O Sun, in such a glorious sky,
So tranquilly declining;

'He cannot leave thee now,
While fresh west winds are blowing,
And all around his youthful brow
Thy cheerful light is glowing!

'Edward, awake, awake –
The golden evening gleams
Warm and bright on Arden's lake –
Arouse thee from thy dreams!

'Beside thee, on my knee,
My dearest friend! I pray
That thou, to cross the eternal sea,
Wouldst yet one hour delay:

'I hear its billows roar –
I see them foaming high;
But no glimpse of a further shore
Has blest my straining eye.

'Believe not what they urge
Of Eden isles beyond;
Turn back, from that tempestuous surge,
To thy own native land.

'It is not death, but pain
That struggles in thy breast –
Nay, rally, Edward, rouse again;
I cannot let thee rest!'

One long look, that sore reproved me
For the woe I could not bear –
One mute look of suffering moved me
To repent my useless prayer:

And, with sudden check, the heaving
Of distraction passed away;
Not a sign of further grieving
Stirred my soul that awful day.

Paled, at length, the sweet sun setting;
Sunk to peace the twilight breeze:
Summer dews fell softly, wetting
40 Glen, and glade, and silent trees.

Then his eyes began to weary,
Weighed beneath a mortal sleep;
And their orbs grew strangely dreary,
Clouded, even as they would weep.

But they wept not, but they changed not,
Never moved, and never closed;
Troubled still, and still they ranged not –
Wandered not, nor yet reposed!

So I knew that he was dying –
50 Stooped, and raised his languid head;
Felt no breath, and heard no sighing,
So I knew that he was dead.

vi [149]. *Song*

The linnet in the rocky dells,
    The moor-lark in the air,
The bee among the heather bells,
    That hide my lady fair:

The wild deer browse above her breast;
    The wild birds raise their brood;
And they, her smiles of love caressed,
    Have left her solitude!

I ween, that when the grave's dark wall
10   Did first her form retain;
They thought their hearts could ne'er recall
    The light of joy again.

They thought the tide of grief would flow
    Unchecked through future years;
But where is all their anguish now,
    And where are all their tears?

Well, let them fight for honour's breath,
    Or pleasure's shade pursue –
The dweller in the land of death
20   Is changed and careless too.

And, if their eyes should watch and weep
    Till sorrow's source were dry,
She would not, in her tranquil sleep,
    Return a single sigh!

Blow, west-wind, by the lonely mound,
    And murmur, summer-streams –
There is no need of other sound
    To soothe my lady's dreams.

vii [163]. *Anticipation*

How beautiful the earth is still,
To thee – how full of happiness!
How little fraught with real ill,
Or unreal phantoms of distress!
How spring can bring thee glory, yet,
And summer win thee to forget
December's sullen time!
Why dost thou hold the treasure fast,
              hen youth is past,
             ar thy prime?

          e thy own compeers,
          d in years,
          ning melt in tears,
          ileless day;
          untried and young,

Before their hearts went wandering wrong,
Poor slaves, subdued by passions strong,
    A weak and helpless prey!

'Because, I hoped while they enjoyed,
20   And, by fulfilment, hope destroyed;
As children hope, with trustful breast,
I waited bliss – and cherished rest.
A thoughtful spirit taught me, soon,
That we must long till life be done;
That every phase of earthly joy
Must always fade, and always cloy:

'This I foresaw – and would not chase
    The fleeting treacheries;
But, with firm foot and tranquil face,
30   Held backward from that tempting race,
Gazed o'er the sands the waves efface,
    To the enduring seas –
There cast my anchor of desire
Deep in unknown eternity;
Nor ever let my spirit tire,
With looking for *what is to be!*

'It is hope's spell that glorifies,
Like youth, to my maturer eyes,
All Nature's million mysteries,
40   The fearful and the fair –
Hope soothes me in the griefs I know;
She lulls my pain for others' woe,
And makes me strong to undergo
    What I am born to bear.

'Glad comforter! will I not brave,
Unawed, the darkness of the grave?
Nay, smile to hear Death's billows rave –
    Sustained, my guide, by thee?
The more unjust seems present fate,
50   The more my spirit swells elate,
Strong, in thy strength, to anticipate
    Rewarding destiny!'

viii [166]. *The Prisoner* (*A Fragment*)

In the dungeon-crypts, idly did I stray,
Reckless of the lives wasting there away;
'Draw the ponderous bars! open, Warder stern!'
He dared not say me nay – the hinges harshly turn.

'Our guests are darkly lodged,' I whisper'd, gazing through
The vault, whose grated eye showed heaven more grey
    than blue;
(This was when glad spring laughed in awaking pride;)
'Aye, darkly lodged enough!' returned my sullen guide.

Then, God forgive my youth; forgive my careless tongue;
10 I scoffed, as chill chains on the damp flag-stones rung:
'Confined in triple walls, art thou so much to fear,
That we must bind thee down and clench thy fetters here?'

The captive raised her face, it was as soft and mild
As sculptured marble saint, or slumbering unwean'd child;
It was so soft and mild, it was so sweet and fair,
Pain could not trace a line, nor grief a shadow there!

The captive raised her hand and pressed it to her brow;
'I have been struck,' she said, 'and I am suffering now;
Yet these are little worth, your bolts and irons strong,
20 And, were they forged in steel, they could not hold me
    long.'

Hoarse laughed the jailer grim: 'Shall I be won to hear;
Dost think, fond, dreaming wretch, that *I* shall grant thy
    prayer?
Or, better still, wilt melt my master's heart with groans?
Ah! sooner might the sun thaw down these granite stones.

'My master's voice is low, his aspect bland and kind,
But hard as hardest flint, the soul that lurks behind;
And I am rough and rude, yet not more rough to see
Than is the hidden ghost that has its home in me.'

About her lips there played a smile of almost scorn,
30 'My friend,' she gently said, 'you have not heard me
        mourn;
When you my kindred's lives, *my* lost life, can restore,
Then may I weep and sue, – but never, friend, before!

'Still, let my tyrants know, I am not doomed to wear
Year after year in gloom, and desolate despair;
A messenger of Hope, comes every night to me,
And offers for short life, eternal liberty.

'He comes with western winds, with evening's wandering
        airs,
With that clear dusk of heaven that brings the thickest
        stars.
Winds take a pensive tone, and stars a tender fire,
40 And visions rise, and change, that kill me with desire.

'Desire for nothing known in my maturer years,
When Joy grew mad with awe, at counting future tears.
When, if my spirit's sky was full of flashes warm,
I knew not whence they came, from sun, or thunder storm.

'But, first, a hush of peace – a soundless calm descends;
The struggle of distress, and fierce impatience ends.
Mute music soothes my breast, unuttered harmony,
That I could never dream, till Earth was lost to me.

'Then dawns the Invisible; the Unseen its truth reveals;
50 My outward sense is gone, my inward essence feels:
Its wings are almost free – its home, its harbour found,
Measuring the gulf, it stoops, and dares the final bound.

'Oh, dreadful is the check – intense the agony –
When the ear begins to hear, and the eye begins to see;
When the pulse begins to throb, the brain to think again,
The soul to feel the flesh, and the flesh to feel the chain.

'Yet I would lose no sting, would wish no torture less,
The more that anguish racks, the earlier it will bless;
And robed in fires of hell, or bright with heavenly shine,
60 If it but herald death, the vision is divine!'

She ceased to speak, and we, unanswering, turned to go –
We had no further power to work the captive woe:
Her cheek, her gleaming eye, declared that man had given
A sentence, unapproved, and overruled by Heaven.

ix [141]. *Hope*

Hope was but a timid friend;
    She sat without the grated den,
Watching how my fate would tend,
    Even as selfish-hearted men.

She was cruel in her fear;
    Through the bars, one dreary day,
I looked out to see her there,
    And she turned her face away!

Like a false guard, false watch keeping,
10   Still in strife, she whispered peace;
She would sing while I was weeping;
    If I listened, she would cease.

False she was, and unrelenting;
    When my last joys strewed the ground,
Even Sorrow saw, repenting,
    Those sad relics scattered round;

Hope, whose whisper would have given
    Balm to all my frenzied pain,
Stretched her wings, and soared to heaven,
20   Went, and ne'er returned again!

x [146]. *A Day Dream*

On a sunny brae, alone I lay
    One summer afternoon;
It was the marriage-time of May
    With her young lover, June.

From her mother's heart, seemed loath to part
    That queen of bridal charms,
But her father smiled on the fairest child
    He ever held in his arms.

The trees did wave their plumy crests,
10   The glad birds carolled clear;
And I, of all the wedding guests,
    Was only sullen there!

There was not one, but wished to shun
    My aspect void of cheer;
The very grey rocks, looking on,
    Asked, 'What do you here?'

And I could utter no reply;
    In sooth, I did not know
Why I had brought a clouded eye
20   To greet the general glow.

So, resting on a heathy bank,
    I took my heart to me;
And we together sadly sank
    Into a reverie.

We thought, 'When winter comes again,
    Where will these bright things be?
All vanished, like a vision vain,
    An unreal mockery!

'The birds that now so blithely sing,
30   Through deserts, frozen dry,
Poor spectres of the perished spring,
    In famished troops, will fly.

'And why should we be glad at all?
    The leaf is hardly green,
Before a token of its fall
    Is on the surface seen!'

Now, whether it were really so,
    I never could be sure;
But as in fit of peevish woe,
40   I stretched me on the moor,

A thousand thousand gleaming fires
    Seemed kindling in the air;
A thousand thousand silvery lyres
    Resounded far and near:

Methought, the very breath I breathed
    Was full of sparks divine,
And all my heather-couch was wreathed
    By that celestial shine!

And, while the wide earth echoing rung
50   To their strange minstrelsy,
The little glittering spirits sung,
    Or seemed to sing, to me.

'O mortal! mortal! let them die;
    Let time and tears destroy,
That we may overflow the sky
    With universal joy!

'Let grief distract the sufferer's breast,
    And night obscure his way;
They hasten him to endless rest,
60   And everlasting day.

'To thee the world is like a tomb,
    A desert's naked shore;
To us, in unimagined bloom,
    It brightens more and more!

'And could we lift the veil, and give
    One brief glimpse to thine eye,
Thou wouldst rejoice for those that live,
    Because they live to die.'

The music ceased; the noonday dream,
    Like dream of night, withdrew;
70
But Fancy, still, will sometimes deem
    Her fond creation true.

xi [150]. *To Imagination*

When weary with the long day's care,
    And earthly change from pain to pain,
And lost and ready to despair,
    Thy kind voice calls me back again:
Oh, my true friend! I am not lone,
While thou canst speak with such a tone!

So hopeless is the world without;
    The world within I doubly prize;
Thy world, where guile, and hate, and doubt,
10
    And cold suspicion never rise;
Where thou, and I, and Liberty,
Have undisputed sovereignty.

What matters it, that, all around,
    Danger, and guilt, and darkness lie,
If but within our bosom's bound
    We hold a bright, untroubled sky,
Warm with ten thousand mingled rays
Of suns that know no winter days?

Reason, indeed, may oft complain
20
    For Nature's sad reality,
And tell the suffering heart how vain
    Its cherished dreams must always be;
And Truth may rudely trample down
The flowers of Fancy, newly-blown:

But, thou art ever there, to bring
    The hovering vision back, and breathe
New glories o'er the blighted spring,
    And call a lovelier Life from Death,
And whisper, with a voice divine,
30   Of real worlds, as bright as thine.

I trust not to thy phantom bliss,
    Yet, still, in evening's quiet hour,
With never-failing thankfulness,.
    I welcome thee, Benignant Power;
Sure solacer of human cares,
And sweeter hope, when hope despairs!

xii [132]. *How Clear She Shines*

How clear she shines! How quietly
    I lie beneath her guardian light;
While heaven and earth are whispering me,
    'Tomorrow, wake, but, dream tonight.'
Yes, Fancy, come, my Fairy love!
    These throbbing temples softly kiss;
And bend my lonely couch above
    And bring me rest, and bring me bliss.

The world is going; dark world, adieu!
10   Grim world, conceal thee till the day;
The heart, thou canst not all subdue,
    Must still resist, if thou delay!

Thy love I will not, will not share;
    Thy hatred only wakes a smile;
Thy griefs may wound – thy wrongs may tear,
    But, oh, thy lies shall ne'er beguile!
While gazing on the stars that glow
    Above me, in that stormless sea,
I long to hope that all the woe
20   Creation knows, is held in thee!

And this shall be my dream tonight;
    I'll think the heaven of glorious spheres
Is rolling on its course of light
    In endless bliss, through endless years;
I'll think, there's not one world above,
    Far as these straining eyes can see,
Where wisdom ever laughed at Love,
    Or Virtue crouched to Infamy;

Where, writhing 'neath the strokes of Fate,
30   The mangled wretch was forced to smile;
To match his patience 'gainst her hate,
    His heart rebellious all the while.
Where Pleasure still will lead to wrong,
    And helpless Reason warn in vain;
And Truth is weak, and Treachery strong;
    And Joy the surest path to Pain;
And Peace, the lethargy of Grief;
    And Hope, a phantom of the soul;
And Life, a labour, void and brief;
40   And Death, the despot of the whole!

xiii [182]. *Sympathy*

There should be no despair for you
    While nightly stars are burning;
While evening pours its silent dew
    And sunshine gilds the morning.
There should be no despair – though tears
    May flow down like a river:
Are not the best beloved of years
    Around your heart for ever?

They weep, you weep, it must be so;
10   Winds sigh as you are sighing,
And Winter sheds his grief in snow
    Where Autumn's leaves are lying:

Yet, these revive, and from their fate
    Your fate cannot be parted:
Then, journey on, if not elate,
    Still, *never* broken-hearted!

xiv [152]. *Plead for Me*

Oh, thy bright eyes must answer now,
When Reason, with a scornful brow,
Is mocking at my overthrow!
Oh, thy sweet tongue must plead for me
And tell, why I have chosen thee!

Stern Reason is to judgment come,
Arrayed in all her forms of gloom:
Wilt thou, my advocate, be dumb?
No, radiant angel, speak and say,
Why I did cast the world away.

Why I have persevered to shun
The common paths that others run,
And on a strange road journeyed on,
Heedless, alike, of wealth and power –
Of glory's wreath and pleasure's flower.

These, once, indeed, seemed Beings Divine;
And they, perchance, heard vows of mine,
And saw my offerings on their shrine;
But, careless gifts are seldom prized,
And *mine* were worthily despised.

So, with a ready heart I swore
To seek their altar-stone no more;
And gave my spirit to adore
Thee, ever-present, phantom thing;
My slave, my comrade, and my king,

10

20

A slave, because I rule thee still;
Incline thee to my changeful will,
And make thy influence good or ill:
A comrade, for by day and night
30   Thou art my intimate delight, –

My darling pain that wounds and sears
And wrings a blessing out from tears
By deadening me to earthly cares;
And yet, a king, though Prudence well
Have taught thy subject to rebel.

And am I wrong to worship, where
Faith cannot doubt, nor hope despair,
Since my own soul can grant my prayer?
Speak, God of visions, plead for me,
40   And tell why I have chosen thee!

xv [130]. *Self-Interrogation*

'The evening passes fast away,
      'Tis almost time to rest;
What thoughts has left the vanished day,
      What feelings, in thy breast?'

'The vanished day? It leaves a sense
      Of labour hardly done;
Of little, gained with vast expense, –
      A sense of grief alone!

'Time stands before the door of Death,
10   Upbraiding bitterly;
And Conscience, with exhaustless breath,
      Pours black reproach on me:

'And though I've said that Conscience lies,
      And Time should Fate condemn;
Still, sad Repentance clouds my eyes,
      And makes me yield to them!'

'Then art thou glad to seek repose?
    Art glad to leave the sea,
And anchor all thy weary woes
20   In calm Eternity?

'Nothing regrets to see thee go –
    Not one voice sobs "farewell",
And where thy heart has suffered so,
    Canst thou desire to dwell?'

'Alas! The countless links are strong
    That bind us to our clay;
The loving spirit lingers long,
    And would not pass away!

'And rest is sweet, when laurelled fame
30   Will crown the soldier's crest;
But, a brave heart, with a tarnished name,
    Would rather fight than rest.'

'Well, thou hast fought for many a year,
    Hast fought thy whole life through,
Hast humbled Falsehood, trampled Fear;
    What is there left to do?'

"Tis true, this arm has hotly striven,
    Has dared what few would dare;
Much have I done, and freely given,
40   But little learnt to bear!'

'Look on the grave, where thou must sleep,
    Thy last, and strongest foe;
It is endurance not to weep,
    If that repose seem woe.

'The long war closing in defeat,
    Defeat serenely borne,
Thy midnight rest may still be sweet,
    And break in glorious morn!'

xvi [159]. *Death*

Death! that struck when I was most confiding
In my certain faith of joy to be –
Strike again, Time's withered branch dividing
From the fresh root of Eternity!

Leaves, upon Time's branch, were growing brightly,
Full of sap, and full of silver dew;
Birds beneath its shelter gathered nightly;
Daily round its flowers the wild bees flew.

Sorrow passed, and plucked the golden blossom;
10 Guilt stripped off the foliage in its pride;
But, within its parent's kindly bosom,
Flowed for ever Life's restoring tide.

Little mourned I for the parted gladness,
For the vacant nest and silent song –
Hope was there, and laughed me out of sadness;
Whispering, 'Winter will not linger long!'

And, behold! with tenfold increase blessing,
Spring adorned the beauty-burdened spray;
Wind and rain and fervent heat, caressing,
20 Lavished glory on that second May!

High it rose – no winged grief could sweep it;
Sin was scared to distance with its shine;
Love, and its own life, had power to keep it
From all wrong – from every blight but thine!

Cruel Death! The young leaves droop and languish;
Evening's gentle air may still restore –
No! the morning sunshine mocks my anguish –
Time, for me, must never blossom more!

Strike it down, that other boughs may flourish
30 Where that perished sapling used to be;
Thus, at least, its mouldering corpse will nourish
That from which it sprung – Eternity.

xvii [105]. *Stanzas to —*

Well, some may hate, and some may scorn,
And some may quite forget thy name;
But my sad heart must ever mourn
Thy ruined hopes, thy blighted fame!
'Twas thus I thought, an hour ago,
Even weeping o'er that wretch's woe;
One word turned back my gushing tears,
And lit my altered eye with sneers.
Then 'Bless the friendly dust,' I said,
'That hides thy unlamented head!
Vain as thou wert, and weak as vain,
The slave of Falsehood, Pride, and Pain, –
My heart has nought akin to thine;
Thy soul is powerless over mine.'

But these were thoughts that vanished too;
Unwise, unholy, and untrue:
Do I despise the timid deer,
Because his limbs are fleet with fear?
Or, would I mock the wolf's death-howl,
Because his form is gaunt and foul?
Or, hear with joy the leveret's cry,
Because it cannot bravely die?
No! Then above his memory
Let Pity's heart as tender be;
Say, 'Earth, lie lightly on that breast
And, kind Heaven, grant that spirit rest!'

xviii [155]. *Honour's Martyr*

The moon is full this winter night;
    The stars are clear, though few;
And every window glistens bright,
    With leaves of frozen dew.

The sweet moon through your lattice gleams
    And lights your room like day;
And there you pass, in happy dreams,
    The peaceful hours away!

While I, with effort hardly quelling
    The anguish in my breast,
Wander about the silent dwelling,
    And cannot think of rest.

The old clock in the gloomy hall
    Ticks on, from hour to hour;
And every time its measured call
    Seems lingering slow and slower:

And oh, how slow that keen-eyed star
    Has tracked the chilly grey!
What, watching yet! how very far
    The morning lies away!

Without your chamber door I stand;
    Love, are you slumbering still?
My cold heart, underneath my hand,
    Has almost ceased to thrill.

Bleak, bleak the east wind sobs and sighs,
    And drowns the turret bell,
Whose sad note, undistinguished, dies
    Unheard, like my farewell!

Tomorrow, Scorn will blight my name,
    And Hate will trample me,
Will load me with a coward's shame –
    A traitor's perjury.

False friends will launch their covert sneers;
    True friends will wish me dead;
And I shall cause the bitterest tears
    That you have ever shed.

The dark deeds of my outlawed race
    Will then like virtues shine;
And men will pardon their disgrace,
40   Beside the guilt of mine.

For, who forgives the accursed crime
    Of dastard treachery?
Rebellion, in its chosen time,
    May Freedom's champion be;

Revenge may stain a righteous sword,
    It may be just to slay;
But, traitor, traitor, – from *that* word
    All true breasts shrink away!

Oh, I would give my heart to death,
50   To keep my honour fair;
Yet, I'll not give my inward faith
    My honour's *name* to spare!

Not even to keep your priceless love,
    Dare I, Beloved, deceive;
This treason should the future prove,
    Then, only then, believe!

I know the path I ought to go;
    I follow fearlessly,
Inquiring not what deeper woe
60   Stern duty stores for me.

So foes pursue, and cold allies
    Mistrust me, every one:
Let me be false in others' eyes,
    If faithful in my own.

xix [115]. *Stanzas*

I'll not weep that thou art going to leave me,
    There's nothing lovely here;
And doubly will the dark world grieve me,
    While thy heart suffers there.

I'll not weep, because the summer's glory
    Must always end in gloom;
And, follow out the happiest story –
    It closes with a tomb!

And I am weary of the anguish
    Increasing winters bear;
Weary to watch the spirit languish
    Through years of dead despair.

So, if a tear, when thou art dying,
    Should haply fall from me,
It is but that my soul is sighing,
    To go and rest with thee.

xx [144]. *My Comforter*

Well hast thou spoken, and yet, not taught
    A feeling strange or new;
Thou hast but roused a latent thought,
A cloud-closed beam of sunshine, brought
    To gleam in open view.

Deep down, concealed within my soul,
    That light lies hid from men;
Yet, glows unquenched – though shadows roll,
Its gentle ray cannot control,
    About the sullen den.

Was I not vexed, in these gloomy ways
        To walk alone so long?
Around me, wretches uttering praise,
Or howling o'er their hopeless days,
        And each with Frenzy's tongue; –

A brotherhood of misery,
        Their smiles as sad as sighs;
Whose madness daily maddened me,
Distorting into agony
20   The bliss before my eyes!

So stood I, in Heaven's glorious sun,
        And in the glare of Hell;
My spirit drank a mingled tone,
Of seraph's song, and demon's moan;
What my soul bore, my soul alone
        Within itself may tell!

Like a soft air, above a sea,
        Tossed by the tempest's stir;
A thaw-wind, melting quietly
30 The snow-drift, on some wintry lea;
No: what sweet thing resembles thee,
        My thoughtful Comforter?

And yet a little longer speak,
        Calm this resentful mood;
And while the savage heart grows meek,
For other token do not seek,
But let the tear upon my cheek
        Evince my gratitude!

xxi [121]. *The Old Stoic*

Riches I hold in light esteem;
        And Love I laugh to scorn;
And lust of fame was but a dream
        That vanished with the morn:

And if I pray, the only prayer
    That moves my lips for me
Is, 'Leave the heart that now I bear,
    And give me liberty!'

Yes, as my swift days near their goal,
    'Tis all that I implore;
In life and death, a chainless soul,
    With courage to endure.

II. Dated Poems

1.

Cold clear and blue the morning heaven
Expands its arch on high
Cold clear and blue Lake Werna's water
Reflects that winter's sky
The moon has set but Venus shines
A silent silvery star

2.

Will the day be bright or cloudy?
Sweetly has its dawn begun
But the heaven may shake with thunder
Ere the setting of the sun

Lady watch Apollo's journey
Thus thy first born's course shall be –
If his beams through summer vapours
Warm the earth all placidly
Her days shall pass like a pleasant dream in sweet
      tranquillity

10   If it darken if a shadow
Quench his rays and summon rain
Flowers may open buds may blossom
Bud and flower alike are vain
Her days shall pass like a mournful story in care and tears
      and pain

If the wind be fresh and free
The wide skies clear and cloudless blue
The woods and fields and golden flowers
Sparkling in sunshine and in dew
Her days shall pass in Glory's light the world's drear desert
      through

3.

Tell me tell me smiling child
What the past is like to thee?
An Autumn evening soft and mild
With a wind that sighs mournfully

Tell me what is the present hour?
A green and flowery spray
Where a young bird sits gathering its power
To mount and fly away

And what is the future happy one?
10 A sea beneath a cloudless sun
A mighty glorious dazzling sea
Stretching into infinity

4.

The inspiring music's thrilling sound
The glory of the festal day
The glittering splendour rising round
Have passed like all earth's joys away

Forsaken by that Lady fair
She glides unheeding through them all
Covering her brow to hide the tear
That still though checked trembles to fall

      She hurries through the outer Hall
10   And up the stairs through galleries dim
      That murmur to the breezes' call
      The night-wind's lonely vesper hymn

5.

      High waving heather 'neath stormy blasts bending
      Midnight and moonlight and bright shining stars
      Darkness and glory rejoicingly blending
      Earth rising to heaven and heaven descending
      Man's spirit away from its drear dungeon sending
      Bursting the fetters and breaking the bars

      All down the mountain sides wild forests lending
      One mighty voice to the life giving wind
      Rivers their banks in the jubilee rending
10   Fast through the valleys a reckless course wending
      Wider and deeper their waters extending
      Leaving a desolate desert behind

      Shining and lowering and swelling and dying
      Changing forever from midnight to noon
      Roaring like thunder like soft music sighing
      Shadows on shadows advancing and flying
      Lightning bright flashes the deep gloom defying
      Coming as swiftly and fading as soon

6.

      Woods you need not frown on me
      Spectral trees that so dolefully
      Shake your heads in the dreary sky
      You need not mock so bitterly

7.

Start not upon the minster wall
Sunshine is shed in holy calm
And lonely though my footsteps fall
The saints shall shelter thee from harm

Shrink not if it be summer noon
This shadow should right welcome be
These stairs are steep but landed soon
We'll rest us long and quietly

What though our path be o'er the dead
10 They slumber soundly in the tomb
And why should mortals fear to tread
The pathway to their future home?

8.

Redbreast early in the morning
Dark and cold and cloudy grey
Wildly tender is thy music
Chasing [the angry] thoughts away

My heart is not enraptured now
My eyes are full of tears
And constant sorrow on my brow
Has done the work of years

It was not hope that wrecked at once
10 The spirit's [early] storm
But a long life of solitude
Hopes quenched and rising thoughts subdued
A bleak November's calm

What woke it then? A little child
Strayed from its father's cottage door
And in the hour of moonlight mild
Laid lonely on the desert moor

———————

I heard it then you heard it too
And seraph sweet it sang to you
20   But like the shriek of misery
That wild wild music wailed to me

9.

Through the hours of yesternight
Hall and gallery blazed with light
Every lamp its lustre showered
On the adorer and the adored
None were sad that entered there
All were loved and all were fair
Some were dazzling like the sun
Shining down at summer noon
Some were sweet as amber even
10   Living in the depth of heaven
Some were soft and kind and gay
Morning's face not more divine
Some were like Diana's day
Midnight moonlight's holy shine

10.

There shines the moon, at noon of night –
Vision of glory – Dream of light!
Holy as heaven – undimmed and pure,
Looking down on the lonely moor –
And lonelier still beneath her ray

That drear moor stretches far away
Till it seems strange that aught can lie
Beyond its zone of silver sky –

Bright moon – dear moon! when years have past
10   My weary feet return at last –
And still upon Lake Elnor's breast
Thy solemn rays serenely rest
And still the Fern-leaves sighing wave
Like mourners over Elbë's grave
And Earth's the same but Oh to see
How wildly Time has altered me!
Am I the being who long ago
Sat watching by that water side
The light of life expiring slow
20   From his fair cheek and brow of pride?
Not oft these mountains feel the shine
Of such a day – as fading then,
Cast from its fount of gold divine
A last smile on the heathery plain
And kissed the far-off peaks of snow
That gleaming on the horizon shone
As if in summer's warmest glow
Stern winter claimed a loftier throne –
And there he lay among the bloom
30   His red blood dyed a deeper hue
Shuddering to feel the ghostly gloom
That coming Death around him threw –
Sickening to think one hour would sever
The sweet, sweet world and him forever
To think that twilight gathering dim
Would never pass away to him –
No – never more! That awful thought
A thousand dreary feelings brought,
And memory all her powers combined
40   And rushed upon his fainting mind.
Wide, swelling woodlands seemed to rise
Beneath soft, sunny, southern skies –
Old Elbë Hall his noble home

Towered 'mid its trees, whose foliage green
Rustled with the kind airs that come
From summer Heavens when most serene
And bursting through the leafy shade
A gush of golden sunshine played;
Bathing the walls in amber light
50   And sparkling in the water clear
That stretched below – reflected bright
The whole wide world of cloudless air –
And still before his spirit's eye
Such well known scenes would rise and fly
Till, maddening with despair and pain
He turned his dying face to me
And wildly cried, 'Oh once again
Might I my native country see!
But once again – one single day!
60   And must it – can it *never* be?
To die – and die so far away
When life has hardly smiled for me –
Augusta – you will soon return
Back to that land in health and bloom
And then the heath alone will mourn
Above my unremembered tomb
For you'll forget the lonely grave
And mouldering corpse by Elnor's wave' –

I I.

The night of storms has passed
The sunshine bright and clear
Gives glory to the verdant waste
And warms the breezy air

And I would leave my bed
Its cheering smile to see
To chase the visions from my head
Whose forms have troubled me

In all the hours of gloom
10   My soul was rapt away
I dreamt I stood by a marble tomb
Where royal corpses lay

It was just the time of eve
When parted ghosts might come
Above their prisoned dust to grieve
And wail their woeful doom

And truly at my side
I saw a shadowy thing
Most dim and yet its presence there
20   Curdled my blood with ghastly fear
And ghastlier wondering

My breath I could not draw
The air seemed ranny
But still my eyes with maddening gaze
Were fixed upon its fearful face
And its were fixed on me

I fell down on the stone
But could [not] turn away
My words died in a voiceless moan
30   When I began to pray

And still it bent above
Its features full in view
It seemed close by and yet more far
Than this world from the farthest star
That tracks the boundless blue

Indeed 'twas not the space
Of earth or time between
But the sea of death's eternity
The gulf o'er which mortality
40   Has never never been

O bring not back again
The horror of that hour
When its lips opened and a sound
Awoke the stillness reigning round
Faint as a dream but the earth shrank
And heaven's lights shivered 'neath its power

    'Woe for the day Regina's pride
    Regina's hope is in the grave
    And who shall rule my land beside
50   And who shall save

    'Woe for the day with gory tears
    My country's sons this day shall rue
    Woe for the day a thousand years
    Can not repair what one shall do

    'Woe for the day' mixed with the wind
    That sad lament was ringing
    It almost broke my heart to hear
    Such dreary dreary singing

12.

I saw thee child one summer's day
Suddenly leave thy cheerful play
And in the green grass lowly lying
I listened to thy mournful sighing

I knew the wish that waked that wail
I knew the source whence sprung those tears
You longed for fate to raise the veil
That darkened over coming years

The anxious prayer was heard and power
10 Was given me in that silent hour
To open to an infant's eye
The portals of futurity

But child of dust the fragrant flowers
The bright blue sky and velvet sod
Were strange conductors to the bowers
Thy daring footsteps must have trod

I watched my time and summer passed
And Autumn waning fleeted by
And doleful winter nights at last
20   In cloudy mourning clothed the sky

And now I'm come this evening fell
Not stormily but stilly drear
A sound sweeps o'er thee like a knell
To banish joy and welcome care

A fluttering blast that shakes the leaves
And whistles round the gloomy wall
And lingering long lamenting grieves
For 'tis the spectre's call

He hears me what a sudden start
30   Sent the blood icy to that heart
He wakens and how ghastly white
That face looks in the dim lamplight

Those tiny hands in vain essay
To thrust the shadowy fiend away
There is a horror on his brow
An anguish in his bosom now

A fearful anguish in his eyes
Fixed strainedly on the vacant air
Heavily bursts in long drawn sighs
40   His panting breath enchained by fear

Poor child if spirits such as I
Could weep o'er human misery
A tear might flow aye many a tear
To see the road that lies before
To see the sunshine disappear
And hear the stormy waters roar
Breaking upon a desolate shore

Cut off from hope in early day
From power and glory cut away
50 But it is doomed and morning's light
Must image forth the scowl of night
And childhood's flower must waste its bloom
Beneath the shadow of the tomb

13.

Sleep not dream not this bright day
Will not cannot last for aye
Bliss like thine is bought by years
Dark with torment and with tears

Sweeter far than placid pleasure
Purer higher beyond measure
Yet alas the sooner turning
Into hopeless endless mourning

I love thee boy for all divine
10 All full of God thy features shine
Darling enthusiast holy child
Too good for this world's warring wild
Too heavenly now but doomed to be
Hell-like in heart and misery

And what shall change that angel brow
And quench that spirit's glorious glow
Relentless laws that disallow
True virtue and true joy below

And blame me not if when the dread
20 Of suffering clouds thy youthful head
If when by crime and sorrow tos[t]
Thy wandering bark is wrecked and los[t]

I too depart I too decline
And make thy path no longer mine
'Tis thus that human minds will turn
All doomed alike to sin and mourn
Yet all with long gaze fixed afar
Adoring virtue's distant star

14.

O God of heaven! the dream of horror
The frightful dream is over now
The sickened heart the blasting sorrow
The ghastly night the ghastlier morrow
The aching sense of utter woe.

The burning tears that would keep welling
The groans that mocked at every tear
That burst from out their dreary dwelling
As if each gasp were life expelling
10   But life was nourished by despair

The tossing and the anguished pining
The grinding teeth and staring eye
The agony of still repining
When not a spark of hope was shining
From gloomy fate's relentless sky

The impatient rage the useless shrinking
From thoughts that yet could not be borne
The soul that was for ever thinking
Till nature maddened tortured sinking
20   At last refused to mourn –

It's over now – and I am free
And the ocean wind is caressing me
The wild wind from that wavy main
I never thought to see again

Bless thee Bright Sea – and glorious dome
And my own world my spirit's home
Bless thee – Bless all – I can not speak
My voice is choked, but not with grief
And salt drops from my haggard cheek
30   Descend like rain upon the heath

How long they've wet a dungeon floor –
Falling on flag-stones damp and grey
I used to weep even in my sleep
The night was dreadful like the day

I used to weep when winter's snow
Whirled through the grating stormily
But then it was a calmer woe
For every thing was drear as me

The bitterest time the worst of all
40   Was that in which the summer sheen
Cast a green lustre on the wall
That told of Fields of lovelier green

Often I've sat down on the ground
Gazing up to that flush scarce seen
Till heedless of the darkness round
My soul has sought a land serene

It sought the arch of heaven divine
The pure blue heaven with clouds of gold
It sought thy Father's home and mine
50   As I remembered it of old

O even now too horribly
Come back the feelings that would swell
When with my face hid on my knee
I strove the bursting groans to quell

I flung myself upon the stone
I howled and tore my tangled hair
And then when the first gush had flown
Lay in unspeakable despair

Sometimes a curse sometimes a prayer
60 Would quiver on my parched tongue
But both without a murmur there
Died in the breast from whence they sprung

And so the day would fade on high
And darkness quench that lonely beam
And slumber mould my misery
Into some strange and spectral dream
Whose phantom horrors made me know
The worst extent of human woe –

But this is past and why return
70 O'er such a past to brood and mourn?
Shake off the fetters break the chain
And live and love and smile again

The waste of youth the waste of years
Departed in that dungeon's thrall
The gnawing grief the hopeless tears
Forget them – O forget them all –

15.

The battle had passed from the height
And still did evening fall
While heaven with its hosts of night
Gloriously canopied all

The dead around were sleeping
On heath and granite grey
And the dying their last watch were keeping
In the closing of the day

＊　＊　＊

How golden bright from earth and heaven
10 The summer day declines
How gloriously o'er land and sea
The parting sunbeam shines

There is a voice in the wind that waves
Those bright rejoicing trees

                *   *   *   *

Not a vapour had stained the breezeless blue
Not a cloud had dimmed the sun
From the time of morning's earliest dew
Till the summer day was done

And all as pure and all as bright
20 The [beam] of evening died
And purer still its parting light
Shone in Lake Elnor's tide

Waveless and calm lies that silent deep
In its wilderness of moors
Solemn and soft the moonbeams sleep
Upon its heathy shores

The deer are gathered to their rest
The wild sheep seek the fold

                *   *   *   *

Only some spires of bright green grass
30 Transparently in sunshine quivering

16.

The sun has set and the long grass now
Waves drearily in the evening wind
And the wild bird has flown from that old grey stone
In some warm nook a couch to find

In all the lonely landscape round
I see no sight and hear no sound
Except the wind that far away
Comes sighing o'er the heathy sea

17.

Lady in your Palace Hall
Once perchance my face was seen
Can no memory now recall
Thought again to what has been

18.

And first an hour of mournful musing
And then a gush of bitter tears
And then a dreary calm diffusing
Its deadly mist o'er joys and cares

And then a throb and then a lightening
And then a breathing from above
And then a star in heaven brightening
The star the glorious star of love

19.

Wind sink to rest in the heather
Thy wild voice suits not me
I would have dreary weather
But all devoid of thee

Sun set from that evening heaven
Thy glad smile wins not mine
If light at all is given
O give me Cynthia's shine

20.

Long neglect has worn away
Half the sweet enchanting smile
Time has turned the bloom to grey
Mould and damp the face defile

But that lock of silky hair
Still beneath the picture twined
Tells what once those features were
Paints their image on the mind

Fair the hand that traced that line
10   'Dearest ever deem me true'
Swiftly flew the fingers fine
When the pen that motto drew

21.

Awaking morning laughs from heaven
On golden summer's forests green
And what a gush of song is given
To welcome in that light serene

A fresh wind waves the clustering roses
And through the open window sighs
Around the couch where she reposes
The lady with the dovelike eyes

With dovelike eyes and shining hair
10   And velvet cheek so sweetly moulded
And hands so soft and white and fair
Above her snowy bosom folded

*   *   *   *

Her sister's and her brother's feet
Are brushing off the scented dew
And she springs up in haste to greet
The grass and flowers and sunshine too

22.

Alone I sat the summer day
Had died in smiling light away
I saw it die I watched it fade
From misty hill and breezeless glade

And thoughts in my soul were rushing
And my heart bowed beneath their power
And tears within my eyes were gushing
Because I could not speak the feeling
The solemn joy around me stealing
In that divine untroubled hour

I asked my self O why has heaven
Denied the precious gift to me
The glorious gift to many given
To speak their thoughts in poetry

Dreams have encircled me I said
From careless childhood's sunny time
Visions by ardent fancy fed
Since life was in its morning prime

But now when I had hoped to sing
My fingers strike a tuneless string
And still the burden of the strain
Is strive no more 'tis all in vain

23. *A. G. A. to A. E.*

Lord of Elbë, on Elbë hill
The mist is thick and the wind is chill
And the heart of thy Friend from the dawn of day
Has sighed for sorrow that thou went away –

Lord of Elbë, how pleasant to me
The sound of thy blithesome step would be
Rustling the heath that, only now
Waves as the night-gusts over it blow

Bright are the fires in thy lonely home
10   I see them far off, and as deepens the gloom
Gleaming like stars through the high forest-boughs
Gladder they glow in the park's repose –

O Alexander! when I return,
Warm as those hearths my heart would burn,
Light as thine own, my foot would fall
If I might hear thy voice in the hall –

But thou art now on a desolate sea –
Parted from Gondal and parted from me –
All my repining is hopeless and vain,
20   Death never yields back his victims again –

24.

The organ swells the trumpets sound
The lamps in triumph glow
And none of all those thousands round
Regards who sleeps below

Those haughty eyes that tears should fill
Glance clearly cloudlessly
Those bounding breasts that grief should thrill
From thought of grief are free

His subjects and his soldiers there
10   They blessed his rising bloom
But none a single sigh can spare
To breathe above his tomb

Comrades in arms I've looked to mark
One shade of feeling swell
As your feet trod above the dark
Recesses of his cell

25.

A sudden chasm of ghastly light
Yawned in the city's reeling wall
And a long thundering through the night
Proclaimed our triumph – Tyrdarum's fall –

The shrieking wind sank mute and mild
The smothering snow-clouds rolled away
And cold – how cold! – wan moonlight smiled
Where those black ruins smouldering lay

'Twas over – all the Battle's madness
10   The bursting fires the cannons' roar
The yells, the groans the frenzied gladness
The death the danger warmed no more

In plundered churches piled with dead
The heavy charger neighed for food
The wounded soldier laid his head
'Neath roofless chambers splashed with blood

I could not sleep through that wild siege
My heart had fiercely burned and bounded
The outward tumult seemed to assuage
20   The inward tempest it surrounded

But . . . cannot bear
And silence whets the tang of pain
I felt the full flood of despair
Returning to my breast again

My couch lay in a ruined Hall
Whose windows looked on the minster-yard
Where chill chill whiteness covered all
Both stone and urn and withered sward

The shattered glass let in the air
30 And with it came a wandering moan
A sound unutterably drear
That made me shrink to be alone

One black yew-tree grew just below
I thought its boughs so sad might wail
Their ghostly fingers flecked with snow
Rattled against an old vault's rail

I listened – no 'twas life that still
Lingered in some deserted heart
O God what caused that shuddering thrill?
40 That anguished agonizing start?

An undefined an awful dream
A dream of what had been before
A memory whose blighting beam
Was flitting o'er me ever more

A frightful feeling frenzy born –
I hurried down the dark oak stair
I reached the door whose hinges torn
Flung streaks of moonshine here and there

I pondered not I drew the bar
50 An icy glory [caught] mine eye
From that wide heaven where every star
Glared like a dying memory

And there the great cathedral rose
Discrowned but most majestic so
It looked down in [serene] repose
On its own realm of buried woe

26.

The old church tower and garden wall
Are black with Autumn rain
And dreary winds foreboding call
The darkness down again

I watched how evening took the place
Of glad and glorious day
I watched a deeper gloom efface
The evening's lingering ray

And as I gazed on the cheerless sky
10   Sad thoughts rose in my mind

27. *Lines*

Far away is the land of rest
Thousand miles are stretched between
Many a mountain's stormy crest
Many a desert void of green

Wasted worn is the traveller
Dark his heart and dim his eye
Without hope or comforter
Faltering faint and ready to die

Often he looks to the ruthless sky
10   Often he looks o'er his dreary road
Often he wishes down to lie
And render up life's tiresome load

But yet faint not mournful man
Leagues on leagues are left behind
Since your sunless course began
Then go on to toil resigned

If you still despair control
Hush its whispers in your breas[t]
You shall reach the final goal
20 You shall win the land of rest

28.

Now trust a heart that trusts in you
And firmly say the word Adieu
Be sure wherever I may roam
My heart is with your heart at home

Unless there be no truth on earth
And vows meant true are nothing worth
And mortal man have no control
Over his own unhappy soul

Unless I change in every thought
10 And memory will restore me nought
And all I have of virtue die
Beneath far Gondal's Foreign sky

The mountain peasant loves the heath
Better than richest plains beneath
He would not give one moorland wild
For all the fields that ever smiled

And whiter brows than yours may be
And rosier cheeks my eyes may see
And lightning looks from orbs divine
20 About my pathway burn and shine

But that pure light changeless and strong
Cherished and watched and nursed so long
That love that first its glory gave
Shall be my pole star to the grave

29.

Sleep brings no joy to me
Remembrance never dies
My soul is given to misery
And lives in sighs

Sleep brings no rest to me
The shadows of the dead
My waking eyes may never see
Surround my bed

Sleep brings no hope to me
10   In soundest sleep they come
And with their doleful imagery
Deepen the gloom

Sleep brings no strength to me
No power renewed [to] brave
I only sail a wilder sea
A darker wave

Sleep brings no friend to me
To soothe and aid to bear
They all gaze on how scornfully
20   And I despair

Sleep brings no wish to knit
My harassed heart beneath
My only wish is to forget
In the sleep of death

30.

Strong I stand though I have borne
Anger hate and bitter scorn
Strong I stand and laugh to see
How mankind have fought with me

Shade of mast'ry I contemn
All the puny ways of men
Free my heart my spirit free
Beckon and I'll follow thee

False and foolish mortal know
10   If you scorn the world's disdain
Your mean soul is far below
Other worms however vain

Thing of Dust – with boundless pride
Dare you ask me for a guide
With the humble I will be
Haughty men are nought to me

31. "Spell bound"

The night is darkening round me
The wild winds coldly blow
But a tyrant spell has bound me
And I cannot cannot go

The giant trees are bending
Their bare boughs weighed with snow
And the storm is fast descending
And yet I cannot go

Clouds beyond clouds above me
10   Wastes beyond wastes below
But nothing drear can move me
I will not cannot go

I'll come when thou art saddest
Laid alone in the darkened room
When the mad day's mirth has vanished
And the smile of joy is banished
From evening's chilly gloom

I'll come when the heart's [real] feeling
Has entire unbiased sway
20   And my influence o'er thee stealing
Grief deepening joy congealing
Shall bear thy soul away

Listen 'tis just the hour
The awful time for thee
Dost thou not feel upon thy soul
A flood of strange sensations roll
Forerunners of a sterner power
Heralds of me

I would have touched the heavenly key
30   That spoke alike of bliss and thee
I would have woke the entrancing song
But its words died upon my tongue
And then I knew that hallowed strain
Could never speak of joy again
And then I felt

32. To a Wreath of Snow

O transient voyager of heaven!
O silent sign of winter skies!
What adverse wind thy sail has driven
To dungeons where a prisoner lies?

Methinks the hands that shut the sun
So sternly from this mourning brow
Might still their rebel task have done
And checked a thing so frail as thou

They would have done it had they known
10   The talisman that dwelt in thee,
For all the suns that ever shone
Have never been so kind to me!

For many a week, and many a day
My heart was weighed with sinking gloom
When morning rose in mourning grey
And faintly lit my prison room,

But angel like, when I awoke,
Thy silvery form so soft and fair
Shining through darkness, sweetly spoke
20   Of cloudy skies and mountains bare

The dearest to a mountaineer
Who, all life long has loved the snow
That crowned her native summits drear,
Better, than greenest plains below –

And voiceless, soulless messenger
Thy presence waked a thrilling tone
That comforts me while thou art here
And will sustain when thou art gone

33. *Song by Julius Angora*

Awake! awake! how loud the stormy morning
Calls up to life the nations resting round;
Arise, Arise, is it the voice of mourning
That breaks our slumber with so wild a sound?

The voice of mourning? Listen to its pealing;
That shout of triumph drowns the sigh of woe;
Each tortured heart forgets its wonted feeling,
Each faded cheek resumes its long-lost glow –

Our souls are full of gladness, God has given
10   Our arms to victory, our foes to death;
The crimson ensign waves its sheet in heaven –
The sea-green Standard lies in dust be[neath].

Patriots, no stain is on your country's glory
Soldiers, preserve that glory bright and free
Let Almedore in peace, and battle gory,
Be still a nobler name for victory!

34. *Lines*

I die but when the grave shall press
The heart so long endeared to thee
When earthly cares no more distress
And earthly joys are nought to me

Weep not, but think that I have past
Before thee o'er a sea of gloom
Have anchored safe and rest at last
Where tears and mourning cannot come

'Tis I should weep to leave thee he[re]
10   On that dark Ocean sailing drear
With storms around and fears before
And no kind light to point the shore

But long or short though life may be
'Tis nothing to eternity
We part below to meet on high
Where blissful ages never die

35.

O mother I am not regretting
To leave this wretched world below
If there be nothing but forgetting
In that dark land to which I go

Yet though 'tis wretched now to languish
Deceived and tired and hopeless here
No heart can quite repress the anguish
Of leaving things that once were dear

Twice twelve short years and all is over
10   And day and night to rise no more
And never more to be a rover
Along the fields the woods the shore

And never more at early dawning
To watch the stars of midnight wane
To breathe the breath of summer morning
And see its sunshine ne'er again

I hear the Abbey bells are ringing
Methinks their chime sound faint and drear
Or else the wind is adverse winging
20   And wafts its music from my ear

The wind the winter night is speaking
Of thoughts and things that should not stay
Mother come near my heart is breaking
I cannot bear to go away

And I *must* go whence no returning
To soothe your grief or calm your care
Nay do not weep that bitter mourning
Tortures my soul with wild despair

No tell me that when I am lying
30   In the old church beneath the stone
You'll dry your tears and check your sighing
And soon forget the spirit gone

You've asked me long to tell what sorrow
Has blanched my cheek and quenched my eye
And we shall sever ere tomorrow
So I'll confess before I die

Ten years ago in last September
Fernando left his home and you
And still I think you must remember
40   The anguish of that last adieu

And well you know how wildly pining
I longed to see his face again
Through all the Autumn's drear declining
Its stormy nights and days of rain

Down on the skirts of Areon's forest
There lies a lone and lovely glade
And there the hearts together nourished
Their first their fatal parting made

The afternoon in softened glory
50   So Bathed each green swell and waving tree
Beyond the broad park spread before me
Stretched far away the boundless sea

And there I stood when he had left me
With ashy cheek but tearless eye
Watching the ship whose sail bereft me
Of life and hope and peace and joy

It past that night I sought a pillow
Of sleepless woe and grieving lone
My soul still hovered o'er the billow
60   And mourned a love for ever flown

Yet smiling bright in recollection
One blissful hour returns to me
One letter told of firm affection
Of safe deliverance from the sea

But not another fearing hoping
Spring winter harvest glided o'er
And time at length brought power for coping
With thoughts I could not once endure

And I would seek in summer's evening
70   The place that saw our last farewell
And there a chain of visions weaving
I'd linger till the curfew bell

36.

Weaned from life and torn away
In the morning of thy day
Bound in everlasting gloom
Buried in a hopeless tomb

Yet upon thy bended knee
Thank the power banished thee
Chain and bar and dungeon wall
Saved thee from a deadlier thrall

Thank the power that made thee part
10   Ere that parting broke thy heart
Wildly rushed the mountain spring
From its source of fern and ling
How invincible its roar
Had its waters won the shore

37.

I'm happiest when most away
I can bear my soul from its home of clay
On a windy night when the moon is bright
And my eye can wander through worlds of light

When I am not and none beside
Nor earth nor sea nor cloudless sky
But only spirit wandering wide
Through infinite immensity

38.

Deep deep down in the silent grave
With none to mourn above

Here with my knee upon thy stone
I bid adieu to feelings gone
I leave with thee my tears and pain
And rush into the world again

O come again what chains withhold
The steps that used so fleet to be –
Come leave thy dwelling dark and cold
10   Once more to visit me

Was it with the fields of green
Blowing flower and budding tree
With the summer heaven serene
That thou didst visit me?

No 'twas not the flowery plain
No 'twas not the fragrant air
Summer skies will come again
But *thou* wilt not be there –

39.

How loud the storm sounds round the Hall!
From arch to arch from door to door
Pillar and roof and granite wall
Rock like a cradle in its roar

That Elm tree by the haunted well
Greets no returning summer skies
Down with a rush the giant fell
And stretched athwart the path it lies

Hardly had passed the funeral train
So long delayed by wind and snow
And how they'll reach the house again
Tomorrow's dawn perhaps will show

40.

What use is it to slumber here:
Though the heart be sad and weary?
What use is it to slumber here
Though the day rise dark and dreary

For that mist may break when the sun is high
And this soul forget its sorrow
And the rosy ray of the closing day
May promise a brighter morrow

41.

O evening why is thy light so sad?
Why is the sun's last ray so cold
Hush our smile is as ever glad
But thy heart is growing old

It's over now I've known it all
I'll hide it in my heart no more
But back again that night recall
And think the fearful vision o'er

10 The evening sun in cloudless shine
Had passed from summer's heaven divine
And dark the shades of twilight grew
And stars were in the depth of blue

And in the heath on mountains far
From human eye and human care
With thoughtful heart and tearful eye
I sadly watched that solemn sky

42.

The wide cathedral Aisles are lone
The vast crowds vanished every one
There can be nought beneath that dome
But the cold tenants of the tomb

O look again for still on high
The lamps are burning gloriously
And look again for still beneath
A thousand thousand live and breathe

All mute as death regard the shrine
10 That gleams in lustre so divine
Where Gondal's monarchs bending low
After the hush of silent prayer
Take in heaven's sight their awful vow
And never dying union swear
King Julius lifts his impious eye
From the dark marble to the sky
Blasts with that Oath his perjured soul
And changeless is his cheek the while
Though burning thoughts that spurn control
20 Kindle a short and bitter smile

As face to face the kinsmen stand
His false hand clasped in Gerald's hand

43.

O hinder me by no delay
My horse is weary of the way
And still his breast must stem the tide
Whose waves are foaming far and wide
Leagues off I heard their thundering roar
As fast they burst upon the shore
A stronger steed than mine might dread
To brave them in their boiling bed

Thus spoke the traveller but in vain
10 The stranger would not turn away
Still clung she to his bridle rein
And still entreated him to stay

44.

Darkness was overtraced on every face
Around clouded with storm and ominous gloom
In Hut or hall smiled out no resting place
There was no resting place but one – the tomb

All our hearts were the mansions of distress
And no one laughed and none seemed free from care
Our children felt their fathers' wretchedness
Our homes one all were shadowed with despair

It was not fear that made the land so sad

45.

Harp of wild and dream like strain
When I touch thy strings
Why dost thou repeat again
Long forgotten things?

Harp in other earlier days
I could sing to thee
And not one of all my lays
Vexed my memory

But now if I awake a note
10   That gave me joy before
Sounds of sorrow from thee float
Changing evermore

Yet still steeped in memory's dyes
They come sailing on
Darkening all my summer skies
Shutting out my sun

46. *Song to A. A.*

This shall be thy lullaby
Rocking on the stormy sea
Though it roar in thunder wild
Sleep stilly sleep my dark haired child

When our shuddering boat was crossing
Elderno lake so rudely tossing
Then 'twas first my nursling smiled
Sleep softly sleep my fair-browed child

Waves above thy cradle break
10   Foamy tears are on thy cheek
Yet the Ocean's self grows mild
When it bears my slumbering child

47.

Why do I hate that lone green dell?
Buried in moors and mountains wild
That is a spot I had loved too well
Had I but seen it when a child

There are bones whitening there in the summer's heat
But it is not for that and none can tell
None but one can the secret repeat
Why I hate that lone green dell

Noble foe I pardon thee
10   All thy cold and scornful pride
For thou wast a priceless friend to me
When my sad heart had none beside

And leaning on thy generous arm
A breath of old times over me came
The earth shone round with a long lost charm
Alas I forgot I was not the same

Before a day – an hour passed by
My spirit knew itself once more
I saw the gilded vapours fly
20   And leave me as I was before

48. *A. G. A. to A. S.*

O wander not so far away!
O love, forgive this selfish tear.
It may be sad for thee to stay
But how can I live lonely here?

The still May morn is warm and bright
Young flowers look fresh and grass is green
And in the haze of glorious light
Our long low hills are scarcely seen –

The woods – even now their small leaves hide
10   The blackbird and the stockdove well
And high in heaven so blue and wide
A thousand strains of music swell –

He looks on all with eyes that speak
So deep, so drear a woe to me!
There is a faint red on his cheek
Not like the bloom I used to see.

Can Death – yes, Death, he is thine own!
The grave must close those limbs around
And hush, for ever hush the tone
20   I loved above all earthly sound.

Well, pass away with the other flowers
Too dark for them, too dark for thee
Are the hours to come, the joyless hours
That Time is treasuring up for me.

If thou hast sinned in this world of care
'Twas but the dust of thy drear abode –
Thy soul was pure when it entered here
And pure it will go again to God –

49. *Gleneden's Dream*

Tell me, watcher, is it winter?
Say how long my sleep has been?
Have the woods I left so lovely,
Lost their robes of tender green?

Is the morning slow in coming?
Is the nighttime loath to go?
Tell me, are the dreary mountains
Drearier still with drifted snow?

10   'Captive, since thou sawest the forest
      All its leaves have died away
      And another March has woven
      Garlands for another May –

      'Ice has barred the Arctic water,
      Soft south winds have set it free
      And once more to deep green valley
      Golden flowers might welcome thee' –

      Watcher, in this lonely prison,
      Shut from joy and kindly air
      Heaven, descending in a vision
20   Taught my soul to do and bear –

      It was night, a night of winter;
      I lay on the dungeon floor,
      And all other sounds were silent –
      All, except the river's roar –

      Over Death, and Desolation,
      Fireless hearths, and lifeless homes
      Over orphans' heart-sick sorrows,
      Over fathers' bloody tombs;

      Over friends that my arms never
30   Might embrace, in love again –
      Memory pondered until madness
      Struck its poignard in my brain –

      Deepest slumber followed raving
      Yet, methought, I brooded still
      Still I saw my country bleeding
      Dying for a Tyrant's will –

      Not because *my* bliss was blasted
      Burned within, the avenging flame –
      Not because my scattered kindred
40   Died in woe, or lived in shame

God doth know, I would have given
Every bosom dear to me
Could that sacrifice have purchased
Tortured Gondal's liberty!

But, that at Ambition's bidding
All her cherished hopes should wane;
That her noblest sons should muster,
Strive, and fight and fall in vain –

Hut and castle, hall and cottage,
50   Roofless, crumbling to the ground –
Mighty Heaven, a glad Avenger
Thy eternal justice found!

Yes, the arm that once would shudder
Even to pierce a wounded deer,
I beheld it, unrelenting,
Choke in blood its sovereign's prayer –

Glorious dream! I saw the city
Blazing in imperial shine;
And among adoring thousands
60   Stood a man of form divine –

None need point the princely victim
Now he smiles with royal pride!
Now his glance is bright as lightning:
Now – the knife is in his side!

Ha, I saw how Death could darken –
Darken that triumphant eye!
His red heart's blood drenched my dagger;
My ear drank his dying sigh!

Shadows come! What means this midnight?
70   O my God, I know it all!
Know the fever-dream is over;
Unavenged the Avengers fall!

50.

None of my kindred now can tell
The features once beloved so well
Those dark brown locks that used to deck
A snowy brow in ringlets small
Now wildly shade my sunburnt neck
And streaming down my shoulders fall

The pure bright red of noble birth
Has deepened to a gipsy glow
And care has quenched the smile of mirth
10   And tuned my heart to welcome woe

Yet you must know in infancy
Full many an eye watched over me
Sweet voices to my slumber sung
My downy couch with silk was hung

And music soothed me when I cried
And when I laughed they all replied
And 'rosy Blanche' how oft was heard
In hall and bower that well-known word

Through gathering summers still caress'd
20   In kingly courts a favourite guest
A Monarch's hand would pour for me
The richest gifts of royalty

But clouds will come too soon they came
For not through age and not through crime
Is Blanche a now forgotten name
True heart and brow unmarked by time
These treasured blessings still are mine

51.

'Twas one of those dark cloudy days
That sometimes come in summer's blaze
When heaven drops not when earth is still
And deeper green is on the hill

52.

Lonely at her window sitting
While the evening stole away
Fitful winds foreboding flitting
Through a sky of cloudy grey

53.

There are two trees in a lonely field
They breathe a spell to me
A dreary thought their dark boughs yield
All waving solemnly

54.

What is that smoke that ever still
Comes rolling down that dark brown hill

55.

Still as she looked the iron clouds
Would part and sunlight shone between
But drearily strange and pale and cold

56.

Away away resign me now
To scenes of gloom and thoughts of fear
I trace the signal on thy brow
Welcome at last though once so drear

57.

It will not shine again
Its sad course is done
I have seen the last ray wane
Of the cold bright sun

58.

None but one beheld him dying
Parting with the parting day
Winds of evening sadly sighing
Bore his soul from earth away

59.

Coldly bleakly drearily
Evening died on Elbë's shore
Winds were in the cloudy sky
Sighing mourning ever more

60.

Old Hall of [Elbë] ruined lonely now
House to which the voice of life shall never more return
Chambers roofless desolate where weeds and ivy grow
Windows through whose broken arches the night winds
    sadly mourn
Home of the departed the long departed dead

61. *Douglas's Ride*

Well, narrower draw the circle round
And hush that organ's solemn sound
And quench the lamp and stir the fire
To rouse its flickering radiance higher;
Loop up the window's velvet veil
That we may hear the night-wind wail –
For wild those gusts and well their chimes
Blend with a song of troubled times –

Song

What rider up Gobelrin's glen
10   Has spurred his straining steed,
And fast and far from living men
Has pressed with maddening speed?

I saw his hoof-prints mark the rock
When swift he left the plain
I heard deep down, the echoing shock
Re-echo back again.

From cliff to cliff, through rock and heath
That coal-black courser bounds;
Nor heeds the river pent beneath,
20   Nor marks how fierce it sounds.

With streaming hair and forehead bare
And mantle waving wide
His master rides; the eagles there
Soar up on every side:

The goats fly by with timid cry
Their realm so rashly won:
They pause – he still ascends on high
They gaze, but he is gone.

O gallant horse hold on thy course!
30   The road is tracked behind –
Spur, rider, spur, or vain thy force
Death comes on every wind.

Roared thunder loud from that pitchy cloud?
[From] it the torrents flow?
Or woke the breeze in the swaying trees
That frown so dark below?

He breathes at last, when the valley is past;
He rests on the grey rock's brow.
What ails thee steed? At thy master's need,
40   Wilt thou prove faithless now?

No, hardly checked, with ears erect,
The charger champed his rein,
Ere his quivering limbs, all foam-beflecked,
Were off like light again.

Hark through the pass, with threatening crash
Comes on the increasing roar!
But what shall brave the deep, deep wave?
The deadly path before?

Their feet are dyed in a darker tide
50   Who dare those dangers drear –
Their breasts have burst through the battle's worst
And why should they tremble here?

Strong hearts they bear and arms as good
To conquer or to fall
They dash into the boiling flood,
They gain the rock's steep wall –

'Now my bold men this one pass more
This narrow chasm of stone
And Douglas – for our sovereign's gore
60   Shall yield us back his own' –

I hear their ever nearing tread
Sound through the granite glen,
There is a tall pine overhead
Laid by the mountain men

That dizzy bridge which no horse could track
Has checked the outlaw's way;
There like a wild beast he turns back
And grimly stands at bay.

Why smiles he so when far below
70   He sees the toiling chase?
The ponderous tree sways heavily
And totters from its place –

They raise their eyes for the sunny skies
Are lost in sudden shade,
But Douglas neither shrinks nor flies –
He need not fly the dead –

62.

For him who struck thy foreign string
I ween this heart hath ceased to care
Then why dost thou such feelings bring
To my sad spirit, old guitar?

It is as if the warm sunlight
In some deep glen should lingering stay
When clouds of tempest and of night
Had wrapped the parent orb away –

It is as if the glassy brook
Should image still its willows fair
Though years ago the woodman's stroke
Laid low in dust their gleaming hair:

Even so, guitar, thy magic tone
Hath moved the tear and waked the sigh
Hath bid the ancient torrent flow
Although its very source is dry!

63.

In dungeons dark I cannot sing
In sorrow's thrall 'tis hard to smile
What bird can soar with broken wing
What heart can bleed and joy the while

64.

The evening sun was sinking down
On low green hills and clustered trees
It was a scene as fair and lone
As ever felt the soothing breeze

That bends the grass when day is gone
And gives the wave a brighter blue
And makes the soft white clouds sail on
Like spirits of ethereal dew

10   Which all the morn had hovered o'er
The azure flowers where they were nursed
And now return to heaven once more
Where their bright glories shone at first

65.

Fall leaves fall die flowers away
Lengthen night and shorten day
Every leaf speaks bliss to me
Fluttering from the autumn tree
I shall smile when wreaths of snow
Blossom where the rose should grow
I shall sing when night's decay
Ushers in a drearier day

66. *Song by Julius Brenzaida*

Geraldine, the moon is shining
With so soft, so bright a ray,
Seems it not that eve, declining
Ushered in a fairer day?

While the wind is whispering only,
Far – across the water borne
Let us, in this silence lonely
Sit beneath the ancient thorn –

Wild the road, and rough and dreary;
10   Barren all the moorland round;
Rude the couch that rests us weary;
Mossy stone and heathy ground –

But when winter storms were meeting
In the moonless midnight dome
Did we heed the tempest's beating
Howling round our spirits' home?

No, that tree, with branches riven
Whitening in the whirl of snow,
As it tossed against the heaven,
20   Sheltered happy hearts below –

And at Autumn's mild returning
Shall our feet forget the way?
And in Cynthia's silver morning,
Geraldine, wilt thou delay?

67. *Song by J. Brenzaida to G. S.*

I knew not 'twas so dire a crime
To say the word, Adieu:
But this shall be the only time
My slighted heart shall sue.

The wild moorside, the winter morn,
The gnarled and ancient tree –
If in your breast they waken scorn
Shall wake the same in me.

I can forget black eyes and brows
10   And lips of rosy charm
If you forget the sacred vows
Those faithless lips could form –

If hard commands can tame your love,
Or prison walls can hold
I would not wish to grieve above
A thing so false and cold –

And there are bosoms bound to mine
With links both tried and strong;
And there are eyes whose lightning shine
20 Has warmed and blessed me long:

Those eyes shall make my only day,
Shall set my spirit free
And chase the foolish thoughts away
That mourn your memory!

68.

Where were ye all? and where wert thou
I saw an eye that shone like thine
But dark curls waved around his brow
And his stern glance was strange to mine

And yet a dreamlike comfort came
Into my heart and anxious eye
And trembling yet to hear his name
I bent to listen watchfully

His voice though never heard before
10 Still spoke to me of years gone by
It seemed a vision to restore
That brought the hot tears to my eye

69.

I paused on the threshold I turned to the sky
I looked on the heaven and the dark mountains round
The full moon sailed bright through that Ocean on high
And the wind murmured past with a wild eerie sound

And I entered the walls of my dark prison-house
Mysterious it rose from the billowy moor

70.

O come with me thus ran the song
The moon is bright in Autumn's sky
And thou hast toiled and laboured long
With aching head and weary eye

71. *F. De Samara to A. G. A.*

Light up thy halls! 'Tis closing day;
I'm drear and lone and far away –
Cold blows on my breast, the north wind's bitter sigh
And oh, my couch is bleak beneath the rainy sky!

Light up thy halls – and think not of me;
That face is absent now, thou hast hated so to see –
Bright be thine eyes, undimmed their dazzling shine,
For never, never more shall they encounter mine!

The desert moor is dark; there is tempest in the air;
10 I have breathed my only wish in one last, one burning prayer –
A prayer that would come forth although it lingered long;
That set on fire my heart, but froze upon my tongue –

And now, it shall be done before the morning rise;
I will not watch the sun ascend in yonder skies.
One task alone remains – thy pictured face to view
And then I go to prove if God, at least, be true!

Do I not see thee now? Thy black resplendent hair;
Thy glory-beaming brow, and smile how heavenly fair!
Thine eyes are turned away – those eyes I would not see;
20   Their dark, their deadly ray would more than madden me

There, go, Deceiver, go! My hand is streaming wet,
My heart's blood flows to buy the blessing – To forget!
Oh could that lost heart give back, back again to thine
One tenth part of the pain that clouds my dark decline!

Oh could I see thy lids weighed down in cheerless woe;
Too full to hide their tears, too stern to overflow;
Oh could I know thy soul with equal grief was torn
This fate might be endured – this anguish might be borne!

How gloomy grows the Night! 'Tis Gondal's wind that
     blows
30   I shall not tread again the deep glens where it rose –
I feel it on my face – Where, wild blast, dost thou roam?
What do we, wanderer, here, so far away from home?

I do not need thy breath to cool my death-cold brow
But go to that far land, where she is shining now;
Tell Her my latest wish, tell Her my dreary doom;
Say, that *my* pangs are past, but Hers are yet to come –

Vain words – vain, frenzied thoughts! No ear can hear me
     call –
Lost in the vacant air my frantic curses fall
And could she see me now, perchance her lip would smile
40   Would smile in careless pride and utter scorn the while!

And yet, for all her hate, each parting glance would tell
A stronger passion breathed, burned in this last farewell –
Unconquered in my soul the Tyrant rules me still –
Life bows to my control, but, *Love* I cannot kill!

72.

When days of Beauty deck the earth
Or stormy nights descend
How well my spirit knows the path
On which it ought to wend

It seeks the consecrated spot
Beloved in childhood's years
The space between is all forgot
Its sufferings and its tears

73.

Still beside that dreary water
Stood he 'neath the cold moon ray
Thinking on the deed of slaughter
On his heart that darkly lay

Soft the voice that broke his dreaming
Stealing through the silent air
Yet before the raven's screaming
He had heard regardless there

Once his name was sweetly uttered
10   Then the echo died away
But each pulse in horror uttered
As the life would pass away

74.

There swept adown that dreary glen
A wilder sound than mountain wind
The thrilling shouts of fighting men
With something sadder far behind

The thrilling shouts they died away
Before the night came greyly down
But closed not with the closing day
The choking sob the tortured moan

Down in a hollow sunk in shade
10 Where dark heath waved in secret gloom
A weary bleeding form was laid
Waiting the death that was to come

75.

O Dream, where art thou now?
Long years have past away
Since last, from off thine angel brow
I saw the light decay –

Alas, alas for me
Thou wert so bright and fair,
I could not think thy memory
Would yield me nought but care!

The sun-beam and the storm,
10 The summer-eve divine,
The silent night of solemn calm,
The full moon's cloudless shine

Were once entwined with thee
But now, with weary pain –
Lost vision! 'tis enough for me –
Thou canst not shine again –

76.

Loud without the wind was roaring
    Through the waned Autumnal sky,
Drenching wet, the cold rain pouring
    Spoke of stormy winters nigh.

    All too like that dreary eve
    Sighed within repining grief –
    Sighed at first – but sighed not long
    Sweet – How softly sweet it came!
    Wild words of an ancient song –
10   Undefined, without a name –

'It was spring, for the skylark was singing.'
Those words they awakened a spell –
They unlocked a deep fountain whose springing
Nor Absence nor Distance can quell.

In the gloom of a cloudy November
They uttered the music of May –
They kindled the perishing ember
Into fervour that could not decay

Awaken on all my dear moorlands
20 The wind in its glory and pride!
O call me from valleys and highlands
To walk by the hill-river's side!

It is swelled with the first snowy weather;
The rocks they are icy and hoar
And darker waves round the long heather
And the fern-leaves are sunny no more

There are no yellow-stars on the mountain,
The blue bells have long died away
From the brink of the moss-bedded fountain,
30 From the side of the wintery brae –

But lovelier than corn-fields all waving
In emerald and scarlet and gold
Are the slopes where the north-wind is raving
And the glens where I wandered of old –

'It was morning; the bright sun was beaming.'
How sweetly that brought back to me
The time when nor labour nor dreaming
Broke the sleep of the happy and free

But blithely we rose as the dusk heaven
40   Was melting to amber and blue –
And swift were the wings to our feet given
While we traversed the meadows of dew.

For the moors, for the moors where the short grass
Like velvet beneath us should lie!
For the moors, for the moors where each high pass
Rose sunny against the clear sky!

For the moors, where the linnet was trilling
Its song on the old granite stone –
Where the lark – the wild skylark was filling
50   Every breast with delight like its own.

What language can utter the feeling
That rose when, in exile afar,
On the brow of a lonely hill kneeling
I saw the brown heath growing there.

It was scattered and stunted, and told me
That soon even that would be gone
It whispered, 'The grim walls enfold me
I have bloomed in my last summer's sun'

But not the loved music whose waking
60   Makes the soul of the Swiss die away
Has a spell more adored and heart-breaking
Than in its half-blighted bells lay –

The spirit that bent 'neath its power
How it longed, how it burned to be free!
If I could have wept in that hour
Those tears had been heaven to me –

Well, well the sad minutes are moving
Though loaded with trouble and pain –
And sometime the loved and the loving
70   Shall meet on the mountains again –

77.

A little while, a little while
The noisy crowd are barred away;
And I can sing and I can smile
A little while I've holiday!

Where wilt thou go my harassed heart?
Full many a land invites thee now;
And places near, and far apart
Have rest for thee, my weary brow –

There is a spot 'mid barren hills
10   Where winter howls and driving rain
But if the dreary tempest chills
There is a light that warms again

The house is old, the trees are bare
And moonless bends the misty dome
But what on earth is half so dear –
So longed for as the hearth of home?

The mute bird sitting on the stone,
The dank moss dripping from the wall,
The garden-walk with weeds o'ergrown
20   I love them – how I love them all!

Shall I go there? or shall I seek
Another clime, another sky.
Where tongues familiar music speak
In accents dear to memory?

Yes, as I mused, the naked room,
The flickering firelight died away
And from the midst of cheerless gloom
I passed to bright, unclouded day –

A little and a lone green lane
30   That opened on a common wide
A distant, dreamy, dim blue chain
Of mountains circling every side –

A heaven so clear, an earth so calm,
So sweet, so soft, so hushed an air
And, deepening still the dreamlike charm,
Wild moor-sheep feeding everywhere –

That was the scene – I knew it well
I knew the pathways far and near
That winding o'er each billowy swell
40   Marked out the tracks of wandering deer

Could I have lingered but an hour
It well had paid a week of toil
But truth has banished fancy's power
I hear my dungeon bars recoil –

Even as I stood with raptured eye
Absorbed in bliss so deep and dear
My hour of rest had fleeted by
And given me back to weary care –

78.

How still, how happy! those are words
That once would scarce agree together
I loved the plashing of the surge –
The changing heaven the breezy weather,

More than smooth seas and cloudless skies
And solemn, soothing, softened airs
That in the forest woke no sighs
And from the green spray shook no tears

How still, how happy! now I feel
10   Where silence dwells is sweeter far
Than laughing mirth's most joyous swell
However pure its raptures are

Come sit down on this sunny stone
'Tis wintery light o'er flowerless moors –
But sit – for we are all alone
And clear expand heaven's breathless shores

I could think in the withered grass
Spring's budding wreaths we might discern
The violet's eye might shyly flash
20   And young leaves shoot among the fern

It is but thought – full many a night
The snow shall clothe those hills afar
And storms shall add a drearier blight
And winds shall wage a wilder war

Before the lark may herald in
Fresh foliage twined with blossoms fair
And summer days again begin
Their glory-haloed crown to wear

Yet my heart loves December's smile
30   As much as July's golden beam
Then let us sit and watch the while
The blue ice curdling on the stream –

79.

The blue bell is the sweetest flower
That waves in summer air
Its blossoms have the mightiest power
To soothe my spirit's care

There is a spell in purple heath
Too wildly, sadly drear
The violet has a fragrant breath
But fragrance will not cheer

The trees are bare, the sun is cold
10 And seldom, seldom seen –
The heavens have lost their zone of gold
The earth its robe of green

And ice upon the glancing stream
Has cast its sombre shade
And distant hills and valleys seem
In frozen mist arrayed –

The blue bell cannot charm me now
The heath has lost its bloom
The violets in the glen below
20 They yield no sweet perfume

But though I mourn the heather-bell
'Tis better far, away
I know how fast my tears would swell
To see it smile today

And that wood flower that hides so shy
Beneath the mossy stone
Its balmy scent and dewy eye
'Tis not for them I moan

It is the slight and stately stem
30 The blossom's silvery blue
The buds hid like a sapphire gem
In sheaths of emerald hue

'Tis these that breathe upon my heart
A calm and softening spell
That if it makes the tear-drop start
Has power to soothe as well

For these I weep, so long divided
Through winter's dreary day
In longing weep – but most when guided
40   On withered banks to stray

If chilly then the light should fall
Adown the dreary sky
And gild the dank and darkened wall
With transient brilliancy

How do I yearn, how do I pine
For the time of flowers to come
And turn me from that fading shine
To mourn the fields of home –

80.

The night was dark yet winter breathed
With softened sighs on Gondal's shore
And though its wind repining grieved
It chained the snow swollen streams no more

How deep into the wilderness
My horse had strayed, I cannot say
But neither morsel nor caress
Would urge him farther on the way

So loosening from his neck the rein
10   I set my worn companion free
And billowy hill and boundless plain
Full soon divided him from me

The sullen clouds lay all unbroken
And blackening round the horizon drear
But still they gave no certain token
Of heavy rain or tempests near

I paused confounded and distressed
Down in the heath my limbs I threw
Yet wilder as I longed for rest
20 More wakeful heart and eyelids grew

It was about the middle night
And under such a starless dome
When gliding from the mountain's height
I saw a shadowy spirit come

Her wavy hair on her shoulders bare
It shone like soft clouds round the moon
Her noiseless feet like melting sleet
Gleamed white a moment then were gone

'What seek you now on this bleak moor's brow
30 Where wanders that form from heaven descending?'
It was thus I said as her graceful head
The spirit above my couch was bending

'This is my home where whirlwinds blow
Where snowdrifts round my path are swelling
'Tis many a year 'tis long ago
Since I beheld another dwelling

'When thick and fast the smothering blast
O'erwhelmed the hunter on the plain
If my cheek grew pale in its loudest gale
40 May I never tread the hills again

'The shepherd had died on the mountainside
But my ready aid was near him then
I led him back o'er the hidden track
And gave him to his native glen

'When tempests roar on the lonely shore
I light my beacon with sea-weeds dry
And it flings its fire through the darkness dire
And gladdens the sailor's hopeless eye

'And the scattered sheep I love to keep
50   Their timid forms to guard from harm
I have a spell and they know it well
And I save them with a powerful charm

'Thy own good steed on his friendless bed
A few hours since you left to die
But I knelt by his side and the saddle untied
And life returned to his glazing eye

'And deem thou not that quite forgot
My mercy will forsake me now
I bring thee care and not Despair
60   Abasement but not overthrow

'To a silent home thy foot may come
And years may follow of toilsome pain
But yet I swear by that Burning Tear
The loved shall meet on its hearth again'

81.

From our evening fireside now,
Merry laugh and cheerful tone,
Smiling eye and cloudless brow,
Mirth and music all are flown:

Yet the grass before the door
Grows as green in April rain;
And as blithely as of yore
Larks have poured their day-long strain.

Is it fear, or is it sorrow
10   Checks the stagnant stream of joy?
Do we tremble that tomorrow
May our present peace destroy?

For past misery are we weeping?
What is past can hurt no more;
And the gracious heavens are keeping
Aid for that which lies before –

One is absent, and for one
Cheerless, chill is our hearthstone –
One is absent, and for him
20   Cheeks are pale and eyes are dim –

Arthur, brother, Gondal's shore
Rested from the battle's roar –
Arthur, brother, we returned
Back to Desmond lost and mourned:

Thou didst purchase by thy fall
Home for us and peace for all;
Yet, how darkly dawned that day –
Dreadful was the price to pay!

Just as once, through sun and mist
30   I have climbed the mountain's breast
Still my gun with certain aim
Brought to earth the fluttering game:

But the very dogs repined,
Though I called with whistle shrill
Listlessly they lagged behind,
Looking backward o'er the hill –

Sorrow was not vocal there:
Mute their pain and my despair
But the joy of life was flown
40   He was gone, and we were lone –

So it is by morn and eve –
So it is in field and hall –
For the absent one we grieve,
One being absent saddens All –

82. *Song*

King Julius left the south country
His banners all bravely flying
His followers went out with Jubilee
But they shall return with sighing

Loud arose the triumphal hymn
The drums were loudly rolling
Yet you might have heard in distance dim
How a passing bell was tolling

The sword so bright from battles won
10 With unseen rust is fretting
The evening comes before the noon
The scarce risen sun is setting

While princes hang upon his breath
And nations round are fearing
Close by his side a daggered Death
With sheathless point stands sneering

That death he took a certain aim
For Death is stony-hearted
And in the zenith of his fame
20 Both power and life departed –

83. *Lines*

The soft unclouded blue of air
The earth as golden-green and fair
And bright as Eden's used to be
That air and earth have rested me

Laid on the grass I lapsed away
Sank back again to childhood's day
All harsh thoughts perished memory mild
Subdued both grief and passion wild

But did the sunshine even now
10 That bathed his stern and swarthy brow
Oh did it wake I long to know
One whisper one sweet dream in hi[m]
One lingering joy that years ago
Had faded – lost in distance di[m]
That iron man was born like me
And he was once an ardent boy
He must have felt in infancy
The glory of a summer sky

Though storms untold his mind have tossed
20 He cannot utterly have lost
Remembrance of his early home
So lost that not a gleam may come

No vision of his mother's face
When she so fondly would set free
Her darling child from her embrace
To roam till eve at liberty –

Nor of his haunts nor of the flowers
His tiny hand would grateful bear
Returning from the darkening bowers
30 To weave into her glossy hair

I saw the light breeze kiss his cheek
His fingers 'mid the roses twined
I watched to mark one transient streak
Of pensive softness shade his mind

The open window showed around
A glowing park and glorious sky
And thick woods swelling with the sound
Of Nature's mingled harmony

Silent he sat. That stormy breast
40 At length, I said has deigned to rest
At length above that spirit flows
The waveless ocean of repose

Let me draw near 'twill soothe to view
His dark eyes dimmed with holy dew
Remorse even now may wake within
And half unchain his soul from sin

Perhaps this is the destined hour
When hell shall lose its fatal power
And heaven itself shall bend above
50 To hail the soul redeemed by love

Unmarked I gazed my idle thought
Passed with the ray whose shine it caught
One glance revealed how little care
He felt for all the beauty there

Oh crime can make the heart grow old
Sooner than years of wearing woe
Can turn the warmest bosom cold
As winter wind or polar snow

84. *To the Blue Bell*

Sacred watcher, wave thy bells!
Fair hill flower and woodland child!
Dear to me in deep green dells –
Dearest on the mountains wild –

Blue bell, even as all divine
I have seen my darling shine –
Blue bell, even as wan and frail
I have seen my darling fail –
Thou hast found a voice for me –
And soothing words are breathed by thee –

Thus they murmur, 'Summer's sun
Warms me till my life is done –
Would I rather choose to die
Under winter's ruthless sky?

'Glad I bloom and calm I fade
Weeping twilight dews my bed
Mourner, mourner dry thy tears.
Sorrow comes with lengthened years!'

85.

I am the only being whose doom
No tongue would ask no eye would mourn
I never caused a thought of gloom
A smile of joy since I was born

In secret pleasure – secret tears
This changeful life has slipped away
As friendless after eighteen years
As lone as on my natal day

There have been times I cannot hide
10   There have been times when this was drear
When my sad soul forgot its pride
And longed for one to love me here

But those were in the early glow
Of feelings not subdued by care
And they have died so long ago
I hardly now believe they were

First melted off the hope of youth
Then Fancy's rainbow fast withdrew
And then experience told me truth
20   In mortal bosoms never grew

'Twas grief enough to think mankind
All hollow servile insincere –
But worse to trust to my own mind
And find the same corruption there

86.

May flowers are opening
And leaves unfolding free
There are bees in every blossom
And birds on every tree

The sun is gladly shining
The stream sings merrily
And I only am pining
And all is dark to me

O – cold cold is my heart
10   It will not cannot rise
It feels no sympathy
With those refulgent skies

Dead dead is my joy
I long to be at rest
I wish the damp earth covered
This desolate breast

If I were quite alone
It might not be so drear
When all hope was gone
20 At least I could not fear

But the glad eyes around me
Must weep as mine have done
And I must see the same gloom
Eclipse their morning sun

If heaven would rain on me
That future storm of care
So their fond hearts were free
I'd be content to bear

Alas as lightning withers
30 The young and aged tree
Both they and I shall fall beneath
The fate we cannot flee

87. *Lines by Claudia*

I did not sleep 'twas noon of day
I saw the burning sunshine fall
The long grass bending where I lay
The blue sky brooding over all

I heard the mellow hum of bees
And singing birds and sighing trees
And far away in woody dell
The Music of the Sabbath bell

I did not dream remembrance still
10   Clasped round my heart its fetters chill
But I am sure the soul is free
To leave its clay a little while
Or how in exile misery
Could I have seen my country smile

In English fields my limbs were laid
With English turf beneath my head
My spirit wandered o'er that shor[e]
Where nought but it may wander more

Yet if the soul can thus return
20   I need not and I will not mourn
And vainly did you drive me far
With leagues of ocean stretched between
My mortal flesh you might debar
But not the eternal fire within

My Monarch died to rule forever
A heart that can forget him never
And dear to me aye doubly dear
Thought shut within the silent tomb
His name shall be for whom I bear
30   This long sustained and hopeless doom

And brighter in the hour of woe
Than in the blaze of victory's pride
That glory shedding star shall glow
For which we fought and bled and died

88.

I know not how it falls on me
This summer evening, hushed and lone
Yet the faint wind comes soothingly
With something of an olden tone

Forgive me if I've shunned so long
Your gentle greeting earth and air
But sorrow withers even the strong
And who can fight against despair

89. *Written on Returning to the P. of I. on the 10th of January 1827*

The busy day has hurried by
And hearts greet kindred hearts once more
And swift the evening hours should fly
But what turns every gleaming eye
So often to the door?

And then so quick away – and why
Does sudden silence chill the room?
And laughter sink into a sigh –
And merry words to whispers die –
10   And gladness change to gloom?

O we are listening for a sound
We know shall ne'er be heard again
Sweet voices in the halls resound;
Fair forms, fond faces gather round
But all in vain – in vain!

Their feet shall never waken more
The echoes in these galleries wide,
Nor dare the snow on the mountain's brow,
Nor skim the river's frozen flow,
20   Nor wander down its side –

They who have been our life – our soul –
Through summer-youth, from childhood's spring –
Who bound us in one vigorous whole
To stand 'gainst Tyranny's control
For ever triumphing –

Who bore the brunt of battle's fray
The first to fight, the last to fall
Whose mighty minds – with kindred ray
Still led the van in Glory's way –
30   The idol chiefs of all –

They, they are gone! not for a while
As golden suns at night decline
And even in death our grief beguile
Foretelling, with a rose-red smile
How bright the morn will shine –

No these dark towers are lone and lorn;
This very crowd is vacancy;
And we must watch and wait and mourn
And half look out for their return;
40   And think their forms we see –

And fancy music in our ear
Such as their lips could only pour
And think we feel their presence near
And start to find they are not here
And never shall be more!

90.

Month after month year after year
My harp has poured a dreary strain –
At length a livelier note shall cheer
And pleasure tune its chords again

What though the stars and fair moonlight
Are quenched in morning dull and grey
They were but tokens of the night
And *this* my soul is day

91.

And now the house dog stretched once more
His limbs upon the glowing floor
The children half resumed their play
Though from the warm hearth scared away
The goodwife left her spinning wheel
And spread with smiles the evening meal
The Shepherd placed a seat and pressed
To their poor fare his unknown guest
And he unclasped his mantle now
10 And raised the covering from his brow
Said 'Voyagers by land and sea
Were seldom feasted daintily'
And checked his host by adding stern
He'd no refinement to unlearn
A silence settled on the room
The cheerful welcome sank to gloom
But not those words though cold and high
So froze their hospitable joy
No – there was something in his face
20 Some nameless thing they could not trace
And something in his voice's tone
Which turned their blood as chill as stone
The ringlets of his long black hair
Fell o'er a cheek most ghastly fair
Youthful he seemed – but worn as they
Who spend too soon their youthful day
When his glance drooped 'twas hard to quell
Unbidden feelings sudden swell
And pity scarce her tears could hide
30 So sweet that brow with all its pride
But when upraised his eye would dart
An icy shudder through the heart
Compassion changed to horror then
And fear to meet that gaze again
It was not hatred's tiger glare
Nor the wild anguish of despair

It was not useless misery
Which mocks at friendship's sympathy
No – lightning all unearthly shone
40 Deep in that dark eye's circling zone
Such withering lightning as we deem
None but a spectre's look may beam
And glad they were when he turned away
And wrapped him in his mantle grey
Leant down his head upon his arm
And veiled from view their basilisk charm

92. *A Farewell to Alexandria*

I've seen this dell in July's shine
As lovely as an angel's dream;
Above, heaven's depth of blue divine;
Around, the evening's golden beam –

I've seen the purple heather-bell
Look out by many a storm-worn stone
And oh, I've known such music swell,
Such wild notes wake these passes lone –

So soft, yet so intensely felt,
10 So low, yet so distinctly heard,
My breath would pause, my eyes would melt
And my tears dew the green heath-sward –

I'd linger here a summer day
Nor care how fast the hours flew by
Nor mark the sun's departing ray
Smile sadly glorious from the sky –

Then, then I might have laid thee down
And deemed thy sleep would gentle be
I might have left thee, darling one
20 And thought thy God was guarding thee!

But now, there is no wandering glow
No gleam to say that God is nigh:
And coldly spreads thy couch of snow
And harshly sounds thy lullaby.

Forests of heather dark and long
Wave their brown branching arms above
And they must soothe thee with their song
And they must shield my child of love!

Alas the flakes are heavily falling
30 They cover fast each guardian crest;
And chilly white their shroud is palling
Thy frozen limbs and freezing breast

Wakes up the storm more madly wild
The mountain drifts are tossed on high –
Farewell unblessed, unfriended child,
I cannot bear to watch thee die!

93.

Come hither child – who gifted thee
With power to touch that string so well?
How daredst thou rouse up thoughts in me
Thoughts that I would – but cannot quell?

Nay chide not lady long ago
I heard those notes in Ula's hall
And had I known they'd waken woe
I'd weep their music to recall

But thus it was one festal night
10 When I was hardly six years old
I stole away from crowds and light
And sought a chamber dark and cold

I had no one to love me there
I knew no comrade and no friend
And so I went to sorrow where
Heaven only heaven saw me bend

Loud blew the wind 'twas sad to stay
From all that splendour barred away
I imaged in the lonely room
20   A thousand forms of fearful gloom

And with my wet eyes raised on high
I prayed to God that I might die
Suddenly in that silence drear
A sound of music reached my ear

And then a note I hear it yet
So full of soul so deeply sweet
I thought that Gabriel's self had come
To take me to my father's home

Three times it rose that seraph-strain
30   Then died nor lived ever again
But still the words and still the tone
Swell round my heart when all alone

94.

Shed no tears o'er that tomb
For there are Angels weeping
Mourn not him whose doom
Heaven itself is mourning
Look how in sable gloom
The clouds are earthward sweeping
And earth receives them home
Even darker clouds returning

Is it when good men die
10   That sorrow wakes above?
Grieve saints when other spirits fly
To swell their choir of love?

Ah no with louder sound –
The golden harp-strings quiver
When good men gain the happy ground
Where they must dwell forever

But he who slumbers there:
His bark will strive no more
Across the waters of despair
20   To reach that glorious shore

The time of grace is past
And mercy scorned and tried
Forsakes to utter wrath at last
The soul so steeled by pride

That wrath will never spare
Will never pity know
Will mock its victim's maddened prayer
Will triumph in his woe

Shut from his Maker's smile
30   The accursed man shall be
Compassion reigns a little while
Revenge eternally –

95.

Mild the mist upon the hill
Telling not of storms tomorrow
No the day has wept its fill
Spent its store of silent sorrow

Oh I'm gone back to the days of youth
I am a child once more
And 'neath my father's sheltering roof
And near the old hall door

I watch this cloudy evening fall
10   After a day of rain
Blue mists sweet mists of summer pall
The horizon's mountain chain

The damp stands in the long green grass
As thick as morning's tears
And dreamy scents of fragrance pass
That breathe of other years

96.

How long will you remain? The midnight hour
Has tolled the last note from [the] minster tower
Come come the fire is dead the lamp burns low
Your eyelids droop a weight is on your brow
Your cold hands hardly hold the useless pen
Come morn will give recovered strength again

No let me linger leave me let me be
A little longer in this reverie
I'm happy now and would you tear away
10   My blissful dream that never comes with day
A vision dear though false for well my mind
Knows what a bitter waking waits behind

Can there be pleasure in this shadowy room
With windows yawning on intenser gloom
And such a dreary wind so bleakly sweeping
Round walls where only you are vigil keeping
Besides your face has not a sign of joy
And more than tearful sorrow fills your eye
Look on those woods look on that heaven lorn
20   And think how changed they'll be tomorrow morn

The dome of heaven expanding bright and blue
The leaves the green grass sprinkled thick with dew
And wet mists rising on the river's breast
And wild birds bursting from their songless nest
And your own children's merry voices chasing
The fancies grief not pleasure has been tracing

Aye speak of these – but can you tell me why
Day breathes such beauty over earth and sky
And waking sounds revive restore again
30   [Dull] hearts that all night long have throbbed in pain

Is it not that the sunshine and the wind
Lure from its self the mourner's woe worn mind
And all the joyous music breathing by
And all the splendour of that cloudless sky

Regive him shadowy gleams of infancy
And draw his tired gaze from futurity

97.

The starry night shall tidings bring
Go out upon the breezy moor
Watch for a bird with sable wing
And beak and talons dripping gore

Look not around look not beneath
But mutely trace its airy way
Mark where it lights upon the heath
Then wanderer kneel thee down and pray

What fortune may await thee there
10   I will not and I dare not tell
But Heaven is moved by fervent prayer
And God is mercy – fare thee well!

98.

It is not pride it is not shame
That makes her leave the gorgeous hall
And though neglect her heart might tame
She mourns not for her sudden fall

'Tis true she stands among the crowd
An unmarked and an unloved child
While each young comrade blithe and proud
Glides through the maze of pleasure wild

And all do homage to their will
And all seem glad their voice to hear
She heeds not that but hardly still
Her eye can hold the quivering tear

What made her weep what made her glide
Out to the park this dreary day
And cast her jewelled chains aside
And seek a rough and lonely way

And down beneath a cedar's shade
On the wet grass regardless lie
With nothing but its gloomy head
Between her and the showery sky

I saw her stand in the gallery long
Watching the little children there
As they were playing the pillars among
And bounding down the marble stair

99.

It was night and on the mountains
Fathoms deep the snow drifts lay
Streams and waterfalls and fountains
Down in darkness stole away

Long ago the hopeless peasant
Left his sheep all buried there
Sheep that through the summer pleasant
He had watched with fondest care

Now no more a cheerful ranger
10   Following pathways known of yore
Sad he stood a wildered stranger
On his own unbounded moor

100.

Fair sinks the summer evening now
In softened glory round my home;
The sky upon its holy brow
Wears not a cloud that speaks of gloom.

The old tower, shrined in golden light,
Looks down on the descending sun –
So gently evening blends with night
You scarce can say that day is done –

And this is just the joyous hour
10   When we were wont to burst away,
To 'scape from labour's tyrant power
And cheerfully go out to play –

Then why is all so sad and lone?
No merry foot-step on the stair –
No laugh – no heart-awaking tone
But voiceless silence everywhere –

I've wandered round our garden-ground
And still it seemed at every turn
That I should greet approaching feet
20   And words upon the breezes borne

In vain – they will not come today
And morning's beam will rise as drear

Then tell me – are they gone for aye
Our sun blinks through the mists of care?

Ah no, reproving Hope doth say
Departed joys 'tis fond to mourn
When every storm that hides their ray
Prepares a more divine return –

101.

Alcona in its changing mood
My soul will sometimes overfly
The long long years of solitude
That 'twixt our time of meeting lie

Hope and despair in turns arise
This doubting dreading heart to move
And now 'mid smiles and bitter sighs
Tell how I fear tell how I love

And now I say 'In Areon Hall' –
10 (Alas that such a dream should come
When well I know whate'er befall
That Areon is no more my home.)

Yet let me say 'In Areon Hall' –
The first faint red of morning shines
And one right gladly to its call
The restless breath of grief resigns

Her faded eye, her pallid face
Would woo the soft awaking wind
All earth is breathing of the peace
20 She long has sought but cannot find

How sweet it is to watch the mist
From that bright silent lake ascend
And high o'er wood and mountain crest
With heaven's grey clouds as greyly blend

How sweet it is to mark those clouds
Break brightly in the rising day
To see the sober veil that shrouds
This summer morning melt away

O sweet to some but not to her
30   Unm[ark]dst once at nature's shrine
She now kneels down a worshipper
A mad adorer, love, to thine

The time is come when hope that long
Revived and sank at length [is o'er]
When faith in him however strong
Dare prompt her to believe no more

The tears which day by day o'erflowed
Their heart deep source begin to freeze
And as she gazes on the road
40   That glances through those spreading trees

No throbbing flutter checks her breath
To mark a horseman hastening by
Her haggard brow is calm as death
And cold like death her dreary eye

102. *Song*

O between distress and pleasure
Fond affection cannot be
Wretched hearts in vain would treasure
Friendship's joys when others flee

Well I know thine eye would never
Smile while mine grieved willingly
Yet I know thine eye forever
Could not weep in sympathy

Let us part the time is over
10 When I thought and felt like thee
I will be an Ocean rover
I will sail the desert sea

Isles there are beyond its billow
Lands where woe may wander free
And beloved thy midnight pillow
Will be soft unwatched by me

Not on each returning morrow
When thy heart bounds ardently
Need'st thou then dissemble sorrow
20 Marking my despondency

Day by day some dreary token
Will forsake thy memory
Till at last all old links broken
I shall be a dream to thee

103.

There was a time when my cheek burned
To give such scornful fiends the lie
Ungoverned nature madly spurned
The law that bade it not defy
O in the days of ardent youth
I would have given my life for truth

For truth, for right, for liberty
I would have gladly, freely died
And now I calmly hear and see
10 The vain man smile the fool deride
Though not because my heart is tame
Though not for fear though not for shame

My soul still chafes at every tone
Of selfish and self-blinded error
My breast still braves the world alone
Steeled as it ever was to terror
Only I know however I frown
The same world will go rolling on

104.

The wind I hear it sighing
With Autumn's saddest sound –
Withered leaves as thick are lying
As spring-flowers on the ground –

This dark night has won me
To wander far away –
Old feelings gather fast upon me
Like vultures round their prey –

Kind were they once, and cherished
10 But cold and cheerless now –
I would their lingering shades had perished
When their light left my brow

'Tis like old age pretending
The softness of a child,
My altered, hardened spirit bending
To meet their fancies wild

Yet could I with past pleasures,
Past woe's oblivion buy –
That by the death of my dearest treasures
20 My deadliest pains might die.

O then another daybreak
Might haply dawn above –
Another summer gild my cheek,
My soul, another love –

105 [xvii]. [*Stanzas to —*]

106.

The wind was rough which tore
That leaf from its parent tree
The fate was cruel which bore
The withering corpse to me

We wander on we have no rest
It is a dreary way

What shadow is it
That ever moves before [my] eyes
It has a brow of ghostly whiteness

107.

That wind I used to hear it swelling
With joy divinely deep
You might have seen my hot tears welling
But rapture made me weep

I used to love on winter nights
To lie and dream alone
Of all the hopes and real delights
My early years had known

And oh above the rest of those
10   That coming time should [bear]
Like heaven's own glorious stars they rose
Still beaming bright and fair

108.

Come, walk with me,
There's only thee
To bless my spirit now –
We used to love on winter nights
To wander through the snow;
Can we not woo back old delights?
The clouds rush dark and wild
They fleck with shade our mountain heights
The same as long ago
10   And on the horizon rest at last
In looming masses piled;
While moonbeams flash and fly so fast
We scarce can say they smiled –

Come walk with me, come walk with me;
We were not once so few
But Death has stolen our company
As sunshine steals the dew –
He took them one by one and we
Are left the only two;
20   So closer would my feelings twine
Because they have no stay but thine –

'Nay call me not – it may not be
Is human love so true?
Can Friendship's flower droop on for years
And then revive anew?
No, though the soil be wet with tears,
How fair soe'er it grew
The vital sap once perished
Will never flow again
30   And surer than that dwelling dread,
The narrow dungeon of the dead
Time parts the hearts of men –'

109.

Heaven's glory shone where he was laid
In life's decline
I turned me from that young saint's bed
To gaze on thine –

It was a summer day that saw
His spirit's flight
Thine parted in a time of awe
A winter-night

110.

Upon her soothing breast
She lulled her little child
A winter sunset in the west
A dreary glory smiled

111.

I gazed within thine earnest eyes
And read the sorrow brooding there
[I saw] thy young breast heave with sighs
And envied such despair

Go to the grave in youth's [first] woe
That doom was written long ago

112. *Written in the Gaaldine Prison Caves to A. G. A.*

Thy sun is near meridian height
And my sun sinks in endless night
But if that night bring only sleep
Then I shall rest, while thou wilt weep.

And say not, that my early tomb
Will give me to a darker doom –
Shall these long, agonizing years
Be punished by eternal tears?

No, *that* I feel can never be;
10   A God of *hate* could hardly bear
To watch, through all eternity,
His own creation's dread despair!

The pangs that wring my mortal breast
Must claim from Justice, lasting rest:
Enough, that this departing breath
Will pass in anguish worse than death.

If I have sinned, long, long ago
That sin was purified by woe –
I've suffered on through night and day;
20   I've trod a dark and frightful way.

Earth's wilderness was round me spread
Heaven's tempests beat my naked head –
I did not kneel: in vain would prayer
Have sought one gleam of mercy there!

How could I ask for pitying love
When that grim concave frowned above
Hoarding its lightnings to destroy
My only and my priceless joy?

They struck and long may Eden shine
30   Ere I would call its glories mine
All Heaven's undreamt felicity
Could never blot the past from me –

No, years may cloud and death may sever
But what is done is done for ever –
And thou false friend, and treacherous guide,
Go sate thy cruel heart with pride –

Go, load my memory with shame;
Speak but to curse my hated name;
My tortured limbs in dungeons bind
40   And spare my life to kill my mind –

Leave me in chains and darkness now
And when my very soul is worn;
When reason's light has left my brow
And madness cannot feel thy scorn;

Then come again – thou wilt not shrink;
I know thy soul is free from fear
The last full cup of triumph drink,
Before the blank of death be there –

Thy raving, dying victim see;
50   Lost, cursed, degraded – all for thee!
Gaze on the wretch – recall to mind
His golden days left long behind.

Does memory sleep in Lethean rest?
Or wakes its whisper in thy breast?
O memory, wake! Let scenes return
That even her haughty heart must mourn!

Reveal, where o'er a lone green wood
The moon of summer pours
Far down from heaven, its silver flood
60   On deep Elderno's shores –

There, lingering in the wild embrace
Youth's warm affections gave
She sits, and fondly seems to trace
His features in the wave –

And while, on that reflected face
Her eyes intently dwell:
'Fernando, sing tonight,' she says,
'The lays I love so well.'

He smiles and sings, though every air
70   Betrays the faith of yesterday:
His soul is glad to cast for her
Virtue and faith and Heaven away.

Well, thou hast paid me back my love!
But, if there be a God above
Whose arm is strong, whose word is true
This hell shall wring thy spirit too!

113.

Far, far away is mirth withdrawn;
'Tis three long hours before the morn
And I watch lonely, drearily –
So come thou shade commune with me

Deserted one! thy corpse lies cold
And mingled with a foreign mould –
Year after year the grass grows green
Above the dust where thou hast been.

I will not name thy blighted name
10   Tarnished by unforgotten shame
Though not because my bosom torn
Joins the mad world in all its scorn –

Thy phantom face is dark with woe
Tears have left ghastly traces there,
Those ceaseless tears! I wish their flow
Could quench thy wild despair.

They deluge my heart like the rain
On cursed Gomorrah's howling plain –
Yet when I hear thy foes deride
20 I must cling closely to thy side –

Our mutual foes – they will not rest
From trampling on thy buried breast –
Glutting their hatred with the doom
They picture thine, beyond the tomb –

But God is not like human kind
Man cannot read the Almighty mind
Vengeance will never torture thee
Nor hunt thy soul eternally

Then do not in this night of grief
30 This time of overwhelming fear
O do not think that God can leave
Forget, forsake, refuse to hear! –

What have I dreamt? He lies asleep
With whom my heart would vainly weep
He rests – and *I* endure the woe
That left his spirit long ago –

114.

It is too late to call thee now –
I will not nurse that dream again
For every joy that lit my brow
Would bring its after-storm of pain –

Besides the mist is half withdrawn,
The barren mountain-side lies bare
And sunshine and awaking morn
Paint no more golden visions there –

Yet ever in my grateful breast
10   Thy darling shade shall cherished be
For God alone doth know how blest
My early years have been in thee!

115 [xix]. [*Stanzas*]

116.

If grief for grief can touch thee,
If answering woe for woe,
If any ruth can melt thee
Come to me now!

I cannot be more lonely,
More drear I cannot be!
My worn heart throbs so wildly
'Twill break for thee –

And when the world despises –
10   When heaven repels my prayer –
Will not mine angel comfort?
Mine idol hear?

Yes by the tears I've poured,
By all my hours of pain
O I shall surely win thee
Beloved, again!

117.

'Tis moonlight summer moonlight
All soft and still and fair
The solemn hour of midnight
Breathes sweet thoughts everywhere

But most where trees are sending
Their breezy boughs on high
Or stooping low are lending
A shelter from the sky

And there in those wild bowers
10   A lovely form is laid
Green grass and dew steeped flowers
Wave gently round her head

118. *The Night-Wind*

In summer's mellow midnight
A cloudless moon shone through
Our open parlour window
And rosetrees wet with dew

I sat in silent musing –
The soft wind waved my hair
It told me Heaven was glorious
And sleeping Earth was fair –

I needed not its breathing
10   To bring such thoughts to me
But still it whispered lowly
'How dark the woods will be! –

'The thick leaves in my murmur
Are rustling like a dream,
And all their myriad voices
Instinct with spirit seem'

I said, 'Go gentle singer,
Thy wooing voice is kind
But do not think its music
20   Has power to reach my mind –

'Play with the scented flower,
The young tree's supple bough –
And leave my human feelings
In their own course to flow'

The Wanderer would not leave me
Its kiss grew warmer still –
'O come,' it sighed so sweetly
'I'll win thee 'gainst thy will –

'Have we not been from childhood friends?
30   Have I not loved thee long?
As long as thou hast loved the night
Whose silence wakes my song?

'And when thy heart is laid at rest
Beneath the church-yard stone
I shall have time enough to mourn
And thou to be alone' –

119.

Companions, all day long we've stood
The wild winds restless blowing
All day we've watched the darkened flood
Around our vessel flowing

Sunshine has never smiled since morn
And clouds have gathered drear
And heavier hearts would feel forlorn
And weaker minds would fear

But look in each young shipmate's eyes
10   Lit by the evening flame
And see how little stormy skies
Our joyous blood can tame

No glance the same expression wears
No lip the same soft smile
Yet kindness warms and courage cheers
Nerves every breast the while

It is the hour of dreaming now
The red fire brightly gleams
And sweetest in a red fire's glow
20 The hour of dreaming seems

I may not trace the thoughts of all
But some I read as well
As I can hear the ocean's fall
And sullen surging swell

Edmund's swift soul is gone before
It threads a forest wide
Whose towers are bending to the shore
And gazing on the tide

And one is there – I know the voice
30 The thrilling stirring tone
That makes his bounding pulse rejoice
Yet makes not *his* alone

Mine own hand longs to clasp her hand
Mine eye to greet her eye
Win white sails, win Zedora's strand
And Ula's Eden sky –

Mary and Flora oft their gaze
Is clouded pensively
And what that earnest aspect says
40 Is all revealed to me

'Tis but two years or little more
Since first they dared that main
And such a night may well restore
That first time back again

The smothered sigh the lingering late
The longed for dreaded hour
The parting at the moss-grown gate
The last look on the tower

50   I know they think of these and then
The evening's gathering gloom
And they alone with foreign men
To guard their cabin room

120.

And like myself lone wholly lone
It sees the day's long sunshine glow
And like myself it makes its moan
In unexhausted woe

Give we the hills our equal prayer
Earth's breezy hills and heaven's blue sea
We ask for nothing further here
But our own hearts and liberty

Ah could my hand unlock its chain
10   How gladly would I watch it soar
And ne'er regret and ne'er complain
To see its shining eyes no more

But let me think that if today
It pines in cold captivity
Tomorrow both shall soar away
Eternally entirely Free

121 [xxi]. [*The Old Stoic*]

122.

Shall Earth no more inspire thee,
Thou lonely dreamer now?
Since passion may not fire thee
Shall Nature cease to bow?

Thy mind is ever moving
In regions dark to thee;
Recall its useless roving –
Come back and dwell with me –

I know my mountain breezes
10   Enchant and soothe thee still –
I know my sunshine pleases
Despite thy wayward will –

When day with evening blending
Sinks from the summer sky,
I've seen thy spirit bending
In fond idolatry –

I've watched thee every hour –
I know my mighty sway –
I know my magic power
20   To drive thy griefs away –

Few hearts to mortals given
On earth so wildly pine
Yet none would ask a Heaven
More like this Earth than thine –

Then let my winds caress thee –
Thy comrade let me be –
Since nought beside can bless thee
Return and dwell with me –

123.

Aye there it is! It wakes tonight
Sweet thoughts that will not die
And feeling's fires flash all as bright
As in the years gone by! –

And I can tell by thine altered cheek
And by thy kindled gaze
And by the words thou scarce dost speak,
How wildly fancy plays –

Yes I could swear that glorious wind
10 Has swept the world aside
Has dashed its memory from thy mind
Like foam-bells from the tide –

And thou art now a spirit pouring
Thy presence into all –
The essence of the Tempest's roaring
And of the Tempest's fall –

A universal influence
From Thine own influence free –
A principle of life intense
20 Lost to mortality –

Thus truly when that breast is cold
Thy prisoned soul shall rise
The dungeon mingle with the mould –
The captive with the skies –

124.

I see around me tombstones grey
Stretching their shadow far away.
Beneath the turf my footsteps tread
Lie low and lone the silent dead –

Beneath the turf – beneath the mould –
Forever dark, forever cold –
And my eyes cannot hold the tears
That memory hoards from vanished years
For Time and Death and Mortal pain
10 Give wounds that will not heal again –
Let me remember half the woe
I've seen and heard and felt below
And heaven itself – so pure and blest
Could never give my spirit rest –
Sweet land of light! thy children fair
Know nought akin to our despair –
Nor have they felt, nor can they tell
What tenants haunt each mortal cell
What gloomy guests we hold within –
20 Torments and madness, tears and sin!
Well – may they live in ecstasy
Their long eternity of joy;
At least we would not bring them down
With us to weep, with us to groan,
No – Earth would wish no other sphere
To taste her cup of sufferings drear;
She turns from Heaven a careless eye
And only mourns that *we* must die!
Ah mother, what shall comfort thee
30 In all this boundless misery?
To cheer our eager eyes a while
We see thee smile, how fondly smile!
But who reads not through that tender glow
Thy deep, unutterable woe?
Indeed no dazzling land above
Can cheat thee of thy children's love –
We all in life's departing shine
Our last dear longings blend with thine;
And struggle still, and strive to trace
40 With clouded gaze thy darling face
We would not leave our native home
For *any* world beyond the Tomb
No – rather on thy kindly breast

Let us be laid in lasting rest
Or waken but to share with thee
A mutual immortality –

125. *Geraldine*

'Twas night, her comrades gathered all
Within their city's rocky wall;
When flowers were closed and day was o'er
Their joyous hearts awoke the more

But lonely in her distant cave
She heard the river's restless wave
Chafing its banks with dreamy flow
Music for mirth, and wail for woe –

Palm trees and cedars towering high
Deepened the gloom of evening's sky
And thick did raven ringlets veil
Her forehead, drooped like lily pale

Yet I could hear my lady sing;
I knew she did not mourn,
For never yet from sorrow's spring
Such witching notes were born

Thus poured she in that cavern wild
The voice of feelings warm
As, bending o'er her beauteous child
She clasped its sleeping form –

'Why sank so soon the summer sun
From our Zedora's skies?
I was not tired, my darling one,
Of gazing in thine eyes –

'Methought the heaven whence thou hast come
Was lingering there awhile
And Earth seemed such an alien home
They did not dare to smile.

'Methought each moment something strange
30   Within their circles shone
And yet, through every magic change
They were Brenzaida's own.

'Methought – what thought I not, sweet love?
My whole heart centred there;
I breathed not but to send above
One gush of ardent prayer.

'Bless it, my gracious God, I cried,
Preserve thy mortal shrine
For thine own sake, be thou its guide
40   And keep it still divine!

'Say, sin shall never blanch that cheek
Nor suffering charge that brow
Speak, in thy mercy maker, speak
And seal it safe from woe!

'Why did I doubt? In God's control
Our mutual fates remain
And pure as now, my angel's soul
Must go to heaven again!'

The revellers in the city slept
50   My lady, in her woodland bed;
I, watching o'er her slumber wept
As one who mourns the dead!

126. *Rosina*

Weeks of wild delirium past –
Weeks of fevered pain,
Rest from suffering comes at last –
Reason dawns again –

It was a pleasant April day
Declining to the afternoon
Sunshine upon her pillow lay
As warm as middle June.

It told her how unconsciously
10   Early spring had hurried by
'Ah Time has not delayed for me!'
She murmured with a sigh.

'Angora's hills have heard their tread
The crimson flag is planted there –
Elderno's waves are rolling red,
While *I* lie fettered here?

'Nay, rather, Gondal's shaken throne
Is now secure and free;
And my King Julius reigns alone,
20   Debtless, alas! to me!'

Loud was the sudden gush of woe
From those who watched around;
Rosina turned, and sought to know
Why burst that boding sound.

'What then, my dreams are false,' she said
'Come maidens, answer me
Has Almedore in battle fled?
Have slaves subdued the free?

'I know it all, he could not bear
30   To leave me dying far away –
He fondly, madly lingered here
And we have lost the day!

'But check those coward sobs, and bring
My robes and smooth my tangled hair:
A noble victory you shall sing
For every hour's despair!

'When will he come? 'Twill soon be night –
He'll come when evening falls –
Oh I shall weary for the light
40   To leave my lonely halls!'

She turned her pallid face aside
As she would seek repose;
But dark Ambition's thwarted pride
Forbade her lids to close –

And still on all who waited by
Oppressive mystery hung;
And swollen with grief was every eye
And chained was every tongue.

They whispered nought, but, 'Lady, sleep,
50   Dear Lady, slumber now!
Had we not bitter cause to weep
While you were laid so low?

'And Hope can hardly deck the cheek
With sudden signs of cheer
When it has worn through many a week
The stamp of anguish drear' –

Fierce grew Rosina's gloomy gaze;
She cried, 'Dissemblers, own,
Exina's arms in victory blaze
60   Brenzaida's crest is down'

'Well, since it must be told, Lady,
Brenzaida's crest *is* down
Brenzaida's sun is set, Lady,
His empire overthrown!

'He died beneath this palace dome –
True hearts on every side –
Among his guards, within his home
Our glorious monarch died

'I saw him fall, I saw the gore
70 From his heart's fountain swell
And mingling on the marble floor
His murderer's life-blood fell –

'And now, 'mid northern mountains lone
His desert grave is made;
And, Lady, of your love, alone
Remains a mortal shade!'

127. *A. S. to G. S.*

I do not weep, I would not weep;
Our Mother needs no tears:
Dry thine eyes too, 'tis vain to keep
This causeless grief for years

What though her brow be changed and cold,
Her sweet eyes closed for ever?
What though the stone – the darksome mould
Our mortal bodies sever?

What though her hand smooth ne'er again
10 Those silken locks of thine –
Nor through long hours of future pain
Her kind face o'er thee shine?

Remember still she is not dead
She sees us Gerald now
Laid where her angel spirit fled
'Mid heath and frozen snow

And from that world of heavenly light
Will she not always bend
To guide us in our lifetime's night
20 And guard us to the end?

Thou know'st she will, and well may'st mourn
That we are left below
But not that she can ne'er return
To share our earthly woe –

128. *H. A. and A. S.*

In the same place, when Nature wore
The same celestial glow;
I'm sure I've seen those forms before
But many springs ago;

And only *he* had locks of light
And *she* had raven hair,
While now, his curls are dark as night
And hers, as morning fair.

Besides, I've dreamt of tears whose traces
10   Will never more depart
Of agony that fast effaces
The verdure of the heart –

I dreamt one sunny day like this
In this peerless month of May
I saw her give the unanswered kiss
As his spirit passed away:

Those young eyes that so sweetly shine
Then looked their last adieu
And pale Death changed that cheek divine
20   To his unchanging hue

And earth was cast above the breast
That beats so warm and free
Where her soft ringlets lightly rest
And move responsively

Then she, upon the covered grave –
The grass grown grave, did lie –
A tomb not girt by Gondal's wave
Nor arched by Gondal's sky.

30 The sod was sparkling bright with dew
But brighter still with tears
That welled from mortal grief, I knew
Which never heals with years –

And if he came not for her woe
He would not now return;
He would not leave his sleep below
When she had ceased to mourn –

O Innocence, that cannot live
With heart-wrung anguish long
Dear childhood's Innocence, forgive,
40 For I have done thee wrong!

The bright rosebuds, those hawthorns shroud
Within their perfumed bower
Have never closed beneath a cloud
Nor bent before a shower –

Had darkness once obscured their sun
Or kind dew turned to rain
No storm-cleared sky that ever shone
Could win such bliss again –

129. *Written in Aspin Castle*

How do I love on summer nights
To sit within this Norman door
Whose sombre portal hides the lights
Thickening above me evermore!

How do I love to hear the flow
Of Aspin's water murmuring low
And hours long listen to the breeze
That sighs in Rockden's waving trees

Tonight, there is no wind to wake
10   One ripple on the lonely lake –
Tonight the clouds subdued and grey
Starlight and moonlight shut away

'Tis calm and still and almost drear
So utter is the solitude;
But still I love to linger here
And form my mood to nature's mood –

There's a wild walk beneath the rocks
Following the bend of Aspin's side
'Tis worn by feet of mountain-flocks
20   That wander down to drink the tide

Never by cliff and gnarled tree
Wound fairy path so sweet to me
Yet of the native shepherds none
In open day and cheerful sun
Will tread its labyrinths alone

Far less when evening's pensive hour
Hushes the bird and shuts the flower
And gives to Fancy magic power
O'er each familiar tone.

30   For round their hearths they'll tell the tale
And every listener swears it true
How wanders there a phantom pale
With spirit-eyes of dreamy blue –

It always walks with head declined
Its long curls move not in the wind
Its face is fair – divinely fair;

But brooding on that angel brow
Rests such a shade of deep despair
As nought divine could ever know

40 How oft in twilight lingering lone
I've stood to watch that phantom rise
And seen in mist and moonlit stone
Its gleaming hair and solemn eyes

The ancient men in secret say
'Tis the first chief of Aspin grey
That haunts his feudal home

But why, around that alien grave
Three thousand miles beyond the wave –
Where his exiled ashes lie
50 Under the cope of England's sky –
Doth he not rather roam?

I've seen his picture in the hall;
It hangs upon an eastern wall
And often when the sun declines
That picture like an angel shines –

And when the moonbeam chill and blue
Streams the spectral windows through
That picture's like a spectre too –

The hall is full of portraits rare;
60 Beauty and mystery mingle there –
At his right hand an infant fair
Looks from its golden frame –

And just like his its ringlets bright
Its large dark eye of shadowy light
Its cheek's pure hue, its forehead white
And like its noble name –

Daughter divine! and could his gaze
Fall coldly on thy peerless face?
And did he never smile to see
70 Himself restored to infancy?

Never part back that golden flow
Of curls, and kiss that pearly brow
And feel no other earthly bliss
Was equal to that parent's kiss?

No; turn towards the western side
There stands Sidonia's deity!
In all her glory, all her pride!
And truly like a god she seems
Some god of wild enthusiast's dreams
80   And this is she for whom he died!
For whom his spirit unforgiven,
Wanders unsheltered shut from heaven
An outcast for eternity –

Those eyes are dust – those lips are clay –
That form is mouldered all away
Nor thought, nor sense, nor pulse, nor breath
The whole devoured and lost in death!

There is no worm, however mean,
That living, is not nobler now
90   Than she – Lord Alfred's idol queen
So loved – so worshipped long ago –

O come away! the Norman door
Is silvered with a sudden shine –
Come leave these dreams o'er things of yore
And turn to Nature's face divine –

O'er wood and wold, o'er flood and fell
O'er flashing lake and gleaming dell
The harvest moon looks down

And when heaven smiles with love and light
100   And earth looks back so dazzling bright
In such a scene, on such a night
Earth's children should not frown –

130 [xv]. [*Self-Interrogation*]

131. *On the Fall of Zalona*

All blue and bright, in glorious light
The morn comes marching on
And now Zalona's steeples white
Glow golden in the sun –

This day might be a festal day;
The streets are crowded all,
And emerald flags stream broad and gay
From turret, tower and wall;

And hark! how music, evermore
10   Is sounding in the sky:
The deep bells boom – the cannon roar,
The trumpets sound on high –

The deep bells boom, the deep bells clash
Upon the reeling air:
The cannon, with unceasing crash
Make answer far and near –

What do those brazen tongues proclaim?
What joyous fête begun –
What offering to our country's fame –
20   What noble victory won?

Go, ask that solitary sire
Laid in his house alone;
His silent hearth without a fire –
His sons and daughters gone –

Go, ask those children, in the street
Beside their mother's door;
Waiting to hear the lingering feet
That they shall hear no more.

Ask those pale soldiers round the gates
30   With famine-kindled eye –
They'll say, 'Zalona celebrates
The day that she must die!'

The charger, by his manger tied
Has rested many a day;
Yet ere the spur have touched his side,
Behold, he sinks away!

And hungry dogs, with wolf-like cry
Unburied corpses tear,
While their gaunt masters gaze and sigh
40   And scarce the feast forbear –

Now, look down from Zalona's wall –
There war the unwearied foe:
If ranks before our cannon fall,
New ranks, forever, grow –

And many a week, unbroken thus,
Their troops, our ramparts hem;
And for each man that fights for us
A hundred fight for them!

Courage and Right and spotless Truth
50   Were pitched 'gainst traitorous crime
We offered all – our age, our youth –
Our brave men in their prime –

And all have failed! the fervent prayers,
The trust in heavenly aid,
Valour and faith and sealed tears
That would not mourn the dead –

Lips, that did breathe no murmuring word;
Hearts, that did ne'er complain
Though vengeance held a sheathed sword
60   And martyrs bled in vain –

Alas, alas, the Myrtle bowers
By blighting blasts destroyed!
Alas, the Lily's withered flowers
That leave the garden void!

Unfolds o'er tower, and waves o'er height,
A sheet of crimson sheen –
Is it the setting sun's red light
That stains our standard green?

Heaven help us in this awful hour!
70   For now might Faith decay –
Now might we doubt God's guardian power
And curse, instead of pray –

He will not even let us die –
Not let us die at home;
The foe must see our soldiers fly
As they had feared the Tomb:

Because, we *dare* not stay to gain
Those longed for, glorious graves –
We dare not shrink from slavery's chain
80   To leave our children slaves!

But when this scene of awful woe
Has neared its final close
As God forsook our armies, so
May He forsake our foes!

132 [xii]. [*How Clear She Shines*]

133. *To A. S. 1830*

Where beams the sun the brightest
In the noons of sweet July?
Where falls the snow the lightest
From bleak December's sky?

Where can the weary lay his head
And lay it safe the while
In a grave that never shuts its dead
From heaven's benignant smile?

Upon the earth in sunlight
10 Spring grass grows green and fair
But beneath the earth is midnight –
Eternal midnight there!

Then why lament that those we love
Escape Earth's dungeon Tomb?
As if the flowers that blow above
Could charm its undergloom –

From morning's faintest dawning
Till evening's deepest shade
Thou wilt not cease thy mourning
20 To know where she is laid;

But if to weep above her grave
Be such a priceless boon
Go, shed thy tears in Ocean's wave
And they will reach it soon.

Yet midst thy wild repining
Mad though that anguish be
Think heaven on her is shining
Even as it shines on thee –

With thy mind's vision pierce the Deep
30 Look how she rests below
And tell me why such blessed sleep
Should cause such bitter woe?

134. *E. G. to M. R.*

Thy Guardians are asleep
So I've come to bid thee rise;
Thou hast a holy vow to keep
Ere yon crescent quit the skies:

Though clouds careering wide
Will hardly let her gleam
She's bright enough to be our guide
Across the mountain-stream –

O waken, Dearest, wake!
10 What means this long delay?
Say, wilt thou not for honour's sake
Chase idle fears away?

Think not of future grief
Entailed on present joy:
An age of woe were only brief
Its memory to destroy –

And neither Hell nor Heaven
Though both conspire at last
Can take the bliss that has been given –
20 Can rob us of the past –

Then, waken, Mary, wake
How canst thou linger now?
For true love's and Gleneden's sake
Arise and keep thy vow!

135.

Had there been falsehood in my breast
No thorns had marred my road
This spirit had not lost its rest
These tears had never flowed

136. *To A. G. A.*

'Thou standest in the greenwood now
The place, the hour, the same –
And here the fresh leaves gleam and glow
And there, down in the lake below
The tiny ripples flame –

'The breeze sings like a summer breeze
Should sing in summer skies
And tower-like rocks and tent-like trees
In mingled glory rise.

10   'But where is he today, today?'
'O question not with me' –
'I will not, Lady, only say
Where may thy lover be?

'Is he upon some distant shore?
Or is he on the sea?
Or is the heart thou dost adore,
A faithless heart to thee?'

'The heart I love, whate'er betide,
Is faithful as the grave
20   And neither foreign lands divide
Nor yet the rolling wave.'

'Then why should sorrow cloud that brow,
And tears those eyes bedim?
Reply this once, is it that thou
Hast faithless been to him?'

'I gazed upon the cloudless moon
And loved her all the night
Till morning came and ardent noon
Then I forgot her light –

30   'No – not forgot, eternally
Remains its memory dear;
But could the day seem dark to me
Because the night was fair?

'I well may mourn that only one
Can light my future sky
Even though by such a radiant sun
My moon of life must die' –

137.

Yes holy be thy resting place
Wherever thou may'st lie
The sweetest winds breathe on thy face
The softest of the sky

And will not guardian Angels send
Kind dreams and thoughts of love
Though I no more may watchful bend
Thy [longed] repose above?

And will not heaven itself bestow
10   A beam of glory there
That summer's grass more green may grow
And summer's flowers more fair?

Farewell farewell 'tis hard to part
Yet loved one it must be
I would not rend another heart
Not even by blessing thee

Go we must break affection's chain
Forget the hopes of years
Nay [grieve] not willest thou remain
20   To waken wilder tears

This [herald] breeze with thee and me
Roved in the dawning day
And thou shouldest be where it shall be
Ere evening far away

138. *A. G. A. to A. S.*

At such a time, in such a spot
The world seems made of light
Our blissful hearts remember not
How surely follows night –

I cannot, Alfred, dream of aught
That casts a shade of woe;
That heaven is reigning in my thought
Which wood and wave and earth have caught
From skies that overflow –

10   That heaven which my sweet lover's brow
Has won me to adore –
Which from his blue eyes beaming now
Reflects a still intenser glow
Than nature's heaven can pour –

I know our souls are all divine
I know that when we die
What seems the vilest, even like thine
A part of God himself shall shine
In perfect purity –

20   But coldly breaks November's day
      Its changes charmless all
      Unmarked, unloved, they pass away
      We do not wish one hour to stay
      Nor sigh at evening's fall

      And glorious is the gladsome rise
      Of June's rejoicing morn
      And who with unregretful eyes
      Can watch the lustre leave its skies
      To twilight's shade forlorn?

30   Then art thou not my golden June,
      All mist and tempest free?
      As shines earth's sun in summer noon
      So heaven's sun shines in thee –

      Let others seek its beams divine
      In cell and cloister drear
      But I have found a fairer shrine
      And happier worship here –

      By dismal rites they win their bliss
      By penance, fasts, and fears –
40   I have one rite – a gentle kiss –
      One penance – tender tears –

      O could it thus forever be
      That I might so adore
      I'd ask for all eternity
      To make a paradise for me,
      My love – and nothing more!

139.

In the earth, the earth thou shalt be laid
A grey stone standing over thee;
Black mould beneath thee spread
And black mould to cover thee –

'Well, there is rest there
So fast come thy prophecy –
The time when my sunny hair
Shall with grass roots twined be'

But cold, cold is that resting place
10   Shut out from Joy and Liberty
And all who loved thy living face
Will shrink from its gloom and thee

'Not so, *here* the world is chill
And sworn friends fall from me
But *there*, they'll own me still
And prize my memory'

Farewell, then, all that love
All that deep sympathy:
Sleep on, heaven laughs above –
20   Earth never misses thee –

Turf-sod and tombstone drear
Part human company
One heart broke, only, there
That heart was worthy thee! –

140. *Rodric Lesley. 1830*

Lie down and rest, the fight is done
Thy comrades to the camp retire;
Gaze not so earnestly upon
The far gleam of the beacon fire.

Listen not to the wind-borne sounds
Of music and of soldiers' cheer;
Thou canst not go – unnumbered wounds
Exhaust thy life and hold thee here –

Had that hand power to raise the sword
10   Which since this morn laid hundreds low
Had that tongue strength to speak the word
That urged thy followers on the foe

Were that warm blood within thy veins
Which now upon the earth is flowing
Splashing its sod with crimson stains
Reddening the pale heath round thee growing

Then Rodric, thou might'st still be turning
With eager eye and anxious breast
To where those signal-lights are burning –
20   To where thy monarch's legions rest –

But never more – Look up and see
The twilight fading from the skies
That last dim beam that sets for thee,
Rodric, for thee shall never rise!

141 [ix]. [*Hope*]

142. *M. G. for the U. S.*

'Twas yesterday at early dawn
I watched the falling snow;
A drearier scene on winter morn
Was never stretched below.

I could not see the mountains round
But I knew by the wild wind's roar
How every drift, in their glens profound
Was deepening ever more –

And then I thought of Ula's bowers
10   Beyond the southern sea
Her tropic prairies bright with flowers
And rivers wandering free –

I thought of many a happy day
Spent in her Eden isle
With my dear comrades, young and gay
All scattered now so far away
But not forgot the while!

Who that has breathed that heavenly air
To northern climes would come
20   To Gondal's mists and moorlands drear
And sleet and frozen gloom?

Spring brings the swallow and the lark
But what will winter bring?
Its twilight noons and evenings dark
To match the gifts of spring?

No, Look with me o'er that sullen main
If thy spirit's eye can see
There are brave ships floating back again
That no calm southern port could chain
30   From Gondal's stormy sea.

O how the hearts of the voyagers beat
To feel the frost-wind blow!
What flower in Ula's gardens sweet
Is worth one flake of snow?

The blast which almost rends their sail
Is welcome as a friend;
It brings them home, that thundering gale
Home to their journey's end:

Home to our souls whose wearying sighs
40   Lament their absence drear
And feel how bright even winter skies
Would shine if they were here!

143. *At Castle Wood*

The day is done – the winter sun
Is setting in its sullen sky
And drear the course that [h]as been run
And dim the hearts that slowly die

No star will light my coming night
No morn of hope for me will shine
I mourn not heaven would blast my sight
And I never longed for [ways] divine

Through Life['s] hard Task I did not ask
10   Celestial aid celestial cheer
I saw my fate [without its] mask
And met it too without a tear

The grief that pressed this [living] breast
Was heavier far than earth can be
And who would dread eternal rest
When labour's hire was agony

Dark falls the fear of this despair
On spirits born for happiness
But I was bred the mate of care
20   The foster child of [sore] distress

No sighs for me, no sympathy,
No wish to keep my soul below
The heart is dead since infancy
Unwept for let the body go

144 [xx]. [*My Comforter*]

145. *A. G. A. to A. S.*

This summer wind, with thee and me
Roams in the dawn of day;
But thou must be where it shall be,
Ere Evening – far away.

The farewell's echo from thy soul
Should not depart before
Hills rise and distant rivers roll
Between us evermore –

I know that I have done thee wrong –
Have wronged both thee and Heaven –
And I may mourn my lifetime long
Yet may not be forgiven –

Repentant tears will vainly fall
To cancel deeds untrue;
But for no grief can I recall
The dreary word – Adieu –

Yet thou a future peace shalt win
Because thy soul is clear;
And I who had the heart to sin
Will find a heart to bear –

Till far beyond earth's frenzied strife
That makes destruction joy
Thy perished faith shall spring to life
And my remorse shall die

146 [x]. [*A Day Dream*]

147. *E. W. to A. G. A.*

How few, of all the hearts that loved,
Are grieving for thee now!
And why should mine, tonight, be moved
With such a sense of woe?

Too often, thus, when left alone
Where none my thoughts can see,
Comes back a word, a passing tone
From thy strange history.

Sometimes I seem to see thee rise
10 A glorious child again –
All virtues beaming from thine eyes
That ever honoured men –

Courage and Truth, a generous breast
Where Love and Gladness lay;
A being whose very Memory blest
And made the mourner gay –

O, fairly spread thy early sail
And fresh and pure and free
Was the first impulse of the gale
20 That urged life's wave for thee!

Why did the pilot, too confiding
Dream o'er that Ocean's foam?
And trust in Pleasure's careless guiding
To bring his vessel home?

For, well, he knew what dangers frowned,
What mists would gather dim,
What rocks and shelves and sands lay round
Between his port and him –

The very brightness of the sun,
30 The splendour of the main,
The wind that bore him wildly on
Should not have warned in vain

An anxious gazer from the shore,
I marked the whitening wave
And wept above thy fate the more
Because I could not save –

It recks not now, when all is over,
But, yet my heart will be
A mourner still, though friend and lover
40   Have both forgotten thee!

148. *The Death of A. G. A.*

Were they shepherds, who sat all day
On that brown mountain-side?
But neither staff nor dog had they;
Nor woolly flock to guide –

They were clothed in savage attire;
Their locks were dark and long;
And at each belt a weapon dire
Like bandit-knives was hung –

One was a woman tall and fair;
10   A princess she might be
From her stately form and her features rare
And her look of majesty –

But oh, she had a sullen frown –
A lip of cruel scorn –
As sweet tears never melted down
Her cheeks since she was born!

'Twas well she had no sceptre to wield,
No subject land to sway;
Fear might have made her vassals yield
20   But Love had been far away –

Yet, Love was even at her feet
In his most burning mood –
That Love which will the Wicked greet
As kindly as the Good –

And he was noble too, who bowed
So humbly by her side –
Entreating, till his eyes o'erflowed,
Her spirit's icy pride –

'Angelica, from my very birth
30   I have been nursed in strife,
And lived upon this weary Earth
A wanderer, all my life;

'The baited tiger could not be
So much athirst for gore,
For men and laws have tortured me
Till I can bear no more –

'The guiltless blood upon my hands
Will shut me out from Heaven
And here, and even in foreign lands
40   I cannot find a haven –

'And in all space, and in all time,
And through Eternity,
To aid a Spirit lost in crime,
I have no hope but thee –

'Yet will I swear, No saint on high
A truer faith could prove –
No angel, from that holy sky,
Could give thee purer love!

'For thee, through never ending years
50   I'd suffer endless pain;
But only give me back my tears
Return my love again!'

Many a time, unheeded, thus
The reckless man would pray;
But something woke an answering flush
On his lady's brow today,
And her eye flashed flame, as she turned to speak,
In concord with her reddening cheek –

'I've known a hundred kinds of love –
60   All made the loved one rue;
And what is thine, that it should prove,
Than other love, more true?

'Listen, I've known a burning heart
To which my own was given
Nay, not in passion; do not start –
Our love was love from heaven:
At least, if heavenly love be born
In the pure light of childhood's morn
Long ere the poison-tainted air
70   From this world's plague-fen rises there:

'That heart was like a tropic sun
That kindles all it shines upon;
And never Magian devotee
Gave worship half so warm as I
And never radiant bow could be
So welcome in a stormy sky
My soul dwelt with her day and night
She was my all sufficing light –
My childhood's mate, my girlhood's guide
80   My only blessing, only pride

'But cursed be the very earth
That gave that fiend her fatal birth!
With her own hand she bent the bow
That laid my best affections low –
Then mocked my grief and scorned my prayers
And drowned my bloom of youth in tears –
Warnings, reproaches, both were vain;
What recked she of another's pain?

My dearer self she would not spare –
90   From Honour's voice she turned his ear:
First made her love his only stay;
Then snatched the treacherous prop away!
Douglas, he pleaded bitterly –
He pleaded as *you* plead to me,
For life-long chains or timeless tomb
Or any, but an Exile's doom –
We both were scorned – both sternly driven
To shelter 'neath a foreign heaven;
And darkens o'er that dreary time
100   A wildering dream of frenzied crime –
I will not now those days recall;
The oath within that caverned hall
And its fulfilment, those you know:
We both together struck the blow:
But – you can never know the pain
That my lost heart did then sustain
When, severed wide by guiltless gore,
I felt that *one* could love no more!
Back maddening thought! – the grave is deep
110   Where my Amedeus lies asleep,
And I have long forgot to weep –

'Now hear me, in these regions wild
I saw today my enemy
Unarmed, as helpless as a child
She slumbered on a sunny lea;
Two friends – no other guard had she;
And they were wandering on the braes;
And chasing in regardless glee,
The wild goat o'er his dangerous ways –
120   My hand was raised – my knife was bare;
With stealthy tread I stole along
But a wild bird sprang from his hidden lair
And woke her with a sudden song:
Yet moved she not; she only raised
Her lids and on the bright sun gazed

And uttered such a dreary sigh
I thought just then she should not die
Since living was such misery –
Now Douglas, for our hunted band –
130   For future joy and former woe
Assist me, with thy heart and hand
To send to hell my mortal foe –
Her friends fall first, that she may drain
A deeper cup of bitterer pain;
Yonder they stand and watch the waves
Dash in among the echoing caves –
Their farewell sight of earth and sea;
Come, Douglas, rise and go with me' –

. . . .

The lark sang clearly overhead
140   And sweetly hummed the Bee
And softly, round their dying bed,
The wind blew from the sea –

Fair Surry would have raised her eyes
To see that water shine;
To see once more in mountain skies
The summer sun decline:

But ever, on her fading cheek,
The languid lid would close
As weary that such light should break
150   Its much-desired repose –

And she was waning fast away –
Even Memory's voice grew dim;
Her former life's eventful day
Had dwindled to a dream:

And hardly could her mind recall
One thought of joy or pain;
That cloud was gathering over all
Which never clears again!

In vain – in vain, you need not gaze
160   Upon those features now!
That sinking head you need not raise,
Nor kiss that pulseless brow –

Let out the grief that chokes your breath;
Lord Lesley, set it free:
The sternest eye, for such a death
Might fill with sympathy.

The tresses o'er her bosom spread
Were by a faint breeze blown;
'Her heart is beating,' Lesley said;
170   'She is not really gone!'

And still that form he fondly pressed,
And still of hope he dreamed
Nor marked how from his own young breast
Life's crimson current streamed –

At last, the sunshine left the ground,
The laden bee flew home,
The deep down sea, with sadder sound
Impelled its waves to foam;

And the corpse grew heavy on his arm,
180   The starry heaven grew dim,
The summer night so mild and warm
Felt wintery chill to him.

A troubled shadow, o'er his eye
Came down, and rested there;
The moors and sky went swimming by
Confused and strange and drear

He faintly prayed, 'Oh, Death, delay
Thy last fell dart to throw
Till I can hear my Sovereign say,
190   The traitors' heads are low!

'God, guard her life, since not to me
That dearest boon was given;
God, bless her arm with victory
Or bless not me with heaven!'

Then came the cry of agony;
The pang of parting pain;
And he had overpassed the sea
That none can pass again.

     .   .   .   .

Douglas leaned above the well;
200 Heather banks around him rose;
Bright and warm the sunshine fell
On that spot of sweet repose –

With the blue heaven bending o'er
And the soft wind singing by
And the clear stream, evermore
Mingling harmony –

On the shady side reclined,
He watched its waters play
And sound and sight had well combined
210 To banish gloom away –

A voice spoke near – 'She'll come,' it said
'And Douglas, thou shalt be
My love, although the very dead
Should rise to rival thee!

'Now, only let thine arm be true
And nerved, like mine, to kill;
And Gondal's royal race shall rue
This day on Elmor Hill!'

They wait not long, the rustling heath
220 Betrays their royal foe;
With hurried step and panting breath
And cheek almost as white as death,
Augusta sprang below –

Yet marked she not where Douglas lay
She only saw the well;
The tiny fountain, churning spray
Within its mossy cell –

'Oh, I have wrongs to pay,' she cried,
'Give life, give vigour now!'
230 And, stooping by the water's side,
She drank its crystal flow.

And brightly, with that draught, came back
The glory of her matchless eye
As, glancing o'er the moorland track,
She shook her head impatiently –

Nor shape, nor shade – the mountain flocks
Quietly feed in grassy dells;
Nor sound, except the distant rocks
Echoing to their bells.

240 She turns – she meets the Murderer's gaze:
Her own is scorched with a sudden blaze –
The blood streams down her brow;
The blood streams through her coal-black hair –
She strikes it off with little care;
She scarcely feels it flow,
For she has marked and known him too
And his own heart's ensanguined dew
Must slake her vengeance now!

False friend! no tongue save thine can tell
250 The mortal strife that then befell:
But, ere night darkened down
The stream in silence sang once more
And, on its green bank, bathed in gore
Augusta lay alone!

False Love! no earthly eye did see,
Yet Heaven's pure eye regarded thee
Where thy own Douglas bled –
How thou didst turn in mockery
From his last hopeless agony
260   And leave the hungry hawk to be
Sole watcher of the dead!

       .   .   .   .   .

Was it a deadly swoon?
Or was her spirit really gone?
And the cold corpse, beneath the moon
Laid like another mass of dust and stone?

The moon was full that night
The sky was almost like the day:
You might have seen the pulse's play
Upon her forehead white;

270   You might have seen the dear, dear sign of life
In her uncovered eye
And her cheek changing in the mortal strife
Betwixt the pain to live and agony to die.

But nothing mutable was there!
The face, all deadly fair,
Showed a fixed impress of keen suffering past,
And the raised lid did show
No wandering gleam below
But a stark anguish, self-destroyed at last –

280   Long he gazed and held his breath,
Kneeling on the blood-stained heath;
Long he gazed those lids beneath
Looking into Death!

Not a word from his followers fell,
They stood by, mute and pale;
That black treason uttered well
Its own heart-harrowing tale –

But earth was bathed in other gore:
There were crimson drops across the moor
290   And Lord Eldred, glancing round
Saw those tokens on the ground:

'Bring him back!' he hoarsely said,
'Wounded is the traitor fled –
Vengeance may hold but minutes brief
And you have all your lives for grief –'

He is left alone – he sees the stars
Their quiet course continuing
And, far away, down Elmor scars
He hears the stream its waters fling:

300   That lulling monotone did sing
Of broken rock and shaggy glen,
Of welcome for the moorcock's wing,
But, not of wail for men!

Nothing in heaven or earth to show
One sign of sympathizing woe –
And nothing but that agony
In her now unconscious eye
To weigh upon the labouring breast
And prove she did not pass at rest –
310   But he who watched, in thought had gone
Retracing back her lifetime flown;
Like sudden ghosts, to memory came
Full many a face, and many a name,
Full many a heart, that in the tomb
He almost deemed might have throbbed again
Had they but known her dreary doom,
Had they but seen their idol there,
A wreck of desolate despair,
Left to the wild birds of the air
320   And mountain winds and rain!
For him – no tear his stern eye shed
As he looked down upon the dead –

'Wild morn' – he thought – 'and doubtful noon;
But yet it was a glorious sun
Though comet-like its course was run:
That sun should never have been given
To burn and dazzle in the heaven
Or night has quenched it far too soon!
And thou art gone – with all thy pride,
330   Thou, so adored, so deified!
Cold as the earth, unweeting now
Of love, or joy, or mortal woe –

'For what thou wert, I would not grieve,
But much, for what thou wert to be –
That life, so stormy and so brief,
That death, has wronged us more than thee!
Thy passionate youth was nearly past
The opening sea seemed smooth at last
Yet vainly flowed the calmer wave
340   Since fate had not decreed to save –
And vain too must the sorrow be
Of those who live to mourn for thee;
But Gondal's foes shall not complain
That thy dear blood was poured in vain!'

149 [vi]. [Song]

150 [xi]. [To Imagination]

151. *D. G. C. to J. A.*

Come, the wind may never again
Blow as now it blows for us
And the stars may never again, shine as now they shine;
Long before October returns
Seas of blood will have parted us
And you must crush the love in your heart
And I, the love in mine!

For face to face will our kindred stand
And as they are so we shall be
10 Forgetting how the same sweet earth has borne and
    nourished all –
One must fight for the people's power
And one for the rights of royalty
And each be ready to give his life to work the other's fall –

The chance of war we cannot shun
Nor would we shrink from our fathers' cause
Nor dread Death more because the hand that gives it may
    be dear
We must bear to see Ambition rule
Over Love, with his iron laws;
Must yield our blood for a stranger's sake and refuse
    ourselves a tear!

20 So, the wind may never again
Blow as now it blows for us
And the stars may never again shine as now they shine
Next October, the cannon's roar
From hostile ranks may be urging us –
Me to strike for your life's blood and you to strike for
    mine –

152 [xiv]. [*Plead for Me*]

153 [i]. [*Faith and Despondency*]

154. *From a Dungeon Wall in the Southern College*

'Listen! when your hair like mine
Takes a tint of silver grey,
When your eyes, with dimmer shine,
Watch life's bubbles float away,

'When you, young man, have borne like me
The weary weight of sixty-three
Then shall penance sore be paid
For these hours so wildly squandered
And the words that now fall dead
10 On your ears be deeply pondered
Pondered and approved at last
But their virtue will be past!

'Glorious is the prize of Duty
Though she be a serious power
Treacherous all the lures of Beauty
Thorny bud and poisonous flower!

'Mirth is but a mad beguiling
Of the golden gifted Time –
Love – a demon meteor wiling
20 Heedless feet to gulfs of crime.

'Those who follow earthly pleasure
Heavenly Knowledge will not lead
Wisdom hides from them her treasure,
Virtue bids them evil speed!

'Vainly may their hearts, repenting,
Seek for aid in future years –
Wisdom scorned knows no relenting –
Virtue is not won by tears

'Fain would we your steps reclaim
30   Waken fear and holy shame
And to this end, our council well
And kindly doomed you to a cell
Whose darkness, may perchance, disclose
A beacon-guide from sterner woes' –

So spake my judge – then seized his lamp
And left me in the dungeon damp,
A vault-like place whose stagnant air
Suggests and nourishes despair!

Rosina, this had never been
40   Except for you, my despot queen!
Except for you the billowy sea
Would now be tossing under me
The wind's wild voice my bosom thrill
And my glad heart bound wilder still

Flying before the rapid gale
Those wondrous southern isles to hail
Which wait for my companions free
But thank your passion – not for me!

You know too well – and so do I
50   Your haughty beauty's sovereignty
Yet have I read those falcon eyes –
Have dived into their mysteries –
Have studied long their glance and feel
It is not love those eyes reveal –

They Flash – they burn with lightning shine
But not with such fond fire as mine;
The tender star fades faint and wan
Before Ambition's scorching sun –
So deem I now – and Time will prove
60   If I have wronged Rosina's love –

155 [xviii]. [*Honour's Martyr*]

156 [v]. [*A Death-Scene*]

157 [iii]. [*The Philosopher*]

158 [iv]. [*Remembrance*]

159 [xvi]. [*Death*]

160 [ii]. [*Stars*]

161.

A thousand sounds of happiness
And only one of real distress;
One hardly uttered groan –
But that has hushed all vocal joy,
Eclipsed the glory of the sky
And made me think that misery
Rules in our world alone!

About his face the sunshine glows
And in his hair the south wind blows
10   And violet and wild wood-rose
Are sweetly breathing near

Nothing without suggests dismay
If he could force his mind away
From tracking farther day by day
The desert of Despair –

Too truly agonized to weep
His eyes are motionless as sleep,
His frequent sighs long-drawn and deep
Are anguish to my ear
20 And I would soothe but can I call
The cold corpse from its funeral pall
And cause a gleam of hope to fall
With my consoling tear?

O Death, so many spirits driven
Through this false world, their all had given
To win the everlasting haven
To sufferers so divine –

Why didst thou smite the loved the blest
The ardent and the happy breast
30 That full of hope desired not rest
And shrank appalled from thine?

At least, since thou wilt not restore
In mercy launch one arrow more
Life's conscious Death it wearies sore
It tortures worse than thee –
Enough of storms have bowed his head,
Grant him at last a quiet bed
Beside his early stricken Dead
Even where he yearns to be!

162. *A. E. and R. C.*

Heavy hangs the raindrop
From the burdened spray;
Heavy broods the damp mist
On Uplands far away;

Heavy looms the dull sky,
Heavy rolls the sea –
And heavy beats the young heart
Beneath that lonely tree –

Never has a blue streak
10   Cleft the clouds since morn –
Never has his grim Fate
Smiled since he was born –

Frowning on the infant,
Shadowing childhood's joy,
Guardian angel knows not
That melancholy boy –

Day is passing swiftly
Its sad and sombre prime;
Youth is fast invading
20   Sterner manhood's time –

All the flowers are praying
For sun before they close
And he prays too, unknowing,
That sunless human rose!

Blossoms, that the west wind
Has never wooed to blow
Scentless are your petals
Your dew as cold as snow.

Soul, where kindred kindness
30   No early promise woke
Barren is your beauty
As weed upon the rock –

Wither, Brothers, wither,
You were vainly given –
Earth reserves no blessing
For the unblessed of Heaven!

Child of Delight! with sunbright hair
And seablue seadeep eyes
Spirit of Bliss, what brings thee here
40   Beneath these sullen skies?

Thou shouldest live in eternal spring
Where endless day is never dim
Why, seraph, has thy erring wing
Borne thee down to weep with him?

'Ah, not from heaven am I descended
And I do not come to mingle tears
But sweet is day, though with shadows blended
And though clouded, sweet are youthful years –

'I, the image of light and gladness
50   Saw and pitied that mournful boy
And I swore to take his gloomy sadness
And give to him my beamy joy –

'Heavy and dark the night is closing
Heavy and dark may its biding be
Better for all from grief reposing
And better for all who watch like me –

'Guardian angel, he lacks no longer;
Evil fortune he need not fear:
Fate is strong but Love is stronger
60   And more unsleeping than angel's care' –

163 [vii]. [*Anticipation*]

164. *M. A. Written on the Dungeon Wall – N. C.*

I know that tonight, the wind is sighing,
The soft August wind, over forest and moor
While I in a grave-like chill am lying
On the damp black flags of my dungeon-floor –

I know that the Harvest Moon is shining;
She neither will wax nor wane for me,
Yet I weary, weary, with vain repining,
One gleam of her heaven-bright face to see!

For this constant darkness is wasting the gladness
10   Fast wasting the gladness of life away;
It gathers up thoughts akin to madness
That never would cloud the world of day

I chide with my soul – I bid it cherish
The feelings it lived on when I was free,
But, shrinking it murmurs, 'Let Memory perish
Forget for thy Friends have forgotten thee!'

Alas, I did think that they were weeping
Such tears as I weep – it is not so!
Their careless young eyes are closed in sleeping;
20   Their brows are unshadowed, undimmed by woe –

Might I go to their beds, I'd rouse that slumber,
My spirit should startle their rest, and tell
How hour after hour, I wakefully number
Deep buried from light in my lonely cell!

Yet let them dream on, though dreary dreaming
Would haunt my pillow if *they* were here
And *I* were laid warmly under the gleaming
Of that guardian moon and her comrade star –

Better that I my own fate mourning
30   Should pine alone in the prison-gloom
Than waken free on the summer morning
And feel they were suffering this awful doom

165. *Julian M. and A. G. Rochelle*

Silent is the House – all are laid asleep;
One, alone, looks out o'er the snow-wreaths deep;
Watching every cloud, dreading every breeze
That whirls the wildering drifts and bends the groaning
    trees –

Cheerful is the hearth, soft the matted floor
Not one shivering gust creeps through pane or door
The little lamp burns straight; its rays shoot strong and far
I trim it well to be the Wanderer's guiding-star –

Frown, my haughty sire, chide my angry Dame;
10 Set your slaves to spy, threaten me with shame;
But neither sire nor dame, nor prying serf shall know
What angel nightly tracks that waste of winter snow –

In the dungeon crypts idly did I stray
Reckless of the lives wasting there away;
'Draw the ponderous bars, open Warder stern!'
He dare not say me nay – the hinges harshly turn –

'Our guests are darkly lodged' I whispered gazing through
The vault whose grated eye showed heaven more grey than
    blue;
(This was when glad spring laughed in awaking pride.)
20 'Aye, darkly lodged enough!' returned my sullen guide –

Then, God forgive my youth, forgive my careless tongue!
I scoffed as the chill chains on the damp flagstones rung;
'Confined in triple walls, art thou so much to fear,
That we must bind thee down and clench thy fetters here?'

The captive raised her face; it was as soft and mild
As sculptured marble saint or slumbering, unweaned child
It was so soft and mild, it was so sweet and fair
Pain could not trace a line nor grief a shadow there!

The captive raised her hand and pressed it to her brow
30   'I have been struck,' she said, 'and I am suffering now
Yet these are little worth, your bolts and irons strong
And were they forged in steel they could not hold me
        long' –

Hoarse laughed the jailer grim 'Shall I be won to hear
Dost think fond, dreaming wretch, that *I* shall grant thy
        prayer?
Or better still, wilt melt my master's heart with groans?
Ah sooner might the sun thaw down these granite stones! –

'My master's voice is low, his aspect bland and kind
But hard as hardest flint the soul that lurks behind:
And I am rough and rude, yet, not more rough to see
40   Than is the hidden ghost which has its home in me!'

About her lips there played a smile of almost scorn
'My friend,' she gently said, 'you have not heard me
        mourn
When you my parents' lives – *my* lost life, can restore
Then may I weep and sue, but, *never*, Friend, before!'

Her head sank on her hands, its fair curls swept the ground
The dungeon seemed to swim in strange confusion round –
'Is she so near to death?' I murmured, half aloud
And kneeling, parted back the floating golden cloud

Alas, how former days upon my heart were borne
50   How memory mirrored then the prisoner's joyous morn
Too blithe, too loving Child, too warmly, wildly gay!
Was that the wintry close of thy celestial May?

She knew me and she sighed 'Lord Julian, can it be,
Of all my playmates, you, alone, remember me?
Nay start not at my words, unless you deem it shame
To own from conquered foe, a once familiar name –

'I cannot wonder now at aught the world will do
And insult and contempt I lightly brook from you,
Since those, who vowed away their souls to win my love
60   Around this living grave like utter strangers move!

'Nor has one voice been raised to plead that I might die
Not buried under earth but in the open sky
By ball or speedy knife or headsman's skilful blow –
A quick and welcome pang instead of lingering woe!

'Yet, tell them, Julian, all, I am not doomed to wear
Year after year in gloom and desolate despair;
A messenger of Hope comes every night to me
And offers, for short life, eternal liberty.

'He comes with western winds, with evening's wandering
          airs,
70   With that clear dusk of heaven that brings the thickest
          stars;
Winds take a pensive tone, and stars a tender fire
And visions rise and change which kill me with desire –

'Desire for nothing known in my maturer years
When joy grew mad with awe at counting future tears;
When, if my spirit's sky was full of flashes warm,
I knew not whence they came from sun or thunderstorm;

'But first a hush of peace, a soundless calm descends;
The struggle of distress and fierce impatience ends;
Mute music soothes my breast – unuttered harmony
80   That I could never dream till earth was lost to me.

'Then dawns the Invisible, the Unseen its truth reveals;
My outward sense is gone, my inward essence feels –
Its wings are almost free, its home, its harbour found;
Measuring the gulf it stoops and dares the final bound!

'Oh, dreadful is the check – intense the agony
When the ear begins to hear and the eye begins to see;
When the pulse begins to throb, the brain to think again,
The soul to feel the flesh and the flesh to feel the chain!

'Yet I would lose no sting, would wish no torture less;
90   The more that anguish racks the earlier it will bless;
And robed in fires of Hell, or bright with heavenly shine,
If it but herald Death, the vision is divine' –

She ceased to speak and I, unanswering watched her there
Not daring now to touch one lock of silken hair –
As I had knelt in scorn, on the dank floor I knelt still –
My fingers in the links of that iron hard and chill –

I heard and yet heard not the surly keeper growl;
I saw, yet did not see, the flagstone damp and foul;
The keeper, to and fro, paced by the bolted door
100 And shivered as he walked and as he shivered, swore –

While my cheek glowed in flame, I marked that he did rave
Of air that froze his blood and moisture like the grave –
'We have been two hours good!' he muttered peevishly,
Then, loosing off his belt the rusty dungeon key,

He said, 'You may be pleased, Lord Julian, still to stay
But duty will not let me linger here all day;
If I might go, I'd leave this badge of mine with you
Not doubting that you'd prove a jailer stern and true'

I took the proffered charge; the captive's drooping lid
110 Beneath its shady lash a sudden lightning hid
Earth's hope was not so dead heaven's home was not so
   dear
I read it in that flash of longing quelled by fear

Then like a tender child whose hand did just enfold
Safe in its eager grasp a bird it wept to hold
When pierced with one wild glance from the troubled hazel
   eye
It gushes into tears and lets its treasure fly

Thus ruth and selfish love together striving tore
The heart all newly taught to pity and adore;
If I should break the chain, I felt my bird would go
120 Yet I must break the chain or seal the prisoner's woe –

Short strife what rest could soothe – what peace could visit
   me
While she lay pining there for Death to set her free?
'Rochelle, the dungeons teem with foes to gorge our hate –
Thou art too young to die by such a bitter fate!'

With hurried blow on blow I struck the fetters through
Regardless how that deed my after hours might rue
Oh, I was over-blest by the warm unasked embrace
By the smile of grateful joy that lit her angel face!

And I was over-blest – aye, more than I could dream
130   When, faint, she turned aside from noon's unwonted beam;
When though the cage was wide – the heaven around it
    lay –
Its pinion would not waft my wounded dove away –

Through thirteen anxious weeks of terror-blent delight
I guarded her by day and guarded her by night
While foes were prowling near and Death gazed greedily
And only Hope remained a faithful friend to me –

Then oft with taunting smile, I heard my kindred tell
'How Julian loved his hearth and sheltering roof-tree well;
How the trumpet's voice might call the battle-standard
    wave
140   But Julian had no heart to fill a patriot's grave.'

And I, who am so quick to answer sneer with sneer;
So ready to condemn to scorn a coward's fear
I held my peace like one whose conscience keeps him dumb
And saw my kinsmen go – and lingered still at home.

Another hand than mine, my rightful banner held
And gathered my renown on Freedom's crimson field
Yet I had no desire the glorious prize to gain –
It needed braver nerve to face the world's disdain –

And by the patient strength that could that world defy;
150   By suffering with calm mind, contempt and calumny;
By never-doubting love, unswerving constancy,
Rochelle, I earned at last an equal love from thee!

166 [viii]. [*The Prisoner* (*A Fragment*)]

167.

No coward soul is mine
No trembler in the world's storm-troubled sphere
I see Heaven's glories shine
And Faith shines equal arming me from Fear

O God within my breast
Almighty ever-present Deity
Life, that in me hast rest
As I Undying Life, have power in thee

Vain are the thousand creeds
10   That move men's hearts, unutterably vain,
Worthless as withered weeds
Or idlest froth amid the boundless main

To waken doubt in one
Holding so fast by thy infinity
So surely anchored on
The steadfast rock of Immortality

With wide-embracing love
Thy spirit animates eternal years
Pervades and broods above,
20   Changes, sustains, dissolves, creates and rears

Though Earth and moon were gone
And suns and universes ceased to be
And thou wert left alone
Every Existence would exist in thee

There is not room for Death
Nor atom that his might could render void
Since thou art Being and Breath
And what thou art may never be destroyed

168.

Why ask to know the date – the clime?
More than mere words they cannot be:
Men knelt to God and worshipped crime,
And crushed the helpless even as we –

But, they had learnt, from length of strife –
Of civil war and anarchy
To laugh at death and look on life
With somewhat lighter sympathy.

It was the autumn of the year,
10   The time to labouring peasants, dear:
Week after week, from noon to noon,
September shone as bright as June –
Still, never hand a sickle held;
The crops were garnered in the field –
Trod out and ground by horses' feet
While every ear was milky sweet;
And kneaded on the threshing-floor
With mire of tears and human gore.
Some said they thought that heaven's pure rain
20   Would hardly bless those fields again:
Not so – the all-benignant skies
Rebuked that fear of famished eyes –
July passed on with showers and dew,
And August glowed in showerless blue;
No harvest time could be more fair
Had harvest fruits but ripened there.

And I confess that hate of rest,
And thirst for things abandoned now,
Had weaned me from my country's breast
30   And brought me to that land of woe.

Enthusiast – in a name delighting,
My alien sword I drew to free
One race, beneath two standards fighting,
For Loyalty, and Liberty –

When kindred strive, God help the weak!
A brother's ruth 'tis vain to seek:
At first, it hurt my chivalry
To join them in their cruelty;
But I grew hard – I learnt to wear
40   An iron front to terror's prayer;
I learnt to turn my ears away
From torture's groans, as well as they.
By force I learnt – what power had I
To say the conquered should not die?
What heart, one trembling foe to save
When hundreds daily filled the grave?
Yet, there *were* faces that could move
A moment's flash of human love;
And there were fates that made me feel
50   I was not to the centre, steel –

I've often witnessed wise men fear
To meet distress which they foresaw;
And seeming cowards nobly bear
A doom that thrilled the brave with awe;

Strange proofs I've seen, how hearts could hide
Their secret with a life-long pride,
And then reveal it as they died –
Strange courage, and strange weakness too,
In that last hour when most are true,
60   And timid natures strangely nerved
To deeds from which the desperate swerved.
These I may tell, but leave them now.
Go with me where my thoughts would go;
Now all today and all last night
I've had one scene before my sight –

Wood-shadowed dales; a harvest moon
Unclouded in its glorious noon;
A solemn landscape, wide and still;
A red fire on a distant hill –
70   A line of fires, and deep below,
Another dusker, drearier glow –

Charred beams, and lime, and blackened stones
Self-piled in cairns o'er burning bones,
And lurid flames that licked the wood
Then quenched their glare in pools of blood –
But yestereve – No! never care;
Let street and suburb smoulder there –
Smoke-hidden, in the winding glen,
They lay too far to vex my ken.

80 Four score shot down – all veterans strong –
One prisoner spared, their leader young –
And he within his house was laid,
Wounded, and weak and nearly dead.
We gave him life against his will;
For he entreated us to kill –
But statue-like we saw his tears –
And harshly fell our captain's sneers!

'Now, heaven forbid!' with scorn he said –
'That noble gore our hands should shed
90 Like common blood – retain thy breath
Or scheme, if thou canst purchase death –
When men are poor we sometimes hear
And pitying grant that dastard prayer;
When men are rich, we make them buy
The pleasant privilege, to die –
O, we have castles reared for kings
Embattled towers and buttressed wings
Thrice three feet thick, and guarded well
With chain, and bolt, and sentinel!
100 We build our despots' dwellings sure;
Knowing they love to live secure –
And our respect for royalty
Extends to thy estate and thee!'

The suppliant groaned; his moistened eye
Swam wild and dim with agony –
The gentle blood could ill sustain
Degrading taunts, unhonoured pain.
Bold had he shown himself to lead;
Eager to smite and proud to bleed –

110   A man amid the battle's storm;
       An infant in the after calm.

       Beyond the town his mansion stood
       Girt round with pasture-land and wood;
       And there our wounded soldiers lying
       Enjoyed the ease of wealth in dying:

       For him, no mortal more than he
       Had softened life with luxury;
       And truly did our priest declare
       'Of good things he had had his share.'

120   We lodged him in an empty place,
       The full moon beaming on his face
       Through shivered glass, and ruins, made
       Where shell and ball the fiercest played.
       I watched his ghastly couch beside
       Regardless if he lived or died –
       Nay, muttering curses on the breast
       Whose ceaseless moans denied me rest:

       'Twas hard, I know, 'twas harsh to say,
       'Hell snatch thy worthless soul away!'
130   But then 'twas hard my lids to keep
       Through this long night, estranged from sleep.
       Captive and keeper, both outworn,
       Each in his misery yearned for morn;
       Even though returning morn should bring
       Intenser toil and suffering.

       Slow, slow it came! Our dreary room
       Grew drearier with departing gloom;
       Yet as the west wind warmly blew
       I felt my pulses bound anew,
140   And turned to him – nor breeze, nor ray
       Revived that mould of shattered clay,
       Scarce conscious of his pain he lay –
       Scarce conscious that my hands removed
       The glittering toys his lightness loved –
       The jewelled rings, and locket fair

Where rival curls of silken hair,
Sable and brown revealed to me
A tale of doubtful constancy.

'Forsake the world without regret,'
150   I murmured in contemptuous tone;
'The world, poor wretch, will soon forget
Thy noble name when thou art gone!
Happy, if years of slothful shame
Could perish like a noble name –
If God did no account require
And being with breathing might expire!'
And words of such [contempt] I said,
Cold insults o'er a dying bed,
Which as they darken memory now
160   Disturb my pulse and flush my brow;
I know that Justice holds in store,
Reprisals for those days of gore –
Not for the blood, but for the sin
Of stifling mercy's voice within.
The blood spilt gives no pang at all;
It is my conscience haunting me,
Telling how oft my lips shed gall
On many a thing too weak to be,
Even in thought, my [enemy] –
170   And whispering ever, when I pray,
'God will repay – God will repay!'
He does repay and soon and well
The deeds that turn his earth to hell
The wrongs that aim a venomed dart
Through nature at the Eternal Heart –
Surely my cruel tongue was cursed
I know my prisoner heard me speak
A transient gleam of feeling burst
And wandered o'er his haggard cheek
180   And from his quivering lids there stole
A look to melt a demon's soul
A silent prayer more powerful far
Than any breathed petitions are

Pleading in mortal agony
To mercy's Source but not to me –
Now I recall that glance and groan
And wring my hands in vain distress
Then I was adamantine stone
Nor felt one touch of tenderness –
190 My plunder ta'en I left him there
Without [one breath] of morning air
To struggle with his last despair
Regardless of the wildered cry
Which wailed for death yet wailed to die
I left him there unwatched alone
And eager sought the court below
Where o'er a trough of chiselled stone
An ice cold well did gurgling flow
The water in its basin shed
200 A stranger tinge of fiery red.
I drank and scarcely marked the hue
My food was dyed with crimson too
As I went out a [ragged] child
With wasted cheek and ringlets wild
A shape of fear and misery
Raised up her [helpless] hands to me
And begged her father's face to see
I spurned the piteous wretch away
Thy father's [face] is lifeless clay
210 As thine mayst be ere fall of day
Unless the truth be quickly told
Where thou hast hid thy father's gold
Yet in the intervals of pain
He heard my taunts and moaned again
And mocking moans did I reply
And asked him why he would not die
In noble agony – uncomplaining.
Was it not foul disgrace and shame
To thus disgrace his ancient name?

220 Just then a comrade came hurrying in
    Alas, he cried, sin genders sin
    For every soldier slain they've sworn
    To hang up five come morn.
    They've ta'en of stranglers sixty-three
    Full thirty from one company
    And all my father's family
    And comrade thou hadst only one
    They've ta'en thy all thy little son
    Down at my captive's feet I fell
230 I had no option in despair
    As thou wouldst save thy soul from hell
    My heart's own darling bid them spare
    Or human hate and hate divine
    Blight every orphan flower of thine
    He raised his head – from death beguiled
    He wakened up he almost smiled
    Twice in my arms twice on my knee
    You stabbed my child and laughed at me
    And so, with choking voice he said
240 I trust I hope in God she's dead
    Yet not to thee not even to thee
    Would I return such misery
    Such is that [fearful] grief I know
    I will not cause thee equal woe
    Write that they harm no infant there
    Write that it is my latest prayer
    I wrote – he signed and thus did save
    My treasure from the gory grave
    And O my soul longed wildly then
250 To give his saviour life again.
    But heedless of my gratitude
    The silent corpse before me lay
    And still methinks in gloomy mood
    I see it fresh as yesterday
    The sad face raised imploringly

To mercy's God and not to me –
The last [look] of that agony
I could not rescue him his child
I found alive and tended well
260 But she was full of anguish wild
And hated me like we hate hell
And weary with her savage woe
One moonless night I let her go

169.

Why ask to know what date what clime
There dwelt our own humanity
Power-worshippers from earliest time
Foot-kissers of triumphant crime
Crushers of helpless misery
Crushing down Justice honouring Wrong
If that be feeble this be strong

Shedders of blood shedders of tears
Self-cursers avid of distress
10 Yet Mocking heaven with senseless prayers
For mercy on the merciless

It was the autumn of the year
When grain grows yellow in the ear
Day after day from noon to noon,
That August's sun blazed bright as June

But we with unregarding eyes
Saw panting earth and glowing skies
No hand the reaper's sickle held
Nor bound the ripe sheaves in the field

20 Our corn was garnered months before,
Threshed out and kneaded-up with gore
Ground when the ears were milky sweet
With furious toil of hoofs and feet
I doubly cursed on foreign sod
Fought neither for my home nor God

III. Undated Poems

170.

All day I've toiled but not with pain
In learning's golden mine
And now at eventide again
The moonbeams softly shine

There is no snow upon the ground
No frost on wind or wave
The south wind blew with gentlest sound
And broke their icy grave

'Tis sweet to wander here at night
10   To watch the winter die
With heart as summer sunshine light
And warm as summer's sky

O may I never lose the peace
That lulls me gently now
Though time should change my youthful face
And years should shade my brow

True to myself and true to all
May I be healthful still
And turn away from passion's call
20   And cùrb my own wild will

171.

'Tis evening now the sun descends
In golden glory down the sky
The city's murmur softly blends
With zephyrs breathing gently by

And yet it seems a dreary [morn]
A dark October [morn] to me
And black the piles of rainclouds [borne]
Athwart heaven's stormy canopy

172.

There let thy bleeding branch atone
For every torturing tear
Shall my young sins my sins alone
Be everlasting here?

Who bade thee keep that cursed name
A pledge for memory
As if Oblivion ever came
To breathe its bliss on me

As if through all the wildering maze
10   Of mad hours left behind
I once forgot the early days
That thou wouldst call to mind

173.

What winter floods what showers of spring
Have drenched the grass by night and day
And yet beneath that spectre ring
Unmoved and undiscovered lay

A mute remembrancer of crime
Long lost concealed forgot for years
It comes at last to cancel time
And waken unavailing tears

174.

All hushed and still within the house
Without – all wind and driving rain
But something whispers to my mind
Through rain and [through the] wailing wind
                    – Never again
Never again? Why not again?
Memory has power as real as thine

175.

 Iernë's eyes were glazed and dim
When the castle bell tolled one
She looked around her dungeon grim
The grating cast a doubtful gleam
'Twas one cloud saddened cold moon-beam
Iernë gazed as in a dream
And thought she saw the sun

She thought it was the break of day
The night had been so long

176.

But the hearts that once adored me
Have long forgot their vow
And the friends that mustered round me
Have all forsaken now

'Twas in a dream revealed to me
But not a dream of sleep
A dream of watchful agony
Of grief that would not weep

Now do not harshly turn away

177.

Methinks this heart should rest awhile
So stilly round the evening falls
The veiled sun sheds no parting smile
Nor mirth nor music wakes my Halls

I have sat lonely all the day
Watching the drizzly mist descend
And first conceal the hills in grey
And then along the valleys wend

And I have sat and watched the trees
10   And the sad flowers how drear they blow
Those flowers were formed to feel the breeze
Wave their light leaves in summer's glow

Yet their lives passed in gloomy woe
And hopeless comes its dark decline
And I lament because I know
That cold departure pictures mine

178.

That dreary lake that midnight sky
That wan moon struggling through the cloud
That sullen murmur whispering by
As if it dared not speak aloud
Fall on my heart so sadly now
Wither my joy so lonely

Touch them not they bloom and smile
But their roots are withering all the while
Ah

179.

His land may burst the galling chain
His people may be free again
For them a thousand hopes remain
But hope is dead for him
Soft falls the moonlight on the sea
Whose wild waves play at liberty
And Gondal's wind sings solemnly
Its [native] midnight hymn

Around his prison walls it sings
10   His heart is stirred through all its strings
Because that sound remembrance brings
Of scenes that once have been

His soul has left the storm below
And reached a realm of sunless snow
The region of [unchanging] woe
Made voiceless by despair

And Gerald's land may burst its chain
His subjects may be free again
For them a thousand hopes remain
20   But hope is dead for him
Set is his sun of liberty
Fixed is his earthly destiny
A few years of captivity
And then a captive's tomb

180.

She dried her tears and they did smile
To see her cheeks' returning glow
How little dreaming all the while
That full heart throbbed to overflow

With that sweet look and lively tone
And bright eye shining all the day
They could not guess at midnight lone
How she would weep the time away

181.

Love is like the wild rose briar,
Friendship, like the holly tree
The holly is dark when the rose briar blooms,
But which will bloom most constantly?

The wild rose briar is sweet in spring,
Its summer blossoms scent the air
Yet wait till winter comes again
And who will call the wild-briar fair

Then scorn the silly rose-wreath now
10   And deck thee with the holly's sheen
That when December blights thy brow
He still may leave thy garland green –

182 [xiii]. [*Sympathy*]

IV. Poems of Doubtful Authorship

Often rebuked, yet always back returning
    To those first feelings that were born with me,
And leaving busy chase of wealth and learning
    For idle dreams of things which cannot be:

Today, I will seek not the shadowy region;
    Its unsustaining vastness waxes drear;
And visions rising, legion after legion,
    Bring the unreal world too strangely near.

I'll walk, but not in old heroic traces,
    And not in paths of high morality,
And not among the half-distinguished faces,
    The clouded forms of long-past history.

I'll walk where my own nature would be leading:
    It vexes me to choose another guide:
Where the grey flocks in ferny glens are feeding;
    Where the wild wind blows on the mountain side.

What have those lonely mountains worth revealing?
    More glory and more grief than I can tell:
The earth that wakes *one* human heart to feeling
    Can centre both the worlds of Heaven and Hell.

To the Horse Black Eagle Which I Rode at the Battle of Zamorna

Swart steed of night, thou hast charged thy last
O'er the red war-trampled plain
Now fallen asleep is the battle blast
It is stilled above the slain

Now hushed is the clang of armour bright
Thou wilt never bear me more
To the deadliest press of the gathering fight
Through seas of noble gore

And the cold eyes of midnight skies
10   Shall not pour their light on thee
When the wearied host of the conqueror lies
On a field of victory

Rest now in thy glory noble steed
Rest all thy wars are done
True is the love and high the meed
Thou from thy lord hast won

In daisied lawns sleep peacefully
Dwell by the quiet wave
Till death shall sound his signal cry
20   And call thee to thy grave.

Further Reading

Editions

Poems by Currer, Ellis, and Acton Bell, London: Aylott & Jones, 1846.

Currer Bell (ed.), *Wuthering Heights and Agnes Grey*, London: Smith, Elder & Co., 1850.

Poems of Charlotte, Emily, and Anne Brontë Now for the First Time Printed, New York: Dodd, Mead & Co., 1902.

Clement Shorter (ed.), *The Complete Poems of Emily Brontë*, London: Hodder & Stoughton, 1910.

Arthur C. Benson (ed.), *Brontë Poems: Selections from the Poetry of Charlotte, Emily, Anne, and Branwell Brontë*, London: Smith, Elder & Co., 1915.

Clement Shorter (ed.), *The Complete Poems of Emily Jane Brontë*, arranged and collated, with bibliography and notes by C.W. Hatfield, London: Hodder & Stoughton, 1923.

Thomas J. Wise and John A. Symington (eds.), *The Poems of Emily Jane Brontë and Anne Brontë*, Oxford: Shakespeare Head Press, 1934.

Helen Brown and Joan Mott (eds.), *Gondal Poems by Emily Jane Brontë*, Oxford: Shakespeare Head Press, 1938.

C.W. Hatfield (ed.), *The Complete Poems of Emily Jane Brontë*, New York: Columbia University Press, 1941.

Philip Henderson (ed.), *The Complete Poems of Emily Jane Brontë*, London: The Folio Society, 1951.

Juliet R.V. Barker (ed.), *The Brontës: Selected Poems*, London: Dent, 1985.

Edward Chitham and Tom Winnifrith (eds.), *Selected Brontë Poems*, Oxford: Basil Blackwell, 1985.

Reference

Janet M. Barclay, *Emily Brontë Criticism 1900–1982: An Annotated Check List*, Westport, Connecticut: Meckler Publishing, 1984.

Edward Chitham, *The Poems of Anne Brontë*, London: Macmillan, 1979.

R. W. Crump, *Charlotte and Emily Brontë, 1846–1915: A Reference Guide*, Boston: G. K. Hall & Co., 1982.

Amy G. Foster, *Analytical Index of the Contents of the Brontë Society Transactions, Volume I (1895) – Volume XV (1967) and Index of Authors*, Keighley: Keighley Printers Ltd, 1968.

G. D. Hargreaves, 'The Publishing of *Poems by Currer, Ellis and Acton Bell*', *Brontë Society Transactions* 15 (1969), 294–300.

Index of English Literary Manuscripts, vol. iv (1800–1900), part 1 (Arnold–Gissing), compiled by Barbara Rosenbaum and Pamela White, Mansell Publishing Ltd, 1982.

David R. Isenberg, 'A Gondal Fragment', *Brontë Society Transactions* 14 (1962), 24–6.

Hilda Marsden and Ian Jack (eds.), *Wuthering Heights*, Oxford: Clarendon Press, 1976.

Lorine White Nagel (trans.), *Five Essays Written in French by Emily Jane Brontë*, introduction and notes by Fannie E. Ratchford, Austin: University of Texas Press, 1948.

Victor Neufeldt, *The Poems of Charlotte Brontë*, New York: Garland Publishing, 1985.

Derek Roper, 'The Revision of Emily Brontë's Poems of 1846', *The Library*, Sixth Series 6 (1984), 153–67.

Tom Winnifrith, *The Poems of Patrick Branwell Brontë*, New York: New York University Press, 1983.

Biography and Criticism

Georges Bataille, *Literature and Evil*, trans. Alastair Hamilton, London: Calder & Boyars, 1973.

Jacques Blondel, *Emily Brontë: Expérience spirituelle et création poétique*, Paris: Presses Universitaires de France, 1956.

Harold Bloom (ed.), *Modern Critical Views: The Brontës*, New York: Chelsea House, 1987.

Robert Bridges, 'The Poems of Emily Brontë', in *Collected Essays*, London: Oxford University Press, 1932.

Helen Brown, 'The Influence of Byron on Emily Brontë', *Modern Language Review* 34 (1939), 374–81.

Edward Chitham and Tom Winnifrith, *Brontë Facts and Brontë Problems*, London: Macmillan, 1983.

Edward Chitham, *A Life of Emily Brontë*, Oxford: Basil Blackwell, 1987.

Herbert Dingle, *The Mind of Emily Brontë*, London: Martin, Brian & O'Keefe, 1974.

Katherine Frank, *A Chainless Soul: A Life of Emily Brontë*, London: Hamish Hamilton, 1990.

Rebecca Fraser, *The Brontës: Charlotte Brontë and Her Family*, New York: Crown Publishers, Inc., 1988.

Winifred Gérin, *Emily Brontë: A Biography*, London: Oxford University Press, 1971.

Ian Gregor, *The Brontës: A Collection of Critical Essays*, Englewood Cliffs, N.J.: Prentice-Hall, 1970.

John Hewish, *Emily Brontë: A Critical and Biographical Study*, London: Macmillan, 1969.

Margaret Homans, *Women Writers and Poetic Identity: Dorothy Wordsworth, Emily Brontë, and Emily Dickinson*, Princeton: Princeton University Press, 1980.

F.R. Leavis, 'Reality and Sincerity' (1952), rpt. in *The Living Principle: 'English' as a Discipline of Thought*, London: Chatto & Windus, 1975.

F.R. Leavis, *Revaluation: Tradition and Development in English Poetry*, London: Chatto & Windus, 1936.

C. Day Lewis, 'The Poetry of Emily Brontë', *Brontë Society Transactions* 13 (1965), 83–95.

Lawrence I. Lipking, *Abandoned Women and Poetic Tradition*, Chicago: University of Chicago Press, 1988.

Margaret Maison, 'Emily Brontë and Epictetus', *Notes and Queries*, NS 25 (June 1978), 230–31.

J. Hillis Miller, *The Disappearance of God: Five Nineteenth-Century Writers*, Cambridge, Mass.: Harvard University Press, 1963.

W.D. Paden, *An Investigation of Gondal*, New York: Bookman Associates, 1965.

Fannie E. Ratchford, *The Brontës' Web of Childhood*, New York: Columbia University Press, 1941.

Fannie E. Ratchford, *Gondal's Queen: A Novel in Verse by Emily Jane Brontë*, Austin: University of Texas Press, 1955.

Clement Shorter, *The Brontës and their Circle*, New York: E.P. Dutton, 1917.

Anne Smith (ed.), *The Art of Emily Brontë*, New York: Barnes & Noble, 1976.

Muriel Spark and Derek Stanford, *Emily Brontë, Her Life and Work*, London: Peter Owen, 1953.

Caroline F.E. Spurgeon, *Mysticism in English Literature*, Cambridge: Cambridge University Press, 1913.

Irene Tayler, *Holy Ghosts: The Male Muses of Emily and Charlotte Brontë*, New York: Columbia University Press, 1990.

Mary Visick, *The Genesis of Wuthering Heights*, Hong Kong: Hong Kong University Press, 1958.

Tom Winnifrith, *The Brontës and Their Background: Romance and Reality*, London: Macmillan, 1973.

Jonathan Wordsworth, 'Wordsworth and the Poetry of Emily Brontë', *Brontë Society Transactions* 16 (1972), 85–100.

Acknowledgements

I am grateful to the following libraries that have made manuscripts in their collections available to me, and to the librarians of these collections for their hospitality: the Brontë Parsonage Museum Library, the British Library, the Pierpont Morgan Library, the New York Public Library, the Princeton University Libraries, and the University of Texas at Austin Library. I wish to thank the staff of the Charles E. Shain Library of Connecticut College, particularly Head Reference Librarian Jim MacDonald, for their assistance. I am also indebted to the National Endowment for the Humanities for a Travel-to-Collections grant and a summer stipend, and to Connecticut College for financial support, including an augmented sabbatical grant. Charles Hartman was generous in providing technical support and encouragement.

I am above all grateful to Christopher Ricks, the General Editor of this series, for seeing the need for a new edition of Emily Jane Brontë's poems and for patient, detailed criticism. While working on this edition, I have kept in mind Robert Bridges's review of Clement Shorter's 1910 edition of Brontë's poems: 'That anyone should have kept Emily Brontë's poems in his desk for years, and should then apologize for publishing them, and not take the trouble to print them correctly, is a piece of magnificent insouciance.' I trust that readers will not attribute errors in this edition to the editor's insouciance, and I will be grateful to those who point them out to me.

Appendix 1

A list of poems in their order of appearance in the *Gondal Poems* notebook and the Honresfeld manuscript

(NOTE: Titles of poems appear below exactly as they do in the manuscripts.)

Contents of the Gondal Poems *Notebook*

'There shines the moon, at noon of night' (10)

A. G. A. to A. E.: 'Lord of Elbë, on Elbë hill' (23)

A. G. A. to A. S.: 'At such a time, in such a spot' (138)

To A. G. A.: '"Thou standest in the greenwood now"' (136)

A. G. A. to A. S.: 'This summer wind, with thee and me' (145)

A. G. A. to A. S.: 'O wander not so far away' (48)

To the bluebell –: 'Sacred watcher, wave thy bells' (84)

Written in Aspin Castle –: 'How do I love on summer nights' (129)

Douglases Ride –: 'Well, narrower draw the circle round' (61)

'From our evening fireside now' (81)

Gleneden's Dream: 'Tell me, watcher, is it winter' (49)

Rosina: 'Weeks of wild delirium past' (126)

Song by Julius Brenzaida to G. S.: 'Geraldine, the moon is shining' (66)

Song by J. Brenzaida: 'I knew not 'twas so dire a crime' (67)

Geraldine –: ' 'Twas night, her comrades gathered all' (125)

'For him who struck thy foreign string' (62)

Written in the Gaaldine Prison Caves to A. G. A.: 'Thy sun is near meridian height' (112)

F. De Samara to A. G. A.: 'Light up thy halls! 'Tis closing day' (71)

Written on Returning to the P. of I. on the 10th of January 1827–: 'The busy day has hurried by' (89)

On the fall of Zalona: 'All blue and bright, in glorious light' (131)

A. G. A. The Death of: 'Were they shepherds, who sat all day' (148)

Contents of the Honresfeld Manuscript

The Night-Wind: 'In summer's mellow midnight' (118)
'Riches I hold in light esteem' (xxi [121])
'Aye there it is! It wakes tonight' (123)
'I'll not weep that thou art going to leave me' (xix [115])
'If grief for grief can touch thee' (116)
'O Dream, where art thou now' (75)
'It is too late to call thee now' (114)
'The wind I hear it sighing' (104)
'Love is like the wild rose briar' (181)
'There should be no despair for you' (xiii [182])
'Well, some may hate and some may scorn' (xvii [105])
'Far, far away is mirth withdrawn' (113)
'I see around me tombstones grey' (124)
'"The evening passes fast away"' (xv [130])
Hope: 'Hope was but a timid friend' (ix [141])
My Comforter: 'Well hast thou spoken – and yet not taught' (xx
[144])
'How clear she shines! How quietly' (xii [132])
'On a sunny brae, alone I lay' (x [146])
To Imagination: 'When weary with the long day's care' (xi [150])
'Oh, thy bright eyes must answer now' (xiv [152])
'"Enough of thought, philosopher"' (iii, [157])
'Ah! why, because the dazzling sun' (ii [160])
'Death! that struck when I was most confiding' (xvi [159])
'How beautiful the Earth is still' (vii [163])
'No coward soul is mine' (167)

Appendix 2

Poems as edited by Charlotte Brontë in 1850

(Selections from Poems by Ellis Bell)

A little while, a little while,
    The weary task is put away,
And I can sing and I can smile,
    Alike, while I have holiday.

Where wilt thou go my harassed heart –
    What thought, what scene invites thee now?
What spot, or near or far apart,
    Has rest for thee, my weary brow?

There is a spot, 'mid barren hills,
10   Where winter howls, and driving rain;
But, if the dreary tempest chills,
    There is a light that warms again.

The house is old, the trees are bare,
    Moonless above bends twilight's dome;
But what on earth is half so dear –
    So longed for – as the hearth of home?

The mute bird sitting on the stone,
    The dank moss dripping from the wall,
The thorn-trees gaunt, the walks o'ergrown,
20   I love them – how I love them all!

Still – as I mused – the naked room,
    The alien firelight died away;
And from the midst of cheerless gloom,
    I passed to bright, unclouded day.

A little and a lone green lane
    That opened on a common wide;
A distant, dreamy, dim, blue chain
    Of mountains, circling every side.

A heaven so clear, an earth so calm,
30   So sweet, so soft, so hushed an air;
And – deepening still the dream-like charm –
    Wild moor-sheep feeding everywhere.

That was the scene, I knew it well;
    I knew the turfy pathway's sweep,
That, winding o'er each billowy swell,
    Marked out the tracks of wandering sheep.

Could I have lingered but an hour,
    It well had paid a week of toil;
But Truth has banished Fancy's power:
40   Restraint and heavy task recoil.

Even as I stood with raptured eye,
    Absorbed in bliss so deep and dear,
My hour of rest had fleeted by,
    And back came labour, bondage, care.

The Bluebell

The Bluebell is the sweetest flower
    That waves in summer air:
Its blossoms have the mightiest power
    To soothe my spirit's care.

There is a spell in purple heath
    Too wildly, sadly dear;
The violet has a fragrant breath,
    But fragrance will not cheer.

The trees are bare, the sun is cold,
 And seldom, seldom seen;
The heavens have lost their zone of gold,
 And earth her robe of green.

And ice upon the glancing stream
 Has cast its sombre shade;
And distant hills and valleys seem
 In frozen mist arrayed.

The Bluebell cannot charm me now,
 The heath has lost its bloom;
The violets in the glen below,
 They yield no sweet perfume.

But, though I mourn the sweet Bluebell,
 'Tis better far away;
I know how fast my tears would swell
 To see it smile to-day.

For, oh! when chill the sunbeams fall
 Adown that dreary sky,
And gild yon dank and darkened wall
 With transient brilliancy;

How do I weep, how do I pine
 For the time of flowers to come,
And turn me from that fading shine,
 To mourn the fields of home!

Loud without the wind was roaring
 Through th' autumnal sky;
Drenching wet, the cold rain pouring,
 Spoke of winter nigh.
  All too like that dreary eve,
  Did my exiled spirit grieve.

Grieved at first, but grieved not long,
    Sweet – how softly sweet! – it came;
Wild words of an ancient song,
10   Undefined, without a name.

'It was spring, and the skylark was singing:'
    Those words they awakened a spell;
They unlocked a deep fountain, whose springing,
    Nor absence, nor distance can quell.

In the gloom of a cloudy November,
    They uttered the music of May;
They kindled the perishing ember
    Into fervour that could not decay.

Awaken, o'er all my dear moorland,
20   West-wind, in thy glory and pride!
O! call me from valley and lowland,
    To walk by the hill-torrent's side!

It is swelled with the first snowy weather;
    The rocks they are icy and hoar,
And sullenly waves the long heather,
    And the fern leaves are sunny no more.

There are no yellow stars on the mountain;
    The bluebells have long died away,
From the brink of the moss-bedded fountain;
30   From the side of the wintry brae.

But lovelier than corn-fields all waving
    In emerald, and vermeil, and gold,
Are the heights where the north-wind is raving,
    And the crags where I wandered of old.

It was morning: the bright sun was beaming;
    How sweetly it brought back to me,
The time when nor labour nor dreaming
    Broke the sleep of the happy and free.

But blithely we rose as the dawn-heaven
40   Was melting to amber and blue,
And swift were the wings to our feet given,
    As we traversed the meadows of dew.

For the moors! For the moors, where the short grass
    Like velvet beneath us should lie!
For the moors! For the moors, where each high pass
    Rose sunny against the clear sky!

For the moors, where the linnet was trilling
    Its song on the old granite stone;
Where the lark, the wild sky-lark, was filling
50   Every breast with delight like its own!

What language can utter the feeling
    Which rose, when in exile afar,
On the brow of a lonely hill kneeling,
    I saw the brown heath growing there?

It was scattered and stunted, and told me
    That soon even that would be gone:
It whispered, 'The grim walls enfold me,
    I have bloomed in my last summer's sun.'

But not the loved music whose waking
60   Makes the soul of the Swiss die away,
Has a spell more adored and heartbreaking
    Than, for me, in that blighted heath lay.

The spirit which bent 'neath its power,
    How it longed – how it burned to be free!
If I could have wept in that hour,
    Those tears had been heaven to me.

Well – well; the sad minutes are moving,
    Though loaded with trouble and pain;
And some time the loved and the loving
70   Shall meet on the mountains again!

Shall Earth no more inspire thee,
    Thou lonely dreamer, now?
Since passion may not fire thee,
    Shall nature cease to bow?

Thy mind is ever moving,
    In regions dark to thee;
Recall its useless roving,
    Come back, and dwell with me.

I know my mountain breezes
    Enchant and soothe thee still;
I know my sunshine pleases,
    Despite thy wayward will.

When day with evening blending,
    Sinks from the summer sky,
I've seen thy spirit bending
    In fond idolatry.

I've watched thee every hour;
    I know my mighty sway:
I know my magic power
    To drive thy griefs away.

Few hearts to mortals given,
    On earth so wildly pine;
Yet few would ask a heaven
    More like this earth than thine.

Then let my winds caress thee;
    Thy comrade let me be:
Since nought beside can bless thee,
    Return – and dwell with me.

The Night-Wind

In summer's mellow midnight,
    A cloudless moon shone through
Our open parlour-window,
    And rose-trees wet with dew.

I sat in silent musing;
    The soft wind waved my hair;
It told me heaven was glorious,
    And sleeping earth was fair.

I needed not its breathing
10   To bring such thoughts to me;
But still it whispered lowly,
    'How dark the woods will be!

'The thick leaves in my murmur
    Are rustling like a dream,
And all their myriad voices
    Instinct with spirit seem.'

I said, 'Go, gentle singer,
    Thy wooing voice is kind:
But do not think its music
20   Has power to reach my mind.

'Play with the scented flower,
    The young tree's supple bough,
And leave my human feelings
    In their own course to flow.'

The wanderer would not heed me;
    Its kiss grew warmer still.
'O come!' it sighed so sweetly;
    'I'll win thee 'gainst thy will.

'Were we not friends from childhood?
30   Have I not loved thee long?
As long as thou, the solemn night,
    Whose silence wakes my song?

'And when thy heart is resting
    Beneath the church-aisle stone,
I shall have time for mourning,
    And *thou* for being alone.'

Ay – there it is! it wakes to-night
    Deep feelings I thought dead;
Strong in the blast – quick gathering light –
    The heart's flame kindles red.

'Now I can tell by thine altered cheek,
    And by thine eyes' full gaze,
And by the words thou scarce dost speak,
    How wildly fancy plays.

'Yes – I could swear that glorious wind
10   Has swept the world aside,
Has dashed its memory from thy mind
    Like foam-bells from the tide:

'And thou art now a spirit pouring
    Thy presence into all:
The thunder of the tempest's roaring,
    The whisper of its fall:

'An universal influence,
    From thine own influence free;
A principle of life – intense –
20   Lost to mortality.

'Thus truly, when that breast is cold,
    Thy prisoned soul shall rise;
The dungeon mingle with the mould –
    The captive with the skies.
Nature's deep being, thine shall hold,
Her spirit all thy spirit fold,
    Her breath absorb thy sighs.
Mortal! though soon life's tale is told;
    Who once lives, never dies!'

Love and Friendship

Love is like the wild rose-briar;
    Friendship like the holly-tree.
The holly is dark when the rose-briar blooms,
    But which will bloom most constantly?

The wild rose-briar is sweet in spring,
    Its summer blossoms scent the air;
Yet wait till winter comes again,
    And who will call the wild-briar fair?

Then, scorn the silly rose-wreath now,
10   And deck thee with the holly's sheen,
That, when December blights thy brow,
    He still may leave thy garland green.

The Elder's Rebuke

'Listen! When your hair, like mine,
    Takes a tint of silver grey;
When your eyes, with dimmer shine,
    Watch life's bubbles float away:
When you, young man, have borne like me
The weary weight of sixty-three,
Then shall penance sore be paid
    For those hours so wildly squandered;
And the words that now fall dead
10   On your ear, be deeply pondered –
Pondered and approved at last:
But their virtue will be past!

'Glorious is the prize of Duty,
    Though she be "a serious power";
Treacherous all the lures of Beauty,
    Thorny bud and poisonous flower!

'Mirth is but a mad beguiling
    Of the golden-gifted time;
Love – a demon-meteor, wiling
20   Heedless feet to gulfs of crime.

'Those who follow earthly pleasure,
    Heavenly knowledge will not lead;
Wisdom hides from them her treasure,
    Virtue bids them evil-speed!

'Vainly may their hearts, repenting,
    Seek for aid in future years;
Wisdom, scorned, knows no relenting;
    Virtue is not won by fears.'

Thus spake the ice-blooded elder grey;
30 The young man scoffed as he turned away,
Turned to the call of a sweet lute's measure,
Waked by the lightsome touch of pleasure:
Had he ne'er met a gentler teacher,
Woe had been wrought by that pitiless preacher.

The Wanderer from the Fold

How few, of all the hearts that loved,
    Are grieving for thee now;
And why should mine to-night be moved
    With such a sense of woe?

Too often thus, when left alone,
    Where none my thoughts can see,
Comes back a word, a passing tone
    From thy strange history.

Sometimes I seem to see thee rise,
10   A glorious child, again;
All virtues beaming from thine eyes
    That ever honoured men:

Courage and truth, a generous breast
     Where sinless sunshine lay:
A being whose very presence blest
     Like gladsome summer-day.

O, fairly spread thy early sail,
     And fresh, and pure, and free,
Was the first impulse of the gale
20   That urged life's wave for thee!

Why did the pilot, too confiding,
     Dream o'er that ocean's foam,
And trust in Pleasure's careless guiding
     To bring his vessel home?

For well he knew what dangers frowned,
     What mists would gather, dim;
What rocks, and shelves, and sands, lay round
     Between his port and him.

The very brightness of the sun,
30   The splendour of the main,
The wind that bore him wildly on
     Should not have warned in vain.

An anxious gazer from the shore –
     I marked the whitening wave,
And wept above thy fate the more
     Because – I could not save.

It recks not now, when all is over:
     But yet my heart will be
A mourner still, though friend and lover
40   Have both forgotten thee!

Warning and Reply

In the earth – the earth – thou shalt be laid,
    A grey stone standing over thee;
Black mould beneath thee spread,
    And black mould to cover thee.

'Well – there is rest there,
    So fast come thy prophecy;
The time when my sunny hair
    Shall with grass roots entwined be.'

But cold – cold is that resting-place,
10   Shut out from joy and liberty,
And all who loved thy living face
    Will shrink from it shudderingly.

'Not so. *Here* the world is chill,
    And sworn friends fall from me:
But *there* – they will own me still,
    And prize my memory.'

Farewell, then, all that love,
    All that deep sympathy:
Sleep on: Heaven laughs above,
20   Earth never misses thee.

Turf-sod and tombstone drear
    Part human company;
One heart breaks only – here,
    But that heart was worthy thee!

Last Words

I knew not 'twas so dire a crime
    To say the word, Adieu;
But this shall be the only time
    My lips or heart shall sue.

The wild hill-side, the winter morn,
    The gnarled and ancient tree,
If in your breast they waken scorn,
    Shall wake the same in me.

I can forget black eyes and brows,
10   And lips of falsest charm,
If you forget the sacred vows
    Those faithless lips could form.

If hard commands can tame your love,
    Or strongest walls can hold,
I would not wish to grieve above
    A thing so false and cold.

And there are bosoms bound to mine
    With links both tried and strong;
And there are eyes whose lightning shine
20   Has warmed and blest me long:

Those eyes shall make my only day,
    Shall set my spirit free,
And chase the foolish thoughts away
    That mourn your memory.

The Lady to Her Guitar

For him who struck thy foreign string,
    I ween this heart hath ceased to care;
Then why dost thou such feelings bring
    To my sad spirit – old Guitar?

It is as if the warm sunlight
    In some deep glen should lingering stay,
When clouds of storm, or shades of night
    Have wrapt the parent orb away.

It is as if the glassy brook
10   Should image still its willows fair,
Though years ago the woodman's stroke
          Laid low in dust their Dryad-hair.

Even so, Guitar, thy magic tone
          Hath moved the tear and waked the sigh:
Hath bid the ancient torrent moan,
          Although its very source is dry.

The Two Children

Heavy hangs the rain-drop
          From the burdened spray;
Heavy broods the damp mist
          On uplands far away.

Heavy looms the dull sky,
          Heavy rolls the sea;
And heavy beats the young heart
          Beneath that lonely tree.

Never has a blue streak
10   Cleft the clouds since morn;
Never has his grim fate
          Smiled since he was born.

Frowning on the infant,
          Shadowing childhood's joy;
Guardian-angel knows not
          That melancholy boy.

Day is passing swiftly
          Its sad and sombre prime;
Boyhood sad is merging
20   In sadder manhood's time:

All the flowers are praying
    For sun, before they close,
And he prays too – unconscious –
    That sunless human rose.

Blossom – that the west-wind
    Has never wooed to blow,
Scentless are thy petals,
    Thy dew as cold as snow!

Soul – where kindred kindness,
30   No early promise woke,
Barren is thy beauty,
    As weed upon a rock.

Wither – soul and blossom!
    You both were vainly given:
Earth reserves no blessing
    For the unblessed of heaven!

    – – – – – – –

Child of delight, with sun-bright hair,
    And sea-blue, sea-deep eyes!
Spirit of bliss! What brings thee here,
40   Beneath these sullen skies?

Thou shouldst live in eternal spring,
    Where endless day is never dim;
Why, Seraph, has thine erring wing
    Wafted thee down to weep with him?

'Ah! not from heaven am I descended,
    Nor do I come to mingle tears;
But sweet is day, though with shadows blended;
    And, though clouded, sweet are youthful years.

'I – the image of light and gladness –
50   Saw and pitied that mournful boy,
And I vowed – if need were – to share his sadness,
    And give to him my sunny joy.

'Heavy and dark the night is closing;
    Heavy and dark may its biding be:
Better for all from grief reposing,
    And better for all who watch like me –

'Watch in love by a fevered pillow,
    Cooling the fever with pity's balm;
Safe as the petrel on tossing billow,
60   Safe in mine own soul's golden calm!

'Guardian-angel he lacks no longer;
    Evil fortune he need not fear:
Fate is strong, but love is stronger;
    And *my* love is truer than angel-care.'

The Visionary

Silent is the house: all are laid asleep:
One alone looks out o'er the snow-wreaths deep;
Watching every cloud, dreading every breeze
That whirls the wildering drift, and bends the groaning
    trees.

Cheerful is the hearth, soft the matted floor;
Not one shivering gust creeps through pane or door;
The little lamp burns straight, its rays shoot strong and far:
I trim it well, to be the wanderer's guiding-star.

Frown, my haughty sire! chide, my angry dame!
10 Set your slaves to spy; threaten me with shame:
But neither sire nor dame, nor prying serf shall know,
What angel nightly tracks that waste of frozen snow.

What I love shall come like visitant of air,
Safe in secret power from lurking human snare;
What loves me, no word of mine shall e'er betray,
Though for faith unstained my life must forfeit pay.

Burn, then, little lamp; glimmer straight and clear –
Hush! a rustling wing stirs, methinks, the air:
He for whom I wait, thus ever comes to me;
20   Strange Power! I trust thy might; trust thou my constancy.

Encouragement

I do not weep; I would not weep;
    Our mother needs no tears:
Dry thine eyes, too; 'tis vain to keep
    This causeless grief for years.

What though her brow be changed and cold,
    Her sweet eyes closed for ever?
What though the stone – the darksome mould
    Our mortal bodies sever?

What though her hand smooth ne'er again
10   Those silken locks of thine?
Nor, through long hours of future pain,
    Her kind face o'er thee shine?

Remember still, she is not dead;
    She sees us, sister, now;
Laid where her angel spirit fled,
    'Mid heath and frozen snow.

And, from that world of heavenly light
    Will she not always bend
To guide us in our lifetime's night,
20   And guard us to the end?

Thou knowest she will; and thou may'st mourn
    That *we* are left below:
But not that she can ne'er return
    To share our earthly woe.

Stanzas

Often rebuked, yet always back returning
    To those first feelings that were born with me,
And leaving busy chase of wealth and learning
    For idle dreams of things which cannot be:

To-day, I will seek not the shadowy region,
    Its unsustaining vastness waxes drear;
And visions rising, legion after legion,
    Bring the unreal world too strangely near.

I'll walk, but not in old heroic traces,
10   And not in paths of high morality,
And not among the half-distinguished faces,
    The clouded forms of long-past history.

I'll walk where my own nature would be leading:
    It vexes me to choose another guide:
Where the grey flocks in ferny glens are feeding;
    Where the wild wind blows on the mountain side.

What have those lonely mountains worth revealing?
    More glory and more grief than I can tell:
The earth that wakes *one* human heart to feeling
20   Can centre both the worlds of Heaven and Hell.

No coward soul is mine,
No trembler in the world's storm-troubled sphere:
    I see Heaven's glories shine,
And faith shines equal, arming me from fear.

    O God within my breast,
Almighty, ever-present Deity!
    Life – that in me has rest,
As I – undying Life – have power in thee!

Vain are the thousand creeds
10   That move men's hearts: unutterably vain;
      Worthless as withered weeds,
Or idlest froth amid the boundless main,

      To waken doubt in one
Holding so fast by thine infinity;
      So surely anchored on
The steadfast rock of immortality.

      With wide-embracing love
Thy spirit animates eternal years,
      Pervades and broods above,
20   Changes, sustains, dissolves, creates, and rears.

      Though earth and man were gone,
And suns and universes ceased to be,
      And Thou were left alone,
Every existence would exist in Thee.

      There is not room for Death,
Nor atom that his might could render void:
      Thou – THOU art Being and Breath,
And what THOU art may never be destroyed.

Notes

The headnote to each poem contains the following information:

1. Date of first publication.

2. Date of composition, where this can be established. Where a date of composition is conjectured, or where I have conjecturally assigned a poem a place in the compositional sequence, the reasons for doing so are given. (See Introduction: This Edition, Copy-text and Order.)

3. Location of holographs. To save space, the notes refer to the Honresfeld manuscript and the *Gondal Poems* notebook without repeating information about their location. The *Gondal Poems* notebook is in the British Library; the location of the Honresfeld manuscript is presently unknown.

4. Copy-text used as a basis for this edition. Except in the case of poems published in 1846, the copy-text is the latest holograph version. A complete record of variants of wording in the manuscripts is provided for the poems published in 1846 and for other poems for which more than one holograph survives. The notes identify all holographs and introduce variant readings with a lemma (]). Variants of punctuation are not recorded, except where variants of wording require citation of a whole line in the notes. I have treated 'The Prisoner (A Fragment)' as a special case: the differences between the poem published in 1846 and the poem in manuscript are so considerable as to require treatment as two poems. The version of the poem published in 1846 (no. viii, 'The Prisoner [A Fragment]') appears among the poems published in 1846; the manuscript version of the poem (no. 165, 'Julian M. and A. G. Rochelle') appears among the dated poems not published in 1846.

5. Other relevant data including filaments to other poems by Emily Jane Brontë, *Wuthering Heights*, and Brontë's devoirs, the school essays she wrote in French while she was in Brussels; sources in and relations to other texts, including poems by the other Brontës, poems by earlier writers, and the Bible; biographical contexts; and Gondal contexts. I have made no effort to reconstruct the Gondal narrative, but I have identified Gondal characters wherever possible and cited the other poems in which these characters appear. (See Introduction: This Edition, Gondal.)

6. Profitable commentary by Brontë's editors and critics. Explanatory notes are mainly concerned with matters of meaning (e.g., diction, usage, syntax). I have also considered whether poems are complete and whether there is anything in them that is obscure or incomprehensible.

7. The notes to the poems Charlotte Brontë published in 1850 comment on any interesting aspects of her revisions. Since some of these poems were long familiar to readers only in their 1850 versions, I have gathered them together in Appendix 2. Readers will find there 'The Visionary', a twenty-line poem composed of the first twelve lines of no. 165, 'Julian M. and A. G. Rochelle' (lines 4 and 12 have been slightly revised), and eight lines added by Charlotte Brontë.

Abbreviations

The abbreviations below are used in the notes to identify the location of manuscripts:

BPML   Bronte Parsonage Museum Library
BL   British Library
NYPL   New York Public Library
PML   Pierpont Morgan Library
PUL   Princeton University Libraries (Robert H. Taylor Collection)
UT   University of Texas at Austin (Stark Collection)

The following editions of Emily Brontë's poems are cited as places of publication in the notes and can be identified by their dates of publication:

Poems by Currer, Ellis, and Acton Bell, London: Aylott & Jones, 1846.
Currer Bell (ed.), *Wuthering Heights and Agnes Grey*, London: Smith, Elder & Co., 1850.
Poems of Charlotte, Emily, and Anne Brontë Now for the First Time Printed, New York: Dodd, Mead & Co., 1902.
Clement Shorter (ed.), *The Complete Poems of Emily Brontë*, London: Hodder & Stoughton, 1910.
Arthur C. Benson (ed.), *Brontë Poems: Selections from the Poetry of Charlotte, Emily, Anne, and Branwell Brontë*, London: Smith, Elder & Co., 1915.
Clement Shorter (ed.), *The Complete Poems of Emily Jane Brontë*, arranged and collated, with bibliography and notes by C. W. Hatfield, London: Hodder & Stoughton, 1923.
Thomas J. Wise and John A. Symington (eds.), *The Poems of Emily Jane Brontë and Anne Brontë*, Oxford: Shakespeare Head Press, 1934.
Helen Brown and Joan Mott (eds.), *Gondal Poems by Emily Jane Brontë*, Oxford: Shakespeare Head Press, 1938.
C. W. Hatfield (ed.), *The Complete Poems of Emily Jane Brontë*, New York: Columbia University Press, 1941.

Other works frequently referred to in the notes:

BFBP   Tom Winnifrith and Edward Chitham, *Brontë Facts and Brontë Problems*
BST   *Brontë Society Transactions*
BWC   Fannie Ratchford, *The Brontës' Web of Childhood*
CB   Winifred Gérin, *Charlotte Brontë*
EB   Winifred Gérin, *Emily Brontë*
GQ   Fannie Ratchford, *Gondal's Queen*
H   C. W. Hatfield (ed.), *The Complete Poems of Emily Jane Brontë*
LEB   Edward Chitham, *A Life of Emily Brontë*
OED   *Oxford English Dictionary*
PAB   Edward Chitham (ed.), *The Poems of Anne Brontë: A New Text and Commentary*
PCB   Victor Neufeldt (ed.), *The Poems of Charlotte Brontë*
PPBB   Tom Winnifrith (ed.), *The Poems of Patrick Branwell Brontë*
SBP   Tom Winnifrith and Edward Chitham (eds.), *Selected Brontë Poems*

SP   Juliet R. V. Barker (ed.), *The Brontës: Selected Poems*
WH   Emily Jane Brontë, *Wuthering Heights*

Notes to Poems Published in 1846

The Brontës decided against anonymity and in favour of pseudonymity when they published their poems in 1846. According to Gérin, their choice of the surname Bell may owe something to Arthur Bell Nicholls's recent arrival in Haworth as Patrick Brontë's curate. Gérin finds 'no clue' to the source of 'Ellis', Emily Brontë's personal name (*EB*, pp. 183–4). Maison suggests a source in Ellis Walker, the author of *The Morals of Epictetus*, a poetical translation of Epictetus's *The Enchiridion*, published in 1692 and subsequently in numerous editions (p. 231). It has not hitherto been remarked that Scott dedicates the fifth canto of *Marmion* to George Ellis. *Marmion* is mentioned in *Jane Eyre* and *The Tenant of Wildfell Hall* and was well known to the Brontës. Although there is no indication that any of the Brontës read Frances Burney's *The Wanderer; or, Female Difficulties*, published in 1814, they may have done so. Burney's heroine, who has escaped from Robespierre's France, protects herself from discovery in England by refusing to acknowledge her name. She is called 'Ellis', a name derived from the initials 'L. S.'.

i [153]. *Faith and Despondency*

This poem is in the *Gondal Poems* notebook, where its composition date is given as 6 November 1844. As a conversation about death between an adult and a wiser child, it owes something to Wordsworth's 'We Are Seven'. Its opening stanza may also be indebted to another lyrical ballad, 'The Tables Turned', in which the speaker urges his friend to 'quit your books', although the invitation is to ramble outdoors, not to talk before the fire. In revising this poem for publication, Brontë combined several four-line stanzas into verse paragraphs. Neither paragraph indentations nor the indentations of the last two stanzas are present in the ms.

Title In the ms., the title is 'I.M. to I.G.'. These are minor Gondal characters; it is not unusual for fathers and daughters to bear different family names in Gondal. The daughter's first name is Iernë. A character called Irenë or Iernë also appears in no. 175, an undated fragment.

4 *gathering*] closing.

5 *pensive hours*: compare no. 129, l. 26: 'evening's pensive hour'.

7 *gusts*] blasts.

19 *closes*] gathers.

22 *hopeless*] speechless.

23 *repinings vain*: compare no. 164, l. 7: 'weary, weary with vain repining'.

24 *greet*] see.

25–37: a peculiar account of the contemplations of 'early infancy'.

39 *drear*: a familiar poetic shortening of 'dreary', the word appears thirty-six times in Emily Brontë's poems, and in both *Jane Eyre* and *Villette*, though not in *Wuthering Heights*.

39 *but they are not there*: compare 'We Are Seven', l. 17: 'And where are they? I pray you tell'.

51 *root*] roots.
54 *rest in sleep*] lie asleep.
60 *our Dearest*: the loved ones who have died.
64 *And wiser than thy sire*: this sounds like an aphorism; in 'Love thou thy land, with love far brought' (1842), ll. 71–2, Tennyson refers to 'the boast so often made/That we are wiser than our sires'.
65 *worldly*] coming.
67–70: Brontë's metre and diction recall one of Isaac Watts's best-known hymns, the paraphrase of Psalm 90, vv. 1–5:

> Our God, our help in ages past,
>   Our hope for years to come;
> Our shelter from the stormy blast,
>   And our eternal home:

70 *steadfast*: compare no. 167, l. 16: 'The steadfast rock of Immortality'.

ii [160]. *Stars*

This poem appears towards the end of the Honresfeld ms., where it is dated 14 April 1845. Dingle points out that the rising sun would have flooded Brontë's bedroom, with its window facing east, and that the moon on the previous night would have been on the other side of the house, providing for abundant starlight (appendix). Chitham suggests a relation to Anne's 'While on my lonely couch I lie', written at about the same time (*LEB*, p. 175).

Grove notes the poem's vocabulary as 'other worldly in a Victorian style' and the eroticism that strives to 'transcend the homeliness of the curtained bedroom-setting' (Smith, p. 63). Homans reads the poem as an allegory of the competition between night and day, or two modes of poetry and life, and notes the difficulty of assimilating the night and stars to other masculine figures of imaginative possession in Brontë's poems. The contrast is rather between a 'rich, almost pre-lapsarian undifferentiated sexuality and violently overt sexual opposition' (pp. 158–9). Tayler comments that the 'stars are mothering lights, and unquestionably preferred to the masculine sun' (p. 37). 'Thus Emily's hostile estimate of the virile father ... reflects her resentment of Patrick Brontë, not so much perhaps for surviving his wife's death as for implicitly calling on his daughter to wake and do the same' (p. 39). Compare the image of mother and infant connected by the mother's gaze in no. 125, lines 23–4, with the image of the stars in the second stanza.

Night and day skies also provide an image for faithless love in no. 136. Tayler notes a relation between Brontë's view of night and day and Shelley's in 'The Triumph of Life', where the poet-speaker is unwilling 'to rise and do the sunshine work of the father-world; rather he experiences "a strange trance", "a Vision" which the rest of Shelley's poem describes' (p. 39).

Title untitled in the ms.
2 *our*] my.
2 *joy*: Brontë rhymes 'joy' with 'sky' here and in no. 161, and with 'eye' in nos. 35 and 96; 'joy' more frequently rhymes with 'destroy', and once rhymes with 'cloy' (no. vii). According to Henry Cecil Wyld, the long *i* and *oi* vowel sounds provided 'good rhymes according to the English habits of pronunciation which obtained far into the eighteenth century', and these vowels continued to be pronounced as exact rhymes by early twentieth-century 'provincial and vulgar speakers' (*Studies in English Rhymes from Surrey to Pope*, New York: E.P. Dutton & Co., 1924, p. 73).

4 *desert*: the stress on the first syllable is found archaically in the eighteenth and nineteenth centuries, with the sense of forsaken or abandoned.

5 *glorious eyes*: brilliant, shining, lustrous; compare no. 157, l. 45: 'Had I but seen his glorious eye/ Once light the clouds', where the reference is to a spirit.

12 *petrel*: a small sea-bird with black and white plumage and long wings; the use of the singular (without an article) is peculiar.

17 *dawn*] rise.

23 *elate*: inspired, exultant, flushed (as with success or victory); the word appears three times in the poems; compare no. 163, l. 50 and no. 182, l. 15.

25-8: compare Wordsworth's 'I Wandered Lonely as a Cloud', ll. 1-2 and 19-22:

> For oft, when on my couch I lie
> In vacant or in pensive mood,
> They flash upon that inward eye
> Which is the bliss of solitude;

27 *steep*] bathe.

43 *hostile light*: Brontë's only metaphorical use of 'hostile' in the poems; the word appears once more only, in no. 151, l. 24: 'hostile ranks'.

iii [157]. *The Philosopher*

In the Honresfeld ms., this poem immediately precedes the one above and is dated 3 February 1845. According to Homans, this poem carries the implications of the danger of the 'externality of poetic power one step farther' than 'Plead for Me' (which immediately precedes it in the Honresfeld ms.) by suggesting that there is 'not much difference between a sought-after "spirit" . . . and oblivious death' (p. 115). Blondel cites the visions of Daniel as a possible source for lines 27-40, but sees a closer relation to the mysticism of Plotinus, in which the soul is composed of the body, the reason, and the spirit (pp. 214-15). The 'inky sea' and 'ocean's gloomy night' may be indebted to the 'sunless sea' and 'lifeless ocean' of Coleridge's 'Kubla Khan'. Tayler compares Brontë's 'Gods . . . warring night and day' to Coleridge's '"Ancestral voices, prophesying war" – which may itself allude to Matthew 24:6, where the disciples are told "ye shall hear of wars and rumours of wars" before the Second Coming' (p. 52). Shelley's image of light in 'Adonais' (ll. 462-5) is a likely influence on lines 37-40:

> Life, like a dome of many-coloured glass,
> Stains the white radiance of Eternity
> Until Death tramples it to fragments. – Die,
> If thou wouldst be with that which thou dost seek!

In the ms., the poem is divided into four-line stanzas, except for two six-line stanzas, lines 1-6 and 35-40. Quotation marks surround lines 1-14 and 27-40. The first fourteen lines are attributed to the poet/seer, who addresses the philosopher. The 'sad refrain' mentioned in line 5 would seem to be provided in lines 7-14, which should therefore be attributed to the philosopher. It is imagined by (and so spoken by) the poet/seer. Brontë indents the entire stanza to indicate an embedded speech. The philosopher speaks lines 15-26 and 41-56. The vision of lines 27-40 is attributed to the poet/seer.

Title according to Hatfield, 'The Philosopher's conclusion' is pencilled at the head of the poem, apparently in Emily Brontë's hand (H, p. 221).

7–14: underlined in the ms.

13, 14 *quenchless fires . . . quenchless will*: the only occurrence of 'quenchless' in the poems; compare Byron's *Cain*: 'Nothing can/Quench the mind' (I, 210–11).

17 *Three gods*: 'Specific translation may be impossible; but as a warring threesome they offer a kind of infernal, repudiating parody of the mystery of the Christian Trinity' (Tayler, p. 53).

26 *suffer*] written above 'waken', cancelled.

35 *sent*] bent.

36 *through that*] on that.

37 *kindling*] written above 'lighting', cancelled.

39 *far, far more fair*] the first 'far' is cancelled in the ms., though still legible.

40 *its*] their.

45 *glorious*: brilliant, shining, lustrous; compare no. ii, l. 5.

46 *wilder*: archaic or poetic, to lead or drive astray.

47 *coward cry*: compare 'No coward soul is mine'.

51 *senseless*] lifeless.

53–6] these lines appear to have been added to the poem after it and the poem following it had been transcribed, very likely when the poem was being prepared for publication. Four lines preceding ll. 53–6 are cancelled in the ms. and indecipherable in the photocopy, but Hatfield (p. 222) provides this transcription:

> O for the lid that cannot weep –
> The Breast that needs no breath –
> The tomb that brings eternal sleep –
> For Life's Deliverer, Death!

55 *conquered good, and conquering ill*] vanquished Good, victorious Ill. Brontë may be recalling Shakespeare's Sonnet no. 66, l. 12: 'And captive-good attending Captaine ill'.

iv [158]. *Remembrance*

In the *Gondal Poems* notebook and dated 3 March 1845. Brontë removed the Gondal names from the poem when she published it. This is her culminating poem of loss and mourning among the Gondal and non-Gondal poems. F.R. Leavis called it 'the finest poem in the nineteenth-century part of *The Oxford Book of English Verse*' (*Revaluation*, p. 13) and Barbara Hardy thought it Brontë's 'best love poem. . . . The growth of feeling seems to rely on the powerful syntax which checks, permits, drives, and shapes sharp feeling' (Smith, pp. 117–18). Tayler suggests that 'the final closure that Rosina "Sternly denied", her rhetoric and prosody urgently impel' (p. 32).

'This poem does unmistakably demand to be read in a plangent declamation; in, that is, a rendering that constitutes an overt assertion of emotional intensity' (Leavis, *The Living Principle*, p. 126). Visick notes the possible parallel to Heathcliff's lament for Catherine, whose death precedes his by eighteen years, but Barbara Hardy points out that the speaker is no Heathcliff; 'she joins passionate lament with an unobsessed remembrance, eroded and distracted' (p. 117).

Tayler compares the speaker's 'Sweet Love of youth' to Wordsworth's Lucy; 'both are versions of the Romantic muse in that they bear the traces of the poet's own original divinity, now lost in the world of yoke and custom' (p. 34). Compare also Wordsworth's 'Surprised by Joy'.

C. Day Lewis provides the following commentary on the poem's metre:

The line here is basically a pentameter: but it is pulled out of the ordinary iambic pentameter rhythm and given a different shape by three devices – by putting a stress on the first syllable of each line, by a marked caesura after the second foot, and by the use of feminine rhymes in lines one and three of each stanza. The effect of this rhythm I find extremely powerful, extremely appropriate. It is a dragging effect, as of feet moving in a funeral march; an andante maestoso: it is the *slowest* rhythm I know in English poetry, and the most sombre. (p. 91)

The poem exemplifies Brontë's imaginative use of feminine endings and rhymes. In addition to the usual two-syllable words in which the second syllable is unstressed, there is one extended feminine rhyme (Decembers/remembers), and the pronouns 'thee' and 'me' are unstressed in lines 1, 3, 13, and 15. Words ending in '-ing' provide the most common feminine ending, although Brontë's rhyme of 'suffering' with 'spring' stresses the '-ing'. On the use of feminine endings, compare no. xiii.

Title in the ms., 'R. Alcona to J. Brenzaida'. Julius Brenzaida is Prince of Angora in Gondal, King of Almedore in Gaaldine, and Emperor of Gondal and Gaaldine. According to Ratchford, 'R' stands for Rosina, and Julius is married to Rosina Alcona, who is sometimes called A. G. A. and sometimes Geraldine. Paden disputes Ratchford's conflation of A. G. A., Rosina Alcona, and Geraldine. Ratchford and Paden agree that Julius died or was assassinated and that the poem is a lament for him by Rosina, his lover or wife. The names Rosina and Alcona appear in separate poems, and this is the only occurrence in the poems of an 'R. Alcona'. On the conflation of A. G. A., Rosina Alcona, and Geraldine, see my Introduction: This Edition, Gondal.
   Several meanings of *Remembrance* are relevant: that operation of the mind involved in recalling or recollecting; the surviving memory of a person; a keepsake or token that serves to remind one person of another.
1 *Cold in the earth*: compare Anne's poem 'Night', written 'early in 1845', which has 'Cold in the grave for years has lain/The form it was my bliss to see' (ll. 9–10); both poems echo a line from Moore's *Irish Melodies*: 'When cold in the Earth lies the Friend thou hast loved' (*PAB*, p. 183).
4 *all-severing*] all wearing; compare Branwell's *Sir Henry Tunstall*, ll. 384–7:

> ... a wider sea shall sever
> My form from thine – a longer time – *For ever!*
> Oh! when I am dead and mouldering in my grave,
> Of me at least some dim remembrance have, –

An early version of this poem, a ms. titled *The Wanderer* and dated 31 July 1838, is in the British Library, where it is attributed to Emily Brontë, but Winnifrith disputes T. J. Wise's identification of the handwriting as hers. Extracts from the poem were published in the *Halifax Guardian*, 4 June 1842 (*PPBB*, p. 291).
6 *northern shore*] Angora's shore: Angora is one of four (or more) kingdoms of Gondal.
8 *Thy*] That.
9 *fifteen wild Decembers*: this belongs to a Gondal chronology.
15 *Other desires and other hopes*] Sterner desires and darker Hopes.
17 *later light*] other sun.
18 *second morn*] other star.
28 *mine*: possibly 'thine'; Brontë's *m* and *th* are confusingly alike.

29 *it*: the soul.

29, 31: the 'languish/anguish' rhyme occurs four times in the poems; compare Gray's 'The Progress of Poesy. A Pindaric Ode', ll. 71-2: 'How do your tuneful Echoes languish,/Mute, but to the voice of Anguish?' and Mary Robinson, 'January, 1795', ll. 11-12: 'Balls, where simpering misses languish;/Hospitals, and groans of anguish'.

v [156]. *A Death-Scene*

In the *Gondal Poems* notebook the poem has two dates at the head of the poem: on the left, 2 December 1844 (the date of composition), and on the right and below the initials A.G.A. (identifying the speaker of the poem), September 1826 (placing the poem in a Gondal chronology).

Title the ms. has 'From A D— W— in the N.C.' or 'From a Dungeon Wall in the Northern College'. Compare no. 164, 'M.A. Written on the Dungeon Wall – N.C.'. Anne wrote a poem titled 'Lines inscribed on the wall of a dungeon in the southern P. of I. [Palace of Instruction]' and signed and dated 'Alexander, April, 1826' (H, p. 217). Anne composed her poem on 16 December 1844, two weeks after 'A Death-Scene'.

9 *Edward*] Elbë; Elbë is Alexander, Lord of Elbë, identified by Ratchford as an early lover of A.G.A. and by Paden as her second husband.

11 *Arden's*] written over 'Elnor's'; Elnor also figures in nos. 10 and 15; a likely source for Arden is *As You Like It*.

16 *one*] underlined in the ms.

27 *Edward*] probably Elbë, but the word is heavily scored in the ms. and unreadable.

37 *at length, the*] at last that.

37-42: heavily revised in the ms.

38 *Sunk to peace the twilight breeze*] Sank to peace the gentle breeze.

43 *orbs*] light.

vi [149]. *Song*

This poem is in the *Gondal Poems* notebook and dated 1 May 1844. The initials E.W. above the poem in the ms. identify the speaker as Lord Eldred W., A.G.A.'s friend and faithful retainer. No. 147, composed on 11 March 1844 and titled 'E.W. to A.G.A.', suggests that the woman who is this poem's subject is A.G.A. The 1846 text of the poem agrees with the ms.

1 *linnet*: a common song-bird, grey or brown, except in summer when its breast and crown turn crimson; the linnet appears on the moors in no. 76, l. 47.

2 *moor-lark*: perhaps the bird Brontë calls 'the lark – the wild skylark' in no. 76, where the scene is also the moors.

3 *heather bells*: a kind of heather blooming on the moors near Haworth; several writers have related the imagery of this poem to the 'heath and hare-bells' and 'soft wind breathing through the grass' in Lockwood's description of the three graves in the last paragraph of *Wuthering Heights*.

5 *wild deer*: a feature of the Gondal (not the Haworth) landscape.

9 *ween*: think or surmise, archaic since the seventeenth century (*OED*); this word also appears in no. 62, l. 2.

25: Abraham Shackleton, a resident of Braithwaite, less than three miles from Haworth, recorded weather conditions for a number of years; he records a south-east wind on 1 May 1844 (Dingle, appendix); the poem's west wind therefore has its source in other poems, not in actual conditions pertaining at the time of the poem's composition.

vii [163]. *Anticipation*

The poem is in the Honresfeld ms., where it is dated 2 June 1845. Charlotte Brontë wrote the following comment in the ms.: 'Never was better stuff penned.' The situation described in the poem's first two stanzas, and some of its language, suggest 'My Heart Leaps Up', which Wordsworth uses as the epigraph to his 'Ode: Intimations of Immortality'. Charlotte Brontë alludes to 'My Heart Leaps Up' in *The Professor*. Like 'Faith and Despondency', this poem takes the form of a dialogue, but both speakers are adults; the language in which the second speaker answers is, however, childlike. Tayler (p. 60) identifies 'thy own compeers' with Brontë's siblings, Branwell (about to be dismissed from his post at Thorp Green and already enslaved by his passion for Mrs Robinson), Anne (depressed by her own situation and by Branwell's), and Charlotte (pining after M. Héger). 'How, Emily's poem asks, does one keep up one's blissful spirits in such surroundings?'

1 *still*: yet; also motionless.

4 *unreal*] shadowy; compare no. x, ll. 27–8: 'like a vision vain,/An unreal mockery'.

12 *Equals*] Equal.

14 *clouded, smileless*] dull unlovely; compare Wordsworth's 'Immortality Ode', l. 78: 'And fade into the light of common day'.

15 *untried*] unproved.

16 *went wandering wrong*] were wildly wrung; Chitham connects this line to Anne's suffering over the death of William Weightman, Charlotte's grief over her separation from M. Héger, and Branwell's disappointed passion for Mrs Robinson (*LEB*, p. 178).

22 *waited*: awaited; the only occurrence of this elision in the poems.

23 *A thoughtful spirit*: reflective or meditative; *OED* cites the earliest use of 'thoughtful' to mean 'considerate' or 'kindly' as 1851; compare no. xx, l. 32: 'My thoughtful Comforter'.

26 *Must*] Will.

26 *cloy*: to overload so as to cause loathing (*OED*).

40 *The fearful and the fair*: the sublime and the beautiful, categories used by eighteenth-century landscape theorists.

48 *Sustained, my guide, by thee?*] My guide, sustained by thee?

50 *swells elate*: compare no. ii, l. 23: 'The soul of Nature, sprang, elate'.

52 *Rewarding destiny*: there is only one other reference to destiny in the poems; in no. 179, l. 22, 'earthly destiny' is a periphrasis for death.

viii [166]. *The Prisoner (A Fragment)*

This poem is excerpted from a much longer (152-line) poem in the *Gondal Poems* notebook, which has a composition date of 9 October 1845. This was about the time that Charlotte Brontë discovered a ms. volume of verse by Emily, the impetus for the 1846 volume as a whole. It has been suggested that Charlotte may have been given the opportunity to find her sister's poems only because Emily was copying this recently completed poem into her *Gondal Poems* notebook. For 1846, Emily Brontë selected lines 13–44 and 65–92 of the ms. poem and wrote an

238   NOTES TO PP. 14-15

additional stanza. 'The Visionary', made up of lines 1–12 and eight lines written by Charlotte Brontë, appeared among the seventeen poems by Emily Brontë published by Charlotte Brontë in 1850 together with *Wuthering Heights* and *Agnes Grey* as 'a selection from their literary remains'. (See Appendix 2.) The 152-line poem first became available to readers in 1938, when it appeared in the Shakespeare Head volume titled *Gondal Poems*.

C. Day Lewis calls lines 37–60 'the greatest passage of poetry Emily Brontë wrote' (p. 92). Lines 45–56 have often been read as her fullest account of a mystical experience. Spurgeon, who places Brontë among the 'philosophical mystics' and no. viii among 'the most perfect mystic poems in English', identifies these lines as 'the description – always unmistakable – of the supreme mystic experience, the joy of the outward flight, the pain of the return, and [they] could only have been written by one who in some measure had knowledge of it' (p. 83). Jonathan Wordsworth offers a corrective: 'The astonishing central lines of *The Prisoner* were written by someone accustomed not only to mystical experience, but to the in fact more passionate loss of self in creative identification' (p. 98). Tayler notes that the poem gathers Brontë's 'key terms and images': 'wind, stars, tenderness, darkness; the longing for feelings lost since childhood, the dread of future tears; the celestial realm internalized; the descent of peace onto the fretful spirit; the loss of consciousness and of all earth-awareness; the music (as in Wordsworth) of an eternal silence' (p. 63). In the ms., these lines are succeeded by Julian's liberation of A.G. Rochelle from her prison so that the poem has a romantic ending, but in the 1846 version, the prisoner's only escape is death and the visionary experience that heralds it. For a fuller discussion of the omitted narrative frame, see the note to no. 165 below.

Compare Emily Brontë's devoir titled *Portrait: le Roi Harold avant la Bataille de Hastings*: 'Death alone can gain victory over his arms, and Harold is ready to bend before her, for the touch of that hand is as the jailer who gave him his liberty was to the slave' (my translation).

Title in the ms., 'Julian M. and A.G. Rochelle', minor Gondal characters; in 1846, the poem is marked as a fragment because it has been excerpted from the longer poem, but it is not, therefore, incomplete.
2 *Reckless*: heedless or careless.
28 *that*] which.
31 *kindred's*] parents'.
32] punctuation and capitalization are different in the ms.: 'Then may I weep and sue, but, *never*, Friend, before!'.
33 *Still, let my tyrants know*] Yet, tell them, Julian, all.
33 *wear*: to lose strength, vitality, keenness, sharpness, or intensity, by the decay of time; to waste, diminish, or fade by gradual loss (*OED*).
33–6: compare Acts 12:6–7.
37–8: these lines sustain the basic six-stress line and strong, central caesura, but create an effect of stretching or expansion by including three words with extra syllables, 'evening's', 'wandering', and 'heaven'.
40 *that*] which.
52 stoops, like a bird of prey, and dares the final limit; compare Milton's description of Satan's entry into Eden (*Paradise Lost*, IV, 181–2): 'At one slight bound high overleap'd all bound/Of Hill or highest Wall'; Milton likens Satan to a wolf and a thief, but once within Eden, he perches on the Tree of Life like a cormorant.

ix [141]. *Hope*
In the Honresfeld ms. and dated 18 December 1843. In the 1846 volume, this poem follows Anne's 'If This Be All' and Charlotte's 'Life', which express alternative attitudes towards life, Anne's despairing, Charlotte's hopeful. Anne's poem ends with the following stanza:

> If Life must be so full of care,
>   Then call me soon to Thee;
> Or give me strength enough to bear
>   My load of misery.

Charlotte's begins with the following four lines:

> Life, believe, is not a dream
>   So dark as sages say;
> Oft a little morning rain
>   Foretells a pleasant day.

Emily's 'Hope' reconfigures rather than resolves this difference between her sisters. See also Anne's 'Views of Life', on the same subject, begun early in 1844 (*PAB*, p. 184).

Title titled in pencil in the ms., probably at the time of preparation for publication.
2 *the*] my; cancelled in the ms., probably at the time of publication.
2 *grated den*: dungeon; compare no. viii, l. 16: 'The vault, whose grated eye', and no. 175, ll. 3-4: 'around her dungeon grim/The grating cast a doubtful gleam'.
12 *If*: written in Charlotte Brontë's hand above 'When', cancelled in the ms. Hatfield prints 'When' but suggests 'If' as an alternative (p. 192).
18 *my*] that.

x [146]. *A Day Dream*
In the Honresfeld ms., where its composition date is given as 5 March 1844. Chitham and Winnifrith date the poem 5 March 1845, but offer no explanation (*SBP*, p. 249). They also note the 'influence of the Platonic Shelley' in 'the visionary stanzas', but the poem owes a wide-ranging debt to several Romantic poems, including Wordsworth's 'Immortality Ode', Keats's 'Ode to a Nightingale', and Coleridge's *The Rime of the Ancient Mariner*. The poem's ballad form and diction are influenced by Coleridge's, and its speaker recalls his speaker's situation when she describes herself as a 'wedding guest'. Blondel points out that death in this poem is the apotheosis of life and that Brontë invokes it 'audaciously' and 'violently' (pp. 204-5). The attitude towards death in this poem anticipates Heathcliff's and Catherine's; the scene of the day dream suggests Cathy Linton's image of an earthly heaven, which she opposes to Linton Heathcliff's (*WH*, 2, 10).

Title titled in the ms., probably at the time of preparation for publication.
1 *brae*: a slope or hillside; exclusively northern English or Scottish and pronounced to rhyme with 'away'; see no. 76, ll. 28-30, where Brontë rhymes 'brae' with 'away' and no. 148, ll. 117-19, where she rhymes 'braes' with 'ways'.
3-4: the image specifies the time of year as the end of May.
5-8: the substitution of anapaestic for iambic feet results in three lines with additional syllables.

7 *the fairest child*: May.

12 *sullen*: compare Wordsworth's 'Immortality Ode': 'Oh, evil day! if I were sullen/ While Earth herself is adorning,/This sweet May morning' (ll. 43–5).

16 *What do you here*] 'What do you do here?' Brontë prefers the irregularity of a five-syllable line to the six-syllable line in the ms.

28 *An unreal mockery*: *Macbeth*, III, iv: 'Unreal mock'ry hence'; compare no. vii, l. 4: 'unreal phantoms of distress'.

35 *its*] the; the revision changes the sense of the line.

36 *the*] its.

37 compare 'Resolution and Independence', ll. 50–51: 'Now, whether it were by peculiar grace,/ A leading from above, a something given . . .'

39 *peevish*: perverse or refractory.

41 *gleaming*] glancing.

41–4 compare *The Rime of the Ancient Mariner*, l. 238: 'And a thousand thousand slimy things'.

49 *rung*] rang; both forms of the past tense verb are used in the nineteenth century; *OED* cites Southey, *Joan of Arc*: 'On the batter'd shield/ Rung the loud lance' (1797).

51 *sung*] sang; see note above; *OED* cites Tennyson, 'Mariana': 'The cock sung out an hour ere light' (1830).

52 *Or*: I follow previous editors in emending the 1846 edition, which has 'O', not 'Or', which is the word in the ms. Hatfield does not record the 1846 reading, probably because he agrees with Hargreaves that 'O' is an 'obvious error', overlooked when the Brontës read proof sheets and, later, when they prepared an errata slip (Hargreaves, p. 296).

65: compare the opening lines of Shelley's sonnet, 'Lift not the painted veil which those who live/ Call Life; though unreal shapes be pictured there . . .'.

68 *Because*] not underlined in the ms.

69–70 *the noonday dream/Like dream of night*: contrast no. 96, l. 10: 'My blissful dream, that never comes with day'.

xi [150]. *To Imagination*
In the Honresfeld ms. and dated 3 September 1844. In the ms., this poem is immediately preceded by the poem that follows it in 1846, 'How Clear She Shines'. In 'How Clear She Shines' Brontë apostrophizes Fancy, in 'To Imagination', Imagination. Imagination, 'my true friend', is a more sober faculty than Fancy, 'my Fairy love'. On the dialogue between Reason (l. 19) and Imagination, see also no. i.

Title added in pencil, in the ms.

5 *lone*: this word appears twenty-three times in the poems; this is its only occurrence in a negative construction.

14 *and guilt*] and grief.

16 *untroubled*] unsullied.

17–18: compare no. x, ll. 41–2.

19–20 *complain/For*: express sorrow for; Reason turns the speaker's attention to the 'hopeless . . . world without'.

21–2: Reason asserts the vanity of the 'world within'.

26 *vision*] visions.

30 *real*] written above 'other', cancelled; the reference here is to 'real' or 'other' external worlds that match the speaker's fondest dreams.

33 *dying*] written before 'failing', cancelled.
36 *sweeter*] brighter.
37 *when hope despairs*: no. ix also explores this paradox.

xii [132]. *How Clear She Shines*

In the Honresfeld ms., where it is dated 13 April 1843, this night poem associates Fancy with the moon. According to Shackleton, the moon on this night was waxing full (Dingle, appendix). Barbara Hardy says that 'the dismissal of Joy, Peace, and especially Hope . . . makes the invocation a startling gathering-up of hostility and cynicism' (Smith, p. 112). The cynicism extends to the poem's identification of Death as a 'despot' rather than an agent of release, and connects this poem to the French devoirs Emily Brontë wrote the previous summer, especially *Le Papillon*, which asserts that 'the whole of creation is equally insane' (my translation).

Title untitled in the ms.
2 *guardian*] silver.
8–9: the 'dark' world is not the night world but the 'grim' daylight world.
10 *conceal*] go hide.
12–19: 'Thy' and 'thee' refer to the daylight world.
36 *surest*] shortest.

xiii [182]. *Sympathy*

In the Honresfeld ms., where it is undated. Hatfield assumes a composition date between 29 October and 14 November 1839 from the location of the poem in the ms., but Chitham correctly asserts that no date of composition can be fixed (*SBP*, p. 246). On Brontë's use of feminine endings, see the note to no. iv above.

Title untitled in the ms.
3 *pours*] sheds.
4 *And*] Or.
9 *They weep, you weep, it must be so*: the grammar suggests that the 'They' who weep together with the speaker are 'the best beloved of years', now dead, but 'They' probably refers to the elements of nature, the winds and winter, that mourn in the second stanza.
11 *sheds*] pours; in revising the poem for publication in 1846, Brontë switched the verbs in ll. 3 and 11.
11–12: unlike 'pours', 'sheds' carries the sense of 'casts off' and so prepares for the turn in the final stanza; compare Shelley's 'Ode to the West Wind': 'Thou on whose stream, mid the steep sky's commotion/ Loose clouds like earth's decaying leaves are shed'.
13 *these*] they.
15 *journey on, if not elate*] journey onward not elate.
15 *elate*: compare no. ii, l. 23, and no. vii, l. 50.
16 *Still*] But.

xiv [152]. *Plead for Me*

In the Honresfeld ms., where it is dated 14 October 1844. Brontë made few revisions when she prepared this poem for publication. Like nos. i and xi, this poem represents a colloquy between Reason and Imagination, here a 'God of visions' who is the speaker's 'advocate' in a trial. The triple rhymes in each stanza provide an occasion for the slant rhymes in the first, third, and seventh stanzas.

Title untitled in the ms.

11-15: compare 'Often rebuked, yet always back returning', where the speaker turns away from 'busy chase of wealth and learning' (l. 3).

20 *mine*] not underlined in the ms.

33 *earthly*] real.

37 *nor hope despair*: compare no. xi, l. 36: 'when hope despairs'.

39: the 'God of visions' the speaker worships is identified with 'my own soul' (l. 38).

xv [130]. *Self-Interrogation*

In the Honresfeld ms., where it is dated 23 October 1842 – 6 February 1843. In October of 1842, Emily was still in Brussels where, just five days earlier, she had written her devoir titled *Le Palais de la Mort*. Death was very present to her during this month, when both William Weightman, aged twenty-eight, and Martha Taylor, aged twenty-three, died of cholera. In the devoir, she takes account of the change in circumstances: previously, old age was death's only minister; now death has numerous ministers and thinks of appointing one as his viceroy. The strongest competitors for this office are Ambition and Fanaticism, but Intemperance overwhelms them, arguing that she alone will be able to survive the advance of Civilization. The composition of 'Self-Interrogation' was interrupted; Emily and Charlotte left Brussels on 6 November, after receiving news of their aunt's death; the poem was taken up again some months later in Haworth.

In the 1846 text, the Brontës did not correct the error which resulted in the omission of the quotation marks which mark the transition from one speaking self to another at the end of the first and fourth stanzas, and I have accordingly followed the ms. in restoring them. Despite the ray of hope in the last two lines, this poem is among Brontë's glummest.

Title untitled in the ms.

6 *hardly*: barely; also with difficulty.

13 *I've said*] I think.

15 *sad*] weak.

24 *Canst thou desire to dwell*] Say, wouldst thou longer dwell; cancelled.

40 *But*] Yet.

43 *It is*] 'Twill be.

44 *seem*] be.

45 *war*] fight.

47 *Thy midnight rest*] Thine eventide.

48 *And break in*] Thy night, a.

xvi [159]. *Death*

In the Honresfeld ms., this poem is dated 10 April 1845. Barker identifies this as a Gondal poem, 'possibly relating to Julius Brenzaida's murder', despite Brontë's decision not to transcribe it into the *Gondal Poems* notebook (*SP*, p. 140). Chitham suggests that Brontë is remembering the deaths of her two eldest sisters, Maria and Elizabeth, which occurred twenty years earlier in May and June of 1825 (*SBP*, p. 251). Tayler notes the biblical source of the poem's imagery in Christ's words to his apostles: 'I am the vine and ye are the branches. . . . If a man abide not in me, he is cast forth as a branch, and is withered' (John 15:5–6) (p. 56). According to Tayler, the poem speaks of two deaths, a spiritual death (like that of the Christian's turn from Christ) that results 'from pursuing ambition and violating her fidelity to her mother' and a bodily death, 'a literal disbranching, which is also the only "cure" possible for the spiritually disbranched' (pp. 56-7). But the poem records a spiritual death from which the speaker recovers through love in stanza five, and the death of the beloved (in stanza six), which makes the speaker long for her own death.

Title untitled in the ms.
1 *most confiding*: confident; Brontë uses the word only in this way; see no. 147, l. 21: 'too confiding'.
3 *Time's withered branch*: compare no. 172, 'There let thy bleeding branch atone'; in 'Death', the branch is not divided from the tree but from 'the fresh root of Eternity'; that is, 'Time's withered branch' is the tree, as the 'perished sapling' of the last stanza is a 'bough'.
20 *that*] its.
25 *Cruel*] Heartless; cancelled in the ms., with 'Cruel' written above it, probably when Brontë revised the poem for publication.
30, 32: compare ll. 2, 4, which introduce the 'be/Eternity' rhyme repeated here.

xvii [105]. *Stanzas to* —
In the Honresfeld ms., this poem is dated 14 November 1839. Hatfield notes that the dates of composition and publication indicate that the poem does not refer to Branwell (p. 133), presumably because the Robinson scandal occurred after the poem's composition and Branwell's death after its publication. But Branwell gave up his studies at Bradford and began to take opium in May of 1839, only a few months before his sister wrote this poem. Chitham notes that 'the name of Shelley has been suggested' (*SBP*, p. 246); he suggests it in *BFBP*, where he also conjectures that the 'One word' mentioned in line 7 is 'atheist' (*BFBP*, p. 69). The text published in 1846 agrees with the ms.

Title untitled in the ms.
7 *gushing tears*: compare no. 18, l. 2: 'a gush of bitter tears'; no. 22, l. 7: 'And tears within my eyes were gushing'; and no. 165, l. 116: 'It gushes into tears'.
8 *altered eye*: a stock phrase; compare Scott's *The Lay of the Last Minstrel*, I, 10: 'Nor in her mother's altered eye/Dared she to look for sympathy'.
11 *Vain*: foolish or idle.
17-22: the animal typology anticipates that of *Wuthering Heights*, where Heathcliff is 'a fierce, pitiless, wolfish man' (I, 10, 126) and tells Edgar his 'type is not a lamb, it's a sucking leveret' (I, 11, 141).
17-23: compare Anne's 'Views of Life', ll. 149-59, which formulates questions in the same way; written in 1844, it cannot be a source; 'Views of Life' and Charlotte's 'Parting' immediately precede no. xvii in 1846.
23 *above his memory*: the sense is positional; in several poems, mourners weep 'above' a tomb or grave or buried dust; compare no. 147, l. 35: 'And wept above thy fate the more'.
24 *heart*] eye; cancelled, with 'heart' written above.
25 echoing Pope's 'Elegy to the Memory of an Unfortunate Lady', l. 64: 'And the green turf lie lightly on thy breast'.

xviii [155]. *Honour's Martyr*
In the *Gondal Poems* notebook, where it is dated 21 November 1844.

Title 'M. Douglas to E.R. Gleneden'. Ratchford identifies E.R. Gleneden as Douglas's sweetheart (*GQ*, p. 102); in no. 134, 'E.G. to M.R.', the speaker, a man, is also called Gleneden. A Douglas, who may or may not be M. Douglas, appears in no. 61 and again in no. 148, where he tries to win Angelica's love by assassinating A.G.A.

21 *Without*] Beside.
33 *covert*] venomed.
47 *that*] not underlined; 'Traitor' is capitalized.
52 *name*] not underlined; 'Honour's' is capitalized.
56 *Then, only then*] Gleneden, then.

xix [115]. *Stanzas*

In the Honresfeld ms., this poem is dated 4 May 1840. Chitham thinks it was inspired by Anne's departure for Thorp Green, probably in March (*SBP*, p. 247).

Title untitled in the ms.
4 *there*: the reference is to the 'dark world', which is 'here' in l. 2.
8 *a tomb*] the tomb.
11 *Weary to watch*] I'm sick to see.

xx [144]. *My Comforter*

In the Honresfeld ms., where it is dated 10 February 1844. Brontë does not name the Comforter, which may be Hope, imagined as a light outside a 'grated den' in no. ix, and called 'Glad comforter' in no. vii; or Imagination, which whispers 'Of real worlds, as bright as thine' in no. xi; or a God of visions, the 'radiant angel' of no. xiv.

Title 'My Comforter' appears on the ms.
9 *Its gentle ray cannot control*: this clause ('that' or 'which' has been omitted) modifies 'shadows' (l. 8) and separates the verb 'roll' (l. 8) from the adverbial phrase in l. 10.
12 *alone*] unlit.
17 *Their*] With.
18 *Whose madness daily maddened me*] Their madness daily maddening me.
19 *Distorting*] And turning.
29 *thaw-wind*: a melting wind.
31 *resembles thee*] can match with thee.
32 *thoughtful*: compare no. vii, l. 23.

xxi [121]. *The Old Stoic*

In the Honresfeld ms., where it is dated 1 March 1841. Epictetus was popular in England in the eighteenth and early nineteenth centuries, and several translations and versions of his maxims and discourses were in print. Maison points out that *Letters on the Improvement of the Mind* (1773) by Hester Chapone, an opponent of Stoicism, was a standard textbook in girls' schools and that much of the curriculum at Roe Head, where Brontë was a pupil, was based on it (pp. 230–31). This poem anticipates no. 167.

Title untitled in the ms.

8 *And give me liberty*: Brontë may be remembering the words of Patrick Henry, spoken in 1775, and familiar in the nineteenth century.

11 *In*] Through.

11 *chainless*: the only occurrence of this word in the poems, though actual and metaphorical chains are common; Maison finds references to chained and chainless souls in Epictetus; Brontë may be recalling Shelley's 'chainless winds' ('Mont Blanc', l. 22) and Byron's 'chainless Mind' ('Sonnet on Chillon', l.1).

Notes to Dated Poems

1. First published in 1902, this poem is conjecturally dated 12 July 1836 or earlier on the evidence of the date written above poem no. 2, which follows it in the ms. in the BPML. Lipking notes that this poem, the earliest extant poem by Brontë, 'reproduces the birth of an identity' (p. 98). Lake Werna is apparently a Gondal setting (mentioned only this once in the poems), and the birth may be A. G. A.'s, but it is tempting to read this poem about the dawning of a female star as announcing the poet's birth as well. According to Lipking, the words translated into English as 'The moon has set' were universally known as Sappho's in Brontë's time, although the Lobel-Page edition of Sappho's poems (1974) rejects them (pp. 256-7). Compare no. ii.

2. First published in 1902, this poem is in the BPML. Dated 12 July 1836, the poem is formulated as an incantation or child's game in which the course of the day is taken to predict a female child's destiny.

5 *Apollo's journey*: Brontë's only reference to the sun as Apollo.

13 *vain*: futile.

3. First published in 1902, this poem has been conjecturally assigned a place in the compositional sequence on the basis of the preceding poem in the ms. in the BPML. Hatfield surrounds the lines that follow the questions in each stanza with quotation marks, but these do not appear in the ms. The poem may be closely related to the preceding one, in which a mother looks ahead to her child's future, for the child in this poem contemplates her own past, present, and future, and natural elements again provide the poem's imagery.

11 *dazzling*: in the ms., 'dazzeling'; compare Milton, *Reform*, 'Unlesse God have smitten us with a dazling giddinesse at noon day' (1641).

4. First published in 1902 as a continuation of the poem above, this poem has been conjecturally assigned a place in the compositional sequence on the basis of no. 2, which appears above it in the ms. in the BPML. Hatfield also prints it as a separate poem.

5 *that Lady fair*: the lady is not identified.

11 *breezes'*: the apostrophe does not appear in the ms. and has been added to assist the sense of the line.

5. First published in 1902, incorporating the poem printed below, 'Woods you need not frown on me', this poem is dated 13 December 1836 on the ms. in the BPML. Hatfield also prints nos. 5 and 6 as separate poems.

5 *dungeon*: in the ms., 'dongeon', an obsolete spelling frequent in the poems.

13 *lowering*: or louring, looking threatening or angry. Although the pairing of opposites in this line ('shining', 'lowering'; 'swelling', 'dying') supports this sense of the word, the other sense of lowering as descending is also relevant, especially if Brontë is imagining clouds; compare the oppositions figured in l. 4: 'Earth rising to heaven and heaven descending'.

6. First published in 1902 as a continuation of the poem printed above, this poem is conjecturally placed in the compositional sequence on the basis of the date above no. 5. The copy-text is the ms. in the BPML.

7. First published in 1910, this poem is conjecturally placed in the compositional sequence on the basis of no. 8, which appears directly below it on the ms. leaf, now in the PUL. This is one of the fourteen poems Hatfield printed from transcripts given to him twenty years earlier by Clement Shorter because he was unable to locate the mss. and examine them himself (H, p. 11). The poem was printed as undated in 1910, and Hatfield does not explain why he assigns a composition date between 23 and 28 November 1839 in 1941.

1 Brown cites Byron's 'Lines Inscribed Upon a Cup Formed from a Skull' (1808), l. 1: 'Start not – nor deem my spirit fled' (p. 376).

6 *right*: or 'night'; Hatfield prints 'night's', as does 1910, but there is no 's' in the ms., and Brontë's 'r' and 'n' are difficult to distinguish.

7 *landed*: the tense is odd (a reader might have expected 'landing'), but the sense is that the travellers will come to an ending to their progress or a stage in it, which will be succeeded by rest. The word 'landed' may have been suggested by the 'stairs'; a 'landing' in this sense is 'a platform in which a flight of stairs terminates' or 'a resting place between two flights of stairs' (*OED*). 'Landed' is also grave with the promise of the last stanza's 'tomb'.

8. First published in 1910, this poem appears on a ms. leaf together with no. 7 (above) and no. 9 (below), now in the PUL (see the note to no. 7). The poem is dated February 1837 on the ms.

I follow previous editors in printing these twenty-one lines as a single poem, but I print the short, straight marks that appear in the ms. after the first, third, and fourth stanzas. Brontë regularly uses such marks to separate poems from each other, and it could be argued that what we have here are four poetical fragments rather than one poem. (See my Introduction: This Edition, Poems and Poetical Fragments, for a fuller discussion of the difficulty of fixing the boundaries between poems.) In the ms., the first stanza has a left margin which corresponds to that of no. 7 above, while the rest of the stanzas and no. 9 below have a different left margin. It could also be argued, less plausibly, that nos. 8 and 9 compose a single poem. Paden's division of the poem into two parts of eight and thirteen lines is not supported by the evidence of the ms. The argument in favour of a single twenty-one line poem rests in part on the desire to have an antecedent for 'it' (lines 14 and 18) and in part on the coincident references to 'wildly tender . . . music' in the first stanza and 'wild wild music' in the last.

1 *Redbreast*: the robin; in the ms., 'Red breast' is written as two words.

2 *Dark*: previously read as 'Dank'.

4 *Chasing* [*the angry*] *thoughts away*: previously read as 'Chasing angry thought away', but additional letters and the plural 'thoughts' are clearly present in the ms.; 'angry' is still dubious, though likely; compare no. 67, l. 23: 'And chase the foolish thoughts away'.

9 *It was not hope that wrecked at once*: this line makes no sense if the verb is taken as transitive, so that hope is said to 'wreck' the 'spirit's [early] storm'; but the verb is intransitive, meaning to undergo shipwreck. *OED* cites Milton's *Paradise Regained* ('Honour, glory, and popular praise;/Rocks whereon greatest men have oftest wreck'd') as well as Tennyson's *Becket* ('Holy Church May rock, but will not wreck').

10 *[early] storm*: this phrase has previously been given by editors as 'calm in storm'. Although I am unable to be certain about my reading of the bracketed word, the manuscript makes 'calm in storm' unlikely, and the idea that Hope wrecks 'the spirit's calm in storm' makes no sense. If 'wrecked' is intransitive, l. 10 is in apposition to the preceding one; commas at the ends of both l. 9 and l. 10 would indicate this.

14–17: recalling Wordsworth's 'Lucy Gray', subtitled 'Or Solitude'.

16 *mild*: previously given by editors as 'wild'.

17 *desert*: the stress on the first syllable is found archaically in the eighteenth and nineteenth centuries, with the sense 'forsaken' or 'abandoned'; compare no. ii, l. 4.

9. First published in 1910, this poem is conjecturally placed in the compositional sequence on the basis of no. 8 above, which precedes it on the ms. leaf in the PUL.

13 *Diana's day*: Brontë's only reference to the moon as Diana; compare no. 10, l. 1: 'There shines the moon, at noon of night'.

14 *shine*: previously given by editors as 'shrine'.

10. This poem was first published in facsimile by Virginia Moore in *The Life and Eager Death of Emily Brontë* (1936). It was subsequently published in 1938. The initials A.G.A. appear at the head of the ms. together with a composition date of 6 March 1837, in the *Gondal Poems* notebook. The initials stand for Augusta G. Almeda, whose first name is given in line 63. Ratchford notes that this is the earliest heading found in the poems and the first occurrence of the name of this Gondal heroine (*GQ*, p. 57). Hatfield regularly prints these initials as titles, but I have treated them as signatures only. (See Introduction: This Edition, Titles.) In the ms., two cancelled and illegible lines follow line 66, and quotation marks appear at the start of each of the spoken lines (58–68).

1 *noon of night*: this phrase appears in three of Byron's poems, including *Childe Harold* (3, 229).

4 *lonely moor*: compare Wordsworth's 'Resolution and Independence', l. 147.

8 *zone*: a region or belt of the sky.

11 *Lake Elnor's breast*: Lake Elnor also appears in no. 15; references to 'Elmor Hill' and 'Elmor Scars' appear in no. 148, and the ms. of no. v also refers to Elnor's lake (l. 11).

14 *Elbë's grave*: for Elbë, see the note to no. v, l. 9.

11. First printed in 1902, this poem is in the PML and is dated 10 June 1837. Hatfield follows 1923 in printing the lines beginning 'Woe for the day Regina's pride' as a separate poem. In the ms., Brontë does not divide the last twelve lines from the lines that precede them in any of the usual ways (a short, horizontal mark, a series of spaced crosses, or a new date), but the margin of the lines beginning with 'Woe for the day Regina's pride' is slightly to the left of the margin of the lines that precede them. This may but need not suggest a new poem; it more likely marks the change in voice as the dreamer records the words of the 'shadowy thing' wailing its 'woeful doom'. (See my Introduction: This Edition, Poems and Poetical Fragments.) Chitham notes that there was stormy weather and thunder on the night of 9 June (*LEB*, p. 90).

10 *rapt*: carried away in spirit, not in body; the ms. has 'wrapt', probably a misspelling; 'In all the hours of gloom' (l. 9) may, however, suggest 'wrapt' (or 'wrapped'), meaning concealed or absorbed; compare no. 62, l. 8, where the ms. has 'wrapped', and no. 91, l. 44, where the ms. has 'wrapt': 'And wrapt him in his mantle grey'; the phrase 'the rapt soul' appears in Byron's *English Bards and Scotch Reviewers*, l. 110.

23 *ranny*: 'a north of England colloquialism meaning sharp or keen' (H, p. 37).

28 [*not*]: not in the ms., but the sense of the line requires it; I follow Hatfield in recommending the interpolation.

48 *Regina*: the name does not appear elsewhere in the poems; according to Anne's notes in *A Grammar of General Geography for the Use of Schools and Young Persons*, Regina is Gondal's capital (rpt. *GQ*, p. 18).

50 *save*: despite the shortness of this line, the rhyme suggests it is complete; 'save' appears twice more in the poems in this absolute construction; compare no. 147, l. 36 ('Because I could not save –'); no. 148, l. 340 ('Since fate had not decreed to save –'); and Cowper, *Charity*: 'Oh, 'tis a godlike privilege to save!'.

55 *mixed*: in the ms., 'mixt'; this earlier spelling is not unusual in the seventeenth and eighteenth centuries.

12. First printed in 1902, this poem is in the PML and is dated July 1837. Because this poem is entirely unpunctuated in the ms., I have not added punctuation after 'come' in line 21 and 'me' in line 29, where the sense requires it. Hatfield prints the last four lines of the poem as a separate stanza, but there is no space between lines 49 and 50 in the ms. Tayler connects the account of life's progress in lines 41–53 to that in Wordsworth's 'Immortality Ode': 'the road traveled, the disappearing light, the lost power and glory, even the sound of distant waters breaking against the shore. But Emily's vision is far more dark and comfortless; and again, her journey takes her away from the human community, not toward it' (p. 42).

52–3: compare Gray's *Elegy*, ll. 55–6: 'Full many a flower is born to blush unseen/ And waste its sweetness on the desert air'; the feeling is very different.

13. First printed in 1910, this poem is in the Ashley Library ms. in the BL and is undated there, although both 1910 and 1923 date it 26 July 1837. Hatfield does not explain why he dates this poem 26 July 1839, but the poem on the previous page of the ms. is dated 26 July 1839. The specificity of the date, with the omission of lines 19–22 in 1910, strongly suggests that another ms. version of this poem existed in 1910. Although a '9' may have been misread for a '7', I find insufficient warrant for accepting Hatfield's later date. (See my note on no. 85.)

The Ashley Library ms. is a slim volume containing sixteen poems or poetical fragments and twenty-four pages, which were bound for T. J. Wise. Brontë used these leaves for making fair copies of poems composed between 1837 and 1839, according to Hatfield from about the end of 1839 (p. 25). The poems are in cursive, and many are unpunctuated. In the binding, loose sheets have been pasted to guards, sometimes obliterating characters at the ends of lines; in some cases, pages may have been trimmed before binding with the same consequence. The brackets at the ends of lines 21 and 22 indicate the absence of these letters in the ms. The initials A. A. A. appear at the head of the ms. and mark the poem as a Gondal poem.

21–2: Brontë is probably remembering *Macbeth*, I, iii: 'Though his Barke cannot be lost,/ Yet it shall be Tempest-tost'; Shakespeare's Sonnet no. 116, l. 7, provides a source for Brontë's 'wandering bark'.

14. First printed in 1902, this poem is dated 7 August 1837. The author's initials E. J. B. appear under the date on the ms. in the BPML.

74 *thrall*: in the ms., spelled 'thrawl' (a stand or frame for barrels or milk-pans).

15. First published in 1902, incorporating nos. 16 and 17, this poem was published as four separate poems or poetical fragments in 1923 and 1941. The copy-text is the ms. in the BPML, where the poem is dated August 1837. I discuss my decision to treat these verses as composing a single thirty-line poem in my Introduction: This Edition, Poems and Poetical Fragments. In the ms., crosses (represented by asterisks in this text) mark divisions between sections of the poem; a horizontal mark appears after line 30, and below no. 16 and no. 17, which also appear on the same ms. leaf.

20 [*beam*]: scribbled over a cancelled and illegible word; the reading is uncertain.
22 *Lake Elnor's tide*: see note to no. 10, l. 11.

16. First published in 1902, this poem is in the BPML. The poem's imagery connects it to no. 15, which appears above it on the same ms. leaf; it is conjecturally placed in the compositional sequence on the basis of no. 15.

17. First published in 1902, this poem is in the BPML; it is conjecturally placed in the compositional sequence on the basis of no. 15, which appears above it on the same ms. leaf.

18. First published in 1902, incorporating nos. 19, 20, and 21, this poem is in the BPML and is conjecturally placed in the compositional sequence on the basis of no. 15 above; it appears on the reverse of the same ms. leaf. According to Miles, this poem or poetical fragment contains Brontë's 'first unmasked treatment of the onset of mystical experience' (p. 87).

8 *The star the glorious star of love*: Venus; compare no. 1: 'The moon has set, but Venus shines/A silent silvery star'.

19. First published in 1902, this poem is in the BPML and is conjecturally placed in the compositional sequence on the basis of no. 15 above; it appears below no. 18.

20. First published in 1902, this poem is in the BPML and is conjecturally placed

in the compositional sequence on the basis of no. 15 above; it appears below no. 19. In 1923, it is titled 'The Picture'.

21. First published in 1902, this poem is in the BPML and is conjecturally placed in the compositional sequence on the basis of no. 15 above; it appears below no. 20. The last stanza is separated from the three stanzas that precede it by spaced crosses (represented by asterisks in this text). In 1902, all the poems on this side of the ms. leaf (nos. 18–21) are printed as a single poem; in 1926, all the poems are printed as individual poems. I follow 1926 and Hatfield in printing the quatrain that begins 'Her sister's and her brother's feet' as the conclusion to 'Awaking morning laughs from heaven'. In the ms., the three poems above this one share a larger left margin; they are separated from each other and from no. 21 by short, horizontal marks. A short, horizontal mark also appears under line 16.

The poem contrasts the awaking morning to the unawakened lady with the dovelike eyes, reposing on her couch in a deathlike attitude. The poem is full of stock romantic diction ('forests green', 'velvet cheek', 'snowy bosom').

22. This poem was first published in 1902 and is dated August 1837 on the ms. in the BPML. The ms. indicates that Brontë considered 'gushing' as the rhyme word in both line 5 and line 7. The tail of a 'g' is visible in both places; another letter, probably an 'r', is also visible in both places. Hatfield reads 'gushing' in line 5 and 'rushing' in line 7, but Brontë refers to 'my gushing tears' in no. xvii, line 7, and no. 165, line 116, has 'It gushes into tears'.

23. First published in 1902 as 'Song' from an earlier version in a ms. in the BPML, this poem also survives in the *Gondal Poems* notebook, the copy-text for this edition. In the BPML ms., the poem is cancelled. The Ashley Library ms. in the BL has only the last five lines of the poem. All three ms. versions are dated 19 August 1837.

Title A.G.A. refers to Augusta Geraldine Almeda (see the note to no. 10 above) and A.E. refers to Alexander, Lord of Elbë (see the note to no. v above). The letter 'E', the author's initial, also appears at the head of the poem. The following variant version of the last verse appears in both the BPML and the BL mss.:

> But, thou art now on the desolate sea
> Thinking of Gondal, and grieving for me;
> Longing to be in sweet Elbë again;
> Thinking and grieving and longing in vain.

In the Ashley Library ms., 'the' in line 17 is cancelled and 'a' is written above it. Lines 18–20, as they appear in the *Gondal Poems* notebook, have also been written between the lines in the Ashley Library ms., with one variant in line 20, as noted below.

3 *dawn*] dawning.
8 *Waves*] Moans.
9 *lonely*] noble.
11 *Gleaming*] Shining.
15 *as thine own, my foot*] as thine own steps.
20 *yields*] gives (Ashley Library ms.).

24. First published in 1910, this poem is in the UT. The poem is dated 30 September 1837. According to Ratchford, the poem describes the coronation of A. G. A. in the cathedral where Julius Brenzaida is buried (*GQ*, p. 125).

25. First published in 1910, with no. 171 appended to it. Hatfield treated these two poems, which appear on separate scraps of paper, as distinct in 1941. The ms. of no. 25 was unavailable to Hatfield, and his copy-text was a transcript made from the original ms. by Clement Shorter (see the note to no. 7 above). The copy-text for this poem is the ms. in the PUL; the poem is dated 14 October 1837.

The ms. suggests that the poem was written hastily, and some lines are illegible. There is a cancelled stanza between lines 48 and 49.

4 *Tyrdarum's*: the reading in 1910; it looks more likely in the ms. than 'Tyndarum's', which is Hatfield's reading.

9 *madness*: the word is blotted in the ms.; only the 'm' and 'ss' are legible.

12 *warmed*: Hatfield reads 'alarmed', and adds commas after 'death' and 'danger'.

21–2: only the first and two last words of l. 21 are decipherable; both 1910 and Hatfield print the following obscure version of ll. 21–2, which are heavily scored in the ms. and difficult to decipher:

> But dreams like this I cannot bear,
> And silence whets the fang of pain;

22 *tang*: a 'projecting pointed part or instrument' and *fig.*, 'a sting or pang' (*OED*).

26, 28: Brontë rhymes 'sward' with 'heard' in no. 92, not with 'yard', as here.

29–36: compare the scene of Lockwood's dream (*WH*, I, 3).

39 *that*: Hatfield reads 'the'.

39 *thrill*: Hatfield reads 'shrill'.

49: following this stanza, there is a cancelled stanza with an incomplete fourth line.

50 [*caught*]: an uncertain reading.

52 *Glared*: Hatfield reads 'Stared'.

54 *Discrowned*: deprived of its architectural adornment, perhaps its spire.

55 [*serene*]: an uncertain reading.

26. First published in 1910 from a ms. unavailable to Hatfield (see the note to no. 7 above), now in the PUL, this poem is dated October 1837. Hatfield prints the poem with ellipses at the end to indicate that it is incomplete; no such marks appear in the ms.

3 *foreboding*: used here as an adverb.

27. First published in 1910, this poem is in the Ashley Library ms. in the BL. Brackets at the end of line 18 indicate where characters have been cut off (see the note to no. 13 above). The poem is dated October 1837. Barbara Hardy calls it 'an exhausted poem. . . . Death was always the goal, but it has to be worked for and waited for' (Smith, p. 103).

12 *tiresome*: tedious or, more colloquially, vexing.

28. First published in 1902, this poem is in the BPML and is dated Novem

29. First published in 1902, this poem is in the BPML. The initials A.G.A. appear at the head, immediately following the date of composition, November 1837. (For A.G.A., see the note to no. 10 above.) Though the initials mark the poem as a Gondal poem, Chitham suggests that Brontë may be thinking of her two dead sisters, Maria and Elizabeth: 'Just like Gondal characters, these two children were perpetually called back from the dead . . .' (*LEB*, p. 98).

14 [*to*]: an uncertain reading; Chitham reads 'or'.
15–16: perhaps recalling Cowper's 'The Castaway': 'But I beneath a rougher sea,/ And whelmed in deeper gulfs than he'.
19 *on*: Hatfield reads 'oh'.
21–4: compare *Macbeth*, II, ii: 'Sleep that knits up the ravel'd Sleeve of Care'.

30. First published in 1902, this poem is conjecturally placed in the compositional sequence on the basis of no. 29, which appears above it on the same ms. leaf in the BPML. The stanzas are evenly divided between two speakers; the second speaker is addressed as 'Shade of mast'ry' (l. 5).

14 *ask*: Hatfield reads 'take'.

31. First published in 1902, this poem is in the BPML and is dated November 1837. In 1902 and all subsequent editions of the poems, this poem is treated as three poems, divided where I have marked divisions by a broken line in this edition, although Paden suggests that lines 1–12 and 13–28 form a single poem (p. 15). In the ms., lines 1–12 are centred on the page; the date appears at the right-hand margin. Lines 13–28 and 29–35 appear side by side, lines 13–28 beginning at the left of the page, and lines 29–35 ending at the right of the page. I have treated these thirty-five lines as constituting a single poetic utterance, on the model of no. 162, where 1850 establishes a precedent for paired poems. No. 31 represents a dialogue between a spell-bound lyric speaker in lines 1–12 and a respondent who promises release in lines 13–28. Lines 29–35 mark the lyric speaker's loss of words, inspiration, and faith. The poem is incomplete.

The three sections of this poem differ in metre and in rhyme, and the third section differs more sharply from the first and second than the first and second do from each other. In both lines 1–12 and lines 13–28, Brontë is working with a ballad stanza and a three-stress line; in lines 13–28, an additional line makes a medial couplet and swells the usual four lines to five. The shift to couplets and a regular iambic tetrameter line in lines 29–35 confirms the speaker's loss of inspiration.

Ratchford considers this a Gondal poem; Barker conjectures that the first twelve lines relate 'to an incident when one of the heroines exposes her child to die' (*SP*, p. 121).

e characters and looks like 'rearl'.
ds 'entheal', but suggests 'hallowed' as an alternative

letter has been changed.

, this poem is in the Ashley Library ms. in the BL, e Brontë and dated December 1837. A cancelled draft poem survives on the bottom half of a torn leaf in the ontained the whole poem at the time of transcription.

The text agrees with that of the Ashley Library ms., except that it is unpunctuated. I have added punctuation at the ends of lines 8, 20, and 28, where the Ashley Library ms. leaf has been trimmed in such a way as to obliterate any mark of punctuation there might have been; the punctuation still visible in the rest of the poem leads a reader to expect it in these lines. This is probably a Gondal poem. The reference to a 'rebel task' in line 7 suggests a civil war.

Title *Wreath of Snow*: a bank or drift of snow, chiefly Scottish.
21 *mountaineer*: someone who dwells on a mountain (as in *Comus*, 426), although the word usually refers to a mountain climber by the nineteenth century.
28 *sustain*: the verb is transitive, with 'me' understood as its object.

33. First published in 1902, this poem is in the Ashley Library ms. in the BL and is undated. Another version in a ms. in the BPML is dated December 1837; the whole poem is cancelled in the BPML ms., and the text, which is unpunctuated, agrees with that of the Ashley Library ms. I have added punctuation at the ends of lines 5, 6, and 12, where the Ashley ms. leaf has been trimmed so as to obliterate any mark of punctuation there might have been and where the punctuation still visible in the rest of the poem leads a reader to expect it.

Title Julius Angora, the poem's speaker, is Prince of Angora (in Gondal) and also ruler of Almedore (in Gaaldine). (See the note to no. iv above.) He bears a 'crimson ensign'; a green standard figures in no. 131, 'On the Fall of Zalona'. Ratchford (*GQ*, pp. 93–5) and Hatfield (H, p. 181) identify Gerald Exina as the ruler of Zalona and the bearer of the green standard.

34. First published in 1910, this poem is in the Ashley Library ms. in the BL and is dated December 1837. The bracket at the end of line 9 indicates that the ms. leaf has been cut so as to eliminate the two bracketed letters. (See the note to no. 13 above.)

35. First published in 1902, this poem is in the BPML and is dated 14 December 1837. This is the earliest of three poems that mention Fernando De Samara (see also nos. 71 and 112). Areon refers here to a forest, later to a hall (see no. 101). The speaker of this poem, who addresses one who is 'mother' to her and Fernando, confesses to the bond between them. She is probably the woman with 'faded eye' and 'pallid face' remembered by Fernando in no. 112 ('Written in the Gaaldine Prison Caves to A. G. A.'). Ratchford conjectures plausibly that she is a foster-sister and sweetheart (*GQ*, pp. 133–6) abandoned when Fernando attaches himself to A. G. A. This poem indicates that she is twenty-four, and that she last saw Fernando at the age of fourteen.

18 *chime sound*: Hatfield reads 'chime-sound'; Brontë may have intended an 's' after 'chime' or 'sound'.
25: compare *Hamlet*, III, i: 'The undiscovered Countrey from whose Borne/No Traveller returnes'.
27: the sense requires a mark of punctuation after 'weep'.
29: the sense requires a comma after 'No'.
35 *sever*: be separated, or part; compare Burns, 'Ae Fond Kiss': 'Ae fond kiss, and then we sever.'
56 *joy*: on the pronunciation of 'joy', see the note to no. ii above, l. 2.
57: the sense requires a mark of punctuation after 'past'.
65: the sense requires a mark of punctuation after 'another'.

36. First published in 1910, this poem is in the NYPL and is dated February 1838. The last four lines were printed as a separate fragment in 1923, but as Hatfield notes, the ms. provides no warrant for this. Hatfield prints them as a separate stanza, but there is no space between lines 10 and 11 in the ms. The initials H.G. appear between the month and the year at the top of the ms.; their reference is unknown, and Ratchford is unable to place this poem in the Gondal narrative.

6: Hatfield adds 'that' in brackets between 'power' and 'banished', presumably on the model of l. 9, but the word does not appear in the ms., and is not required for the sense or the metre.

12 *ling*: a kind of heather.

37. First published in 1910, this poem is in the NYPL and is conjecturally placed in the compositional sequence on the basis of no. 36, which appears on the reverse side of the same ms. leaf.

38. First published in 1902, incorporating nos. 39, 40, and 41, this poem is conjecturally placed in the compositional sequence on the basis of no. 42, which is on the reverse side of the ms. in the BPML and has a composition date of March 1838. Hatfield prints this poem as four poetical fragments, separated where I have provided a broken line in this edition. In the ms., the horizontal marks that appear after lines 2, 6, and 10 are shorter than those that separate this poem from other poems on the same leaf, no. 39, no. 40, and what I take to be the first four lines of no. 41, a poem continued on the reverse side. (See my Introduction: This Edition, Poems and Poetical Fragments.)

9 *dark*: Hatfield reads 'dank'.

39. First published in 1902, as part of no. 38, this poem is in the BPML and is conjecturally placed in the compositional sequence on the basis of no. 42.

40. First published in 1902, as part of no. 38, this poem is in the BPML and is conjecturally placed in the compositional sequence on the basis of no. 42.

41. First published in 1902, as two poems, lines 1–4 (as part of no. 38) and lines 5–16 (incorporating nos. 42 and 43), and printed as two poems in 1923 and 1941. The copy-text is the ms. in the BPML, and although the poem is undated, it is conjecturally placed in the compositional sequence on the basis of no. 42. Lines 1–4 appear at the bottom of one side of the ms. leaf, and lines 5–16 appear at the top of the reverse side. Both the metre and the sense of the lines support the hypothesis that they compose a single poem.

42. First published in 1902, this poem is in the BPML and is dated March 1838. The poem describes a vow of union taken by Julius Brenzaida (see the note to no. iv above) and Gerald Exina, both kings in Gondal. The poem also makes clear Julius's intent to betray his vow. Ratchford suggests that Julius's defeat of Exina in no. 33 precedes this vow, and that the imprisonment of Gerald follows it (*GQ*, p. 98).

1 *Aisles*: in the ms., misspelt as 'Isles'.

43. First published in 1902, this poem is in the BPML and is conjecturally placed in the compositional sequence on the basis of no. 42, which appears above it.

44. First published in 1910, this poem is in the PUL, and is dated May 1838. The ms. was unavailable to Hatfield (see the note to no. 7 above). The poem is unfinished. Compare no. 168.

3 *smiled out*: Hatfield reads 'there was'.
9: Hatfield adds an ellipsis.

45. First published in 1910, this poem is in the PUL, and is conjecturally placed in the compositional sequence on the basis of no. 44, which appears above it.

46. First printed in 1902 from the draft cancelled in the ms. in the BPML. The copy-text for this poem is the Ashley Library ms. in the BL. Both mss. show a composition date of May 1838. The 'dark haired child' A.A. does not appear in any other poem. In the draft, the child is 'bright haired', and the name 'Blanche' appears next to the date.

4 *my dark*] thou bright.
5 *shuddering*] shivering.
8 *my fair-browed*] thou Fairbrowed.
12 *bears*] clasps; the sense is carries, sustains, or gives birth to.

47. First published in 1902, this poem is in the BPML and is dated 9 May 1838. The initials A.G.A. appear at its head. (For A.G.A., see the note to no. 10.)

48. First published in 1902, this poem is in the *Gondal Poems* notebook and is dated 20 May 1838. An earlier draft version survives in the Ashley Library ms. in the BL. All but the first stanza is cancelled in this ms. A.S. has been identified as Lord Alfred S. of Aspin Castle. Two other poems, nos. 138 and 145, bear the same title. Stanford cites the 'Immortality Ode' as a source for the poem's theology (p. 174); Brontë may also be recalling the opening stanzas of 'Resolution and Independence', which mention the music of the stockdove.

Title] Lines by A.G.A. to A.S.
6 *Young flowers look fresh*] Sweet flowers are fresh.
9 *The woods*] Our woods.
9 *small*] young.
10 *stockdove*] throstle.
17 *Can*: Hatfield prints 'Call', but notes that the *Gondal Poems* notebook has 'Can'; the Ashley Library ms. also has 'Can'.
18 *must*] shall.

49. First published by Clement Shorter in *Charlotte Brontë and Her Circle* (1896), pp. 154-7, and in an edition of the poems, in a slightly different version, in 1923. The poem is in the *Gondal Poems* notebook and is dated 21 May 1838. Gleneden may be Arthur Gleneden (*GQ*, p. 113). An E.R. Gleneden, probably his sister, is addressed in no. xviii; in no. 81, the speaker is an R. Gleneden, who speaks of a brother named Arthur; in no. 134, 'E.G. to M.R.', the speaker is an E. Gleneden. The author's initial, 'E', appears next to the date at the head of the ms.

21 *of*: Hatfield reads 'in'.

50. First published in 1910, the copy-text for this poem is the ms. in the PUL; the poem is dated June 1838. The name 'Blanche' appears only in a draft version of no. 46.

9 *has*: my emendation; the ms. has 'is'.

51. First published in 1902, this poetical fragment is in the BPML and is dated June 1838. The same ms. leaf also includes nos. 52 to 60 inclusive.

52. First published in 1902, this poetical fragment is in the BPML and is conjecturally placed in the compositional sequence on the basis of no. 51 above it.

53. First published in 1902, this poetical fragment is in the BPML and is conjecturally placed in the compositional sequence on the basis of no. 51 above it.

54. First published in 1902, this poetical fragment is in the BPML and is conjecturally placed in the compositional sequence on the basis of no. 51 above it.

55. First published in 1902, this poetical fragment is in the BPML and is conjecturally placed in the compositional sequence on the basis of no. 51 above it.

1 *iron clouds*: the phrase has a source in Dryden's translation of Virgil's *Georgics*, I, 630.

56. First published in 1902, this poetical fragment is in the BPML and is conjecturally placed in the compositional sequence on the basis of no. 51 above it.

57. First published in 1902, this poetical fragment is in the BPML and is conjecturally placed in the compositional sequence on the basis of no. 51 above it.

58. First published in 1902, this poetical fragment is in the BPML and is conjecturally placed in the compositional sequence on the basis of no. 51 above it.

59. First published in 1902, this poetical fragment is in the BPML and is conjecturally placed in the compositional sequence on the basis of no. 51 above it.

2 *Elbë*: see the note to no. v above.

60. First published in 1902, this poem is in the BPML and is conjecturally placed in the compositional sequence on the basis of no. 51 above it.

1 [*Elbë*]: see the note to no. v above.

61. First published in 1902, with the 'Song' as a separate poem, this poem is in the *Gondal Poems* notebook and is dated 11 July 1838. Douglas also appears in no. 148. Ratchford reads no. 61 as the narrative sequel to no. 148, an account of the pursuit of Douglas after his murder of A. G. A. (*GQ*, p. 153).

9 *Gobelrin's glen*: the name does not appear elsewhere in the poems.
34 [*From*]: the word is illegible in the ms.
39 *What ails thee steed?*: probably familiar to Brontë in at least three versions: the closest is Peacock's *Rhododaphne* (1818), canto 1: 'What ails thee, stranger' (*Works*, vii, 13); Peacock is a possible source for Keats's 'La Belle Dame Sans Merci' (1819): 'O what can ail thee, wretched wight', as is Coleridge's 'Christabel' (1816): 'And what can ail the mastiff bitch?' (l. 53).
66 *checked*: Hatfield reads 'choked'.
71-6: Ratchford suggests that Douglas starts an avalanche that kills his pursuers.

62. First published in 1850, this poem, dated 30 August 1838, is the earliest of the seventeen poems Charlotte Brontë included in her 'selection from their literary remains'. In 1850, Charlotte Brontë titled it 'The Lady to Her Guitar'; the title appears above the poem in the ms. in Charlotte Brontë's hand. Charlotte Brontë slightly altered four lines, substituting 'Dryad-hair' for 'gleaming hair' in line 12. The copy-text is the *Gondal Poems* notebook.

2 *ween*: surmise; 'the word seems to have gone out of general use in the 17th century' (*OED*); Brontë uses it only twice in the poems, here and in no. vi.
8 *wrapped*: this is the ms. reading; probably a pun on 'rapt'; see the note to no. 11, l. 10, above.
14, 15 *Hath*: Hatfield reads 'Has', although Charlotte Brontë prints 'Hath', which is in the ms.

63. First published in 1910, this poem is in the NYPL and is undated. The ms. contains no. 63, no. 64, no. 65, and a draft version of the first ten lines of no. 76 on one side, and on the reverse no. 72, no. 73, no. 74, and a variant draft of no. 97. The dated poems are no. 64 (either 23 September 1836 or 23 September 1838), the draft version of the first ten lines of no. 76 (November 1838), and the draft version of no. 97 (November 1838). This poem is conjecturally placed in the compositional sequence on the basis of no. 64, which in turn is conjecturally dated 1838 rather than 1836 by the presence on this ms. leaf of drafts of nos. 76 and 97, dated 1838.
   In the ms., the poem has the name 'Arthur Ex' and the designation 'To —' at its head. 'Arthur Ex' probably stands for 'Arthur Exina' (H, p. 81); the name 'Marcius' is pencilled below the dash. These names do not appear elsewhere in the poems.

64. First published in 1910, this poem is in the NYPL and is dated 23 September 1836 or 23 September 1838. 1910 and 1923 date the poem 23 September 1836, but Hatfield gives 23 September 1838 as its date. (See the note to no. 63 above.) At the bottom of the poem, two As appear, separated by crosses.

65. First published in 1910, this poem is conjecturally placed in the compositional sequence on the basis of no. 64 above it on the ms. in the NYPL.

5 *wreaths of snow*: banks or drifts of snow (chiefly Scottish).
8 *Ushers in a drearier day*: compare no. 66 below, l. 4: 'Ushered in a fairer day'.

66. First published in 1902, this poem is in the *Gondal Poems* notebook and is
dated 17 October 1838. In September, Brontë assumed a position as a teacher at
Law Hill, where she remained until the following March. The words 'To G.S.'
appear below the title. Both nos. 66 and 67 are addressed by Julius Brenzaida (see
note to no. iv) to Geraldine S. Geraldine's initial suggests that she is the wife of
Lord Alfred S.; according to Ratchford, Geraldine is A. G. A.'s middle name, and
A. G. A. and Geraldine are one (*GQ*, p. 82). Geraldine appears once more in the
poems; her name provides the title for no. 125. See my Introduction: This
Edition, Gondal.

1 *Geraldine*: the likely internal rhyme suggests that the name is pronounced to
rhyme with 'shine', as in Coleridge's 'Christabel' and Scott's *The Lay of the Last
Minstrel*.
4 *Ushered in a fairer day*: compare no. 65, l. 8, above: 'Ushers in a drearier day'.

67. First published in 1850, this poem is in the *Gondal Poems* notebook
immediately after no. 66; it has the same composition date (17 October 1838) and
a close title. Charlotte Brontë wrote the words 'Love's Farewell' under the title in
the ms., but she titled the poem 'Last Words' in 1850.

23: compare no. 8, l. 4: 'Chasing [the angry] thoughts away'.

68. First published in 1902, this poem is in the BPML and is dated October
1838; the initials A. G. A. are written below the date. (For A. G. A., see the note to
no. 10 above.)

69. First published in 1902, this poem is in the BPML and is undated. It is
conjecturally placed in the compositional sequence on the basis of no. 68, which
appears above it in the same ms. Chitham suggests that it may have been written
on 2 November, a night on which there was a full moon, and that the 'dark prison
house' refers to Law Hill (*LEB*, p. 110).

70. First published in 1902, this poem is in the BPML and is undated. It is
conjecturally placed in the compositional sequence on the basis of no. 68, which
appears above it in the same ms. This lyric may also express Brontë's unhappiness
at Law Hill. As a poet, she was unusually prolific during the months of October
and November, early in her stay at Law Hill. Her imagination was drawn to Gondal
subjects and, in nos. 69 and 70, to lament her own weariness and confinement.

71. First published in 1902, this poem is in the *Gondal Poems* notebook and is
dated 1 November 1838. Chitham reports a heavy rain early in the day followed
by hail and a strong wind, though not a north wind (*LEB*, p. 111).
  For Fernando De Samara, see the notes to nos. 35 and 112. This poem follows
no. 112 in the Gondal chronology and tells the story of Fernando's suicide. It
includes a physical description of A. G. A.: 'black resplendent hair' and eyes that
may be dark in colour.

9 *desert moor*: see the note to no. 8, l. 17, where this phrase also appears.

72. First published in 1910, this poem is in the NYPL and is conjecturally placed in the compositional sequence on the basis of a draft version of no. 97, on the same side of the ms. (See the note to no. 63 above.) No. 72 is separated from no. 73 by a row of five crosses.

8 *tears*: possibly 'fears'.

73. First published in 1910, this poem is in the NYPL and is conjecturally placed in the compositional sequence on the basis of a draft version of no. 97 on the same side of the ms. (See the note to no. 63 above.) Beneath no. 73, there is a sketch of hills with a sunrise or sunset.

74. First published in 1910, this poem is in the NYPL and is conjecturally placed in the compositional sequence on the basis of a draft version of no. 97 on the same side of the ms. (See the note to no. 63 above.)

75. First published in 1902, this poem is in the Honresfeld ms. and is dated 5 November 1838. A cancelled version of the first twelve lines survives in the Ashley Library ms. in the BL and bears the same date. Compare no. 12, another poem about 'Lost vision'.

3 *thine*] thy.

76. First published in 1850, this poem is in the Honresfeld ms., where it is dated 11 November 1838. The first ten lines of the poem survive in a ms. in the NYPL, where they are dated November 1838 (see note to no. 63). There are no differences, apart from punctuation, between these ten lines and the Honresfeld ms. version. Chitham's preference for the looser date over the more specific one because weather conditions on 11 November were not consistent with the description of the weather in the poem (*SBP*, p. 243) assumes a dependence on external circumstances more exact than is necessary or likely. The poem was written while Brontë was away from Haworth and teaching at Law Hill. Chitham reads it autobiographically, and remarks that the reference to 'exile afar' in line 52 exaggerates: Halifax (where Law Hill was located) was ten miles from Haworth. The mood of this poem, which may have autobiographical elements, is, however, very close to that of no. 63, a Gondal poem appearing in the same ms.

According to Chitham, lines 11 and 35 'appear to be quotations from an actual "ancient song"' that has not been identified (*SBP*, p. 243); according to Homans, the song is 'the voice of the speaker's own memory, and its imagined externality expresses the poet's surprise at finding a voice of her own' (p. 134).

Charlotte Brontë altered nineteen lines when she published this poem in 1850. Lines 2 and 4 appear to have been altered so as to produce a three-stress rather than a four-stress line; line 6 is altered so as to produce an exact rhyme, 'grieve' instead of 'grief'; the colours of the corn-fields in line 32 are given as 'emerald, and vermeil, and gold' rather than 'emerald and scarlet and gold'. The words of the ancient song in line 11 are slightly changed: 'It was spring, and the skylark was singing.'

8 *it*: the 'ancient song' (l. 9).
30 *brae*: see the note to no. x, l. 1, above.
47 *linnet*: see the note to no. vi, l. 1, above.

49 *wild skylark*: perhaps the bird Brontë calls the 'moor-lark' in no. vi, l. 2.

59-60: the Swiss, who were invaded and occupied by the French in 1798, symbolized liberty for Wordsworth. He writes of the voices of the sea and the mountains as their 'chosen Music, Liberty!' in 'Thought of a Briton on the Subjugation of Switzerland' (1807). Brontë may also be recalling 'The Swiss Emigrant's Return', a poem by Charlotte Brontë, which appears in one of the Glass Town tales, *The Foundling* (31 May–27 June 1833):

> Yet to my spirit more sweet is the sound
> Than the music which floats over vine-covered France ... (ll. 17–18)

77. First published in 1850, this poem is in the Honresfeld ms. and is dated 4 December 1838. This poem, like nos. 76, 78, and perhaps 79, was written during Brontë's stay at Law Hill. The setting may explain the poem's references to the 'noisy crowd' (her pupils) and to a 'holiday'. Chitham notes that the setting described in lines 29–32 and the deer mentioned in line 40 belong to Gondal, not Haworth (*SBP*, p. 243).

Charlotte Brontë also titled this poem 'Stanzas' in 1850. She omitted lines 21–4, which make the transition from thoughts of home to thoughts of 'Another clime', probably Gondal, and altered thirteen other lines.

4 *holiday*: I have modernized the spelling, although Brontë's own spelling in the ms., 'holyday', may be significant; until the sixteenth century, 'holy day' and 'holiday' are used interchangeably to refer to a consecrated day or to a day of recreation and suspension of ordinary occupations (*OED*); in 1850, Charlotte Brontë printed 'holiday'.

22: although the mark in the ms. at the end of this line looks like a full stop, a comma would make better sense.

78. First published in 1902, this poem is in the Honresfeld ms. and is dated 7 December 1838. Chitham finds the reference to 'blue ice' in line 32 inconsistent with the 'sunny stone' in line 13 and with the fine weather reported on 7 December by Shackleton, the Keighley meteorologist. This poem was also written at Law Hill. Charlotte Brontë's handwriting on the ms. suggests that she considered this poem for publication in 1850. The contrast between a happy stillness and a 'joyous swell' anticipates that between Linton Heathcliff's heaven, an 'ecstasy of peace', and Catherine Linton's, a 'glorious jubilee' (*WH*, II, 10).

8 *tears*: the pronunciation of the word is uncertain; Brontë most frequently rhymes 'tears' with 'years', but she rhymes 'tears' with 'prayers' in nos. 131, 148, and 169, and with 'cares' in no. 18; compare the rhyming of 'moors' with 'shores' (ll. 14 and 16). According to Wyld, all these rhymes were 'good in their day – that is, the words paired together might be pronounced so as to rhyme, without eccentricity, or departure from a current usage'. He cites Shakespeare's rhyming of 'swears' and 'tears', Cowley's of 'prayer' and 'hear', 'there' and both 'tear' and 'despair', and Dryden's of 'spares' and 'tears' (*Studies in English Rhymes from Surrey to Pope*, New York: E. P. Dutton & Co., 1924, pp. 66–7).

29-30: the accent was commonly on the first syllable of 'July' as late as Dr Johnson's time; 'the modern English pronunciation is abnormal and unexplained' (*OED*); compare no. 92, l. 1, where the accent is on the first syllable of 'July'; also Scott's *The Lay of the Last Minstrel*: 'Alike to him was time, or tide,/December's snow, or July's pride' (I, 21).

32: Brown notes Byron: 'The blue flames curdle o'er the hearth' ('Oscar of Alva', l. 184); the image of ice curdling complicates the relation of stillness to motion.

79. First published in 1850 with the title 'The Bluebell', this poem is in the Honresfeld ms. and is dated 18 December 1838. Charlotte Brontë omitted lines 25–40 in 1850 and altered six other lines. Although Charlotte Brontë printed 'blue-bell' as one word in 1850, Emily Brontë is inconsistent in writing 'blue bell' as both two words (in the Honresfeld ms. and the Ashley Library ms. of no. 84, also about the blue bell) and one word (in the *Gondal Poems* notebook ms. of no. 84). *OED* gives 'blue bell' and 'blue-bell', and I have therefore preferred the two-word form.

There is some confusion about which flower Brontë has in mind. The blue bell is either a species of *Campanula*, which grows in summer and autumn and is called 'the blue bell of Scotland and of the north of England', or a species of *Scillanutans*, or wild hyacinth, which flowers in the spring and is more usually called the blue bell in the south of England (*OED*). Chitham observes that the Brontës usually refer to the harebell (by which he seems to mean the blue bell of Scotland) as the bluebell, but that the flower here is the 'true blue bell' or wild hyacinth (*SBP*, p. 244). The poem, however, refers to summer bloom, and Brontë likely has the *Campanula* or blue bell of Scotland in mind.

6 *drear*: Hatfield reads 'dear'; the first 'r' in the word is visible but may have been cancelled, although another stray vertical line on the ms. suggests a slip of the pen.

21 *heather-bell*: a name given to *Erica tetralix* and sometimes to *E. cinerca*.

25 *that wood flower*: the violet.

26 *the*] or 'its'; one word is superimposed on the other.

80. First published in 1902, this poem is in the BPML, where it is dated 12 January 1839. Chitham points out that the temperature rose to 50 degrees on 12 January (*LEB*, p. 117). There are no quotation marks in the ms. to mark the speech of the poem's speaker and the 'shadowy spirit', but I follow Hatfield in adding them. I have also added a question mark at the end of line 30.

9–10: in l. 55, the spirit implicitly rebukes the rider, who has loosened his horse's rein but not unsaddled him, and 'left [him] to die', not set him free.

25, 27: Brown cites Byron's *The Giaour*:

> Her hair in hyacinthine flow . . .
> Had swept the marble where her feet
> Gleamed whiter than the mountain sleet . . . (ll. 496–501)

52 *a powerful charm*] written above 'my single arm', cancelled.

53 *Thy*] written above 'Your', cancelled.

81. First published in 1902 with the title 'The Absent One', added by the Reverend A. B. Nicholls when he transcribed it. This poem is in the *Gondal Poems* notebook, where it is dated 17 April 1839; a cancelled version of lines 1–3 and 34–44 survives in the Ashley Library ms. in the BL. Hatfield suggests that the intervening lines were written on separate leaves, now missing. In the *Gondal Poems* notebook, the words 'By R. Gleneden' appear above the poem, and in the Ashley Library ms., the words 'Lines by R. G.' also appear, but the poem

probably reflects Brontë's feelings about Anne's absence. Anne left home for her post as governess at Blake Hall about a week before it was written. Brontë may also be anticipating Charlotte's leaving home the following month to assume her post as governess at Stonegappe.

According to Ratchford, R. Gleneden is E.R. Gleneden; E.R. Gleneden is addressed by her sweetheart, M. Douglas, in no. xviii (in the ms., the poem is headed 'M. Douglas to E.R. Gleneden'). Arthur Gleneden, who is named as the absent brother in this poem, may be the speaker of no. 49, 'Gleneden's Dream'. R. Gleneden may be a sister, also called E.R. Gleneden, or a brother, R. Gleneden; the references to battle and hunting suggest the latter. Ratchford also conjectures that E.R. Gleneden mourns her brother Arthur in no. 118 (*GQ*, p. 113).

4: the pairing of mirth and music is traditional; compare Herbert's 'The Pearl', l. 24.

24 *Desmond*: the name occurs only once in the poems.

35 *Listlessly they*] Tay and Carlo.

38 *pain*] woe.

82. First published in 1910, this poem is in the Ashley Library ms. in the BL and is dated 20 April 1839. Julius is Julius Brenzaida (see the note to no. iv above). The poem uses a conventional ballad stanza, with alternating masculine and feminine endings. Compare no. 126, also a ballad about Julius's last battle, defeat, and death.

This poem and those written later in the spring of 1839 may also reflect Brontë's thoughts about Branwell's situation. After what Gérin calls a 'propitious outset', his career as a portrait painter in Bradford 'was ending in failure'. Although Branwell did not return home until mid-May, in March Charlotte was writing 'Henry Hastings', a story about a young woman who is faithful to her disgraced brother, though she knows he is an 'unredeemed villain' (*CB*, pp. 136–7).

1 *country*: the wrenched accent is conventional in folk ballads; compare no. 126, which twice wrenches the accent on 'Lady' (ll. 61 and 63).

83. First published in 1910, this poem is in the Ashley Library ms. in the BL and is dated 28 April 1839. For its possible connection to the life of Branwell Brontë, see the note to no. 82 above. Miles suggests that 'ardent' (l. 16) punningly refers to Branwell's red hair (Smith, p. 72). Brackets around letters at the ends of lines 12 and 14 indicate where the ms. leaf has been trimmed (see the note to no. 13 above).

7: the sense requires a mark of punctuation between 'perished' and 'memory'.

51: the sense requires a mark of punctuation after 'gazed'.

84. First published in 1902, this poem survives both in the *Gondal Poems* notebook and, in a cancelled version, in the Ashley Library ms. in the BL. It is dated 9 May 1839. In the *Gondal Poems* notebook, the initials A.G.A. appear together with the title, and the signature 'by A.G.A.' also appears under the title 'To a Blue Bell' in the Ashley Library ms. (For A.G.A., see the note to no. 10 above.)

On the blue bell, and Brontë's spelling of the word, see the note to no. 79

above. She probably has the blue bell of Scotland in mind here also, since the flower blooms in summer, but the wild hyacinth is more appropriately called a 'woodland child'.

9 *Thou hast found a voice for me*] Lift thy head and speak to me.
10 *And soothing words*] Soothing thoughts.
11 *murmur*] whisper.
12 *Warms me till my life is done*] 'Lights my course commenced and done', revised to 'Lights me till my life is done'.
14 *ruthless*] stormy.
16 *Weeping twilight dews my bed*] Dews of heaven are round me shed.

85. First published in 1910, this poem is in the PUL and is clearly dated 17 May 1839, as in both 1910 and 1923. The ms. was not available to Hatfield, who printed the poem from a transcript, dating it 17 May 1837 instead of 17 May 1839, presumably because the speaker gives her age as eighteen and Brontë was eighteen in 1837. C. Day Lewis, accepting Hatfield's dating of the poem, reads it as evidence that Brontë's Methodist upbringing and her own reading of Cowper had convinced her she was damned (p. 86). The mood of this poem is closely related to that of no. 86, written about a week later, and is sustained in no. 87, a Gondal poem. Lewis notes that the 'struggle of the soul against predestined doom is one form which the freedom motif takes in Emily Brontë's work. Another is the theme of exile' (p. 87).

2 *eye*] written above a cancelled word, probably 'heart'.
6 *This changeful life*: compare no. ii, l. 11: 'my changeful dreams'.
14 *not subdued*: other suggestions are 'that subdued' (1910) and 'since subdued' (Hatfield), but the ms. clearly has 'not subdued'; compare no. 8, l. 12: 'Hopes quenched and rising thoughts subdued'.
21 *think*] written above 'know', cancelled.
21 *mankind*] written above 'my kind', cancelled.

86. First published in 1910, this poem is in the NYPL and is dated 25 May 1839. In the ms., the signature E J Brontë appears at the bottom of the poem. The opening two stanzas are reminiscent of Wordsworth's 'Resolution and Independence'.

12 *refulgent*: radiant, brilliantly gleaming.

87. First published in 1910, this poem is in the Ashley Library ms. in the BL and is dated 28 May 1839. Both in this poem and in no. 129, Brontë refers to Gondal characters who have been exiled to England and whose spirits return to Gondal, their home country.

Title the name 'Claudia' does not appear elsewhere in the poems.
17: the bracket indicates that the letter 'e' is missing from the ms. leaf (see the note to no. 13 above).
28 *Thought*: the sense is obscure, although the word is clear in the ms.; Hatfield reads 'Though'; 1910 has 'Thoughts'.

88. First published in 1910, followed by the first five lines of no. 89, which appear on the reverse side of the ms. in the NYPL. The poem is dated 8 June 1839 and suggests a lifting of depressed spirits.

89. First published in 1902, the poem is in the *Gondal Poems* notebook and is dated 14 June 1839. Two variant drafts of the first five and six lines appear in a ms. (a torn fragment) in the NYPL. The first five lines are cancelled by lines drawn across them; neither variant is dated. Once again, the poem may reflect Emily's sense of her sisters' absence from Haworth; both Anne and Charlotte had been away since spring.

Title The Palace of Instruction is also referred to in the title of a poem by Anne, 'Lines inscribed on the Wall of a Dungeon in the Southern P of I [Palace of Instruction]' (*PAB*, p. 106). Anne's poem, composed on 16 December 1844, and Emily's no. 89 and no. v, composed two weeks earlier, bear Gondal dates that suggest that Emily and Anne had worked out a narrative chronology for 1826–7: April 1826 (Anne's poem); September 1826 (no. v, which has the title 'From a D— W— [Dungeon Wall] in the N.C. [North College]' in the *Gondal Poems* notebook); and 10 January 1827 (no. 89).

1 *busy day has hurried*] hours of day have glided (cancelled draft ms.); busy day has glid'd by.
3 *swift the evening hours should fly*] voices murmur cheerily (cancelled draft ms.).
5 *the door*] the unopened door (both draft mss.).
32–5: the sense is that 'golden suns at night decline/ And even in [their] death' beguile our grief by foretelling 'How bright the morn will shine'.

90. First published in 1910, this poem is in the PUL and is dated 18 June 1839.

7 *were*: Hatfield, who did not have access to the ms. of this poem, prints 'are'.

91. First published in 1902, this poem is in the PML and is dated 12 July 1839. The author's name, E. J. Brontë, appears to the left of the date at the head of the poem. The 'unknown guest' is Byronic; his 'basilisk charm' anticipates Heathcliff's (*WH*, II, 3).

13–14: these lines have been added in the right-hand margin, and are written in even tinier print than the rest of the poem.
44 *wrapped*: 'wrapt' in the ms.; compare Shelley's 'To Night', l. 8: 'Wrap thy form in a mantle grey'.

92. First published in May 1860 in the *Cornhill Magazine*, with the title 'The Outcast Mother'. The poem has a composition date of 12 July 1839 in the *Gondal Poems* notebook. According to both Paden and Ratchford, the speaker is A. G. A. Ratchford identifies Alexandria's father as Julius Brenzaida (p. 120). Paden identifies him as Lord Alfred S.; born after the death of Alexander, Alexandria is named after him by A. G. A. in expiation, according to Paden (p. 46). The poem tells the story of a mother's abandonment of her child, whose death she spares herself the distress of watching.

1 *July's shine*: the accent is on the first syllable; see the note to no. 78 above.
12 *sward*: the rhyme may be exact, like all the other rhymes in this poem; compare no. 25, where 'sward' rhymes with 'yard'.
17 *thee*] 'me', cancelled.
18 *thy*] 'my', cancelled.
20 *thy*] 'my', cancelled.

93. First published in 1902, this poem is in the BPML and is dated 19 July 1839. The author's name, Emily Jane Brontë, appears at the bottom of the poem. The following lines appear in the left-hand margin, perpendicular to the poem itself:

> Alas that she
> would bid adieu
> To all the hopes her childhood knew
> Hushed is the harp

3 *daredst*: as in the ms.; Hatfield reads 'darest', but the sense is clearly past ('dared' or 'durst').
6 *Ula's hall*: Ula is a province or kingdom in Gaaldine; no. 119 refers to 'Ula's Eden sky' (l. 36) and no. 142 to 'Ula's bowers/Beyond the southern sea' (ll. 9–10).
27 *Gabriel's self*: the archangel Gabriel.

94. First published in 1910, this poem is in the Ashley Library ms. in the BL and is dated 26 July 1839. Approaching her twenty-first birthday (30 July), Brontë imagines the death of a despairing sinner, doomed to eternal woe. Chitham associates the 'man over whose tomb we are enjoined not to weep' with Shelley (*LEB*, p. 134). The initial 'H' appears above the poem at the left-hand margin.

31 *Compassion*] 'For mercy', written above; neither word is cancelled.
32 *Revenge*] 'But hate', written above; neither word is cancelled.

95. First published in 1910, this poem is in the PUL. The last digit of the date, which has been read as 27 July 1839, is blotted, but the ink and script are like those Brontë used for other poems also in the Taylor Collection and clearly dated 1839.

96. First printed in 1902, this poem is in the BPML and is dated 12 August 1839. There are sketches to the left and right sides of the poem in the ms., including a winged serpent and a frond or feather. Hatfield prints quotation marks, which are not in the ms., to indicate that this is a dialogue between two speakers whose voices alternate. Chitham claims that the interlocutor 'must be' Charlotte Brontë (*LEB*, p. 123), but the reference to children in line 25 works against this reading.

2 [*the*]: overwritten.
7 *No let me linger leave me let me be*] above this line, the following uncancelled, redundant line appears in the ms.: 'No leave me let me linger yet 'tis long'.
17 *joy*: on the pronunciation of 'joy', see the note to no. ii, l. 2, above.
23–5: according to Chitham, the river and children signal a move into the Gondal world (*LEB*, p. 123).
30 [*Dull*]: only the first letter of this word, either 'D' or 'T', is legible; Hatfield reads 'The'; Chitham reads 'Dull'.
35 *Regive*: restore; the word 'Regive' and the phrase 'Regive him' have been written several times on the ms. below the poem; the 'shadowy gleams of infancy' are reminiscent of Wordsworth. Brontë may also be recalling Tennyson's 'Ode to Memory' (1830), where the 'infinity/futurity' rhyme appears (ll. 33 and 36). Although Brontë's speaker clings to a 'blissful dream that never comes with day' (l. 10), Tennyson's poem celebrates a power that comes 'with the morning mist,/ And with the evening cloud' (ll. 21–2).

97. First published in 1910, this poem is in the PUL and is dated 13 August 1839. Two stanzas, apparently an early draft beginning of this poem, survive on a torn leaf in the NYPL. They are dated November 1838 and cancelled. The first stanza differs from the first stanza of the later version by only one word. Hatfield printed the second stanza in 1941:

> It will perch on a heathy swell
> Against the light of the coming moon
> Then poor wretch thy misery tell
> Thou shalt have the wished for boon

1 *tidings*] comfort.

98. First published in 1910, without the first two stanzas, as a continuation of no. 97 above. The poem as a whole was first published in 1923. The poem is undated on the ms., a torn scrap of paper in the NYPL, but Hatfield follows 1923 in assigning 13 August 1839 as the date of composition. The assignment of so specific a date in 1923 suggests the existence at that time of another ms. or the rest of the torn leaf on which the poem now survives. The relation of no. 98 to no. 97, which has the same composition date and metre, is not clear. In the NYPL ms., the first two stanzas of no. 98 are slightly indented.

1-4: compare Byron's *Childe Harold's Pilgrimage*, 'To Inez', i, 845-8:

> It is not love, it is not hate,
>   Nor low Ambition's honours lost,
> That bids me loathe my present state,
>   And fly from all I priz'd the most:

99. This poem was first published in 1902. Hatfield places it just ahead of no. 135, which appears below it in the ms. in the BPML and is dated 26 July 1843 there. Paden suggests that these two poems form a single poem (p. 15), but the ms. does not support this conjecture. No. 99 appears on the same side of the ms. leaf as no. 135, but it is upside down, and the style of its writing is very different from that of no. 135, which resembles that of no. 137, 'Yes holy be thy resting place', the poem on the reverse side of the leaf. No. 99 bears no date, but the style of its writing corresponds to that of a list of Gondal characters on the same side of the ms. leaf and upside down. This list is dated 21 August. Isenberg says 'it is more than likely' that the list belongs to the same year as no. 135, but Chitham argues for a date of 1839 because 'the writing style of the Gondal list . . . is that of 1839', even though Brontë packed the scrap of paper containing it and no. 99 and took it to Belgium in 1842 (*LEB*, p. 129).

The following cancelled lines appear in the ms. between the first and the second stanzas:

> Cold and wild the wind was blowing
> Keen and clear the heaven above
> But though countless stars were glowing
> Absent was the star of love

100. First published in 1902, this poem is in the Honresfeld ms., where it is dated 30 August 1839. In late August of 1839, Anne was still at Blake Hall, and

Charlotte took a brief holiday with Ellen Nussey. All but the last two words of the first two lines of the poem are cancelled in the ms. and revised as indicated; the cancelled words are illegible. Revisions in lines 25 and 27 (see below) are probably in Charlotte Brontë's hand, and suggest that she considered publishing this poem in 1850. Lines 7–24 are lightly crossed through, and this revision is also more likely Charlotte's than Emily's.

25 *Ah no*: 'Be still', probably in Charlotte Brontë's hand.
27 *their ray*: 'its ray', probably in Charlotte Brontë's hand.

101. First published in *BST* 9:3:48 (1938), this poem is in the BPML. It is dated 6 September 1839. Commas have been added in lines 17 and 32, where there are spaces in the ms. indicating pauses. The reference to Areon Hall (identified as the home of Fernando De Samara in no. 35) suggests that the speaker of this poem is also Fernando. His references to a woman with a 'faded eye' and 'pallid face' recall the speaker of no. 35, whose cheek is 'blanched' and whose eye is 'quenched' by sorrow. This poem is the basis for Ratchford's claim that Alcona is A. G. A., since Fernando addresses A. G. A. as his seductress in no. 112, and Alcona as his seductress in this poem (*GQ*, pp. 26–7). (See my Introduction: This Edition, Gondal.) Brackets in lines 30 and 34 indicate uncertain readings.

1 *Alcona*: Hatfield marks the name as an apostrophe by adding a comma after it.
4 *That 'twixt our time of meeting lie*: the reference would seem to be to the time that lies between the present and an earlier time when the speaker was with Alcona.
9 *Areon*: Hatfield reads 'Areon'; Brown and Mott read 'Arvon' (p. 161); the word is certainly 'Areon' in its earlier appearance in no. 35.
12 *my home*: or 'thy home'.

102. First published in 1910, this poem is in the Ashley Library ms. in the BL. It is dated 15 October 1839.

1 *between*: the sense is of a shifting relation to distress and pleasure.
2 *Fond*: doting or foolish.
12 *desert*: empty; see the note to no. 8, l. 17, above.
16 *me*] written above 'thee', cancelled.

103. First published in 1910, this poem is in the NYPL and is dated October 1839. The poem is unpunctuated in the ms., but I have added commas in lines 7 and 8, where spaces in the ms. indicate pauses.

104. First published in 1902, this poem is in the Honresfeld ms., where it is dated 29 October 1839. Homans says the poem ends with 'a vacant optimism' (p. 140).

9 *Kind*: friendly or benevolent; also natural.
24 *My soul, another love* –: the sense is ambiguous; either the soul gilds another love, or another love gilds the soul, or the soul simply loves another.

105. See note to no. xvii above.

106. This poem is first published in 1910; Hatfield follows the ms. in separating the first four from the remaining five lines by several dates (1 October, 7 July, and

13 January). The poem is in the NYPL and is dated 23 November 1839. It is written in an angular script very different from the handwriting of the other poems in this collection of mss. Brontë has in mind two of Shelley's poems, 'Ode to the West Wind' and 'Mutability'. The rough wind, the 'ghostly whiteness', and the 'corpse' all appear in Shelley's famous autumnal ode; Brontë's syntax and diction, as well as her subject, suggest 'Mutability':

> We rest. – A dream has power to poison sleep;
>   We rise. – One wandering thought pollutes the day . . .
> It is the same! –

4 *The*: Hatfield reads 'Its'.
8 [*my*]: unclear in the ms.

107. First published in 1902, this poem is in the BPML. It is dated 28 November 1839. This is the third in a series of poems about the wind, all written in the month between 29 October and 28 November 1839. Brontë selected 'Well, some may hate, and some may scorn', written two weeks earlier, for publication in 1846 as no. xvii.

7 *hopes*: Hatfield reads 'rare'; 'hopes' is written above the same word, cancelled.
10 [*bear*]: difficult to decipher in the ms.

108. First published in 1902, this poem is in the *Gondal Poems* notebook and is undated. It was published as dated in 1923 (between 28 November and 14 December 1839), presumably on the basis of another ms. that no longer survives. Hatfield conjectured a date of composition between 11 March and 1 May 1844, probably on the basis of the poem's placement in the notebook.

109. First published in 1910, together with nos. 110 and 111, but separated from them by a line. This poem is in the NYPL, and is dated 19 December 1839. Hatfield suggests that the ms. containing no. 109 and the ms. containing both nos. 110 and 111 compose a single leaf, with the portion of the leaf containing no. 109 as the upper part.

110. First published in 1910, incorporating nos. 109 and 111, the ms. is in the NYPL. The poem bears no composition date, but it is conjecturally placed in the compositional sequence on the basis of no. 109 above. A short, horizontal mark separates no. 110 from no. 111; these poetical fragments are closely related.

2 *lulled*: soothed, or induced to sleep.

111. First published in 1910, as a part of nos. 109 and 110, with a line dividing 109 from 110 and the last two lines of 111 from the rest of the poem. This poem is in the NYPL; for its conjectural placement in the compositional sequence, see the note to no. 110 above. The 'I' of the poem may be the mother who is described comforting her infant child in no. 110. The brackets around words indicate that they are difficult to decipher.

112. First published in August 1897 in *The Woman at Home*. The poem is in the *Gondal Poems* notebook and is dated 6 January 1840. The speaker's name, F. De Samara, appears on the ms., together with the title. He is Fernando De Samara,

who made his earliest appearance in no. 35; Ratchford plausibly conjectures that he is the speaker of no. 101. According to Anne's notes, Gaaldine is 'a large island newly discovered in the South Pacific' (rpt. in *GQ*, p. 18). In contrast to Gondal, it has a tropical climate.

Lines 4-12 consider and reject the doctrine of eternal damnation, as does no. 113, written three months later. The French devoir titled *Le Papillon*, written on 11 August 1842, offers a related statement of the religious conviction expressed here:

> God is the god of justice and mercy; then assuredly, each pain that he inflicts on his creatures, be they human or animal, rational or irrational, each suffering of our unhappy nature is only a seed [*semence*] for that divine harvest which will be gathered when sin having spent its last drop of poison, Death having discharged its last arrow, both will expire on the funeral pyre of a universe in flames, and leave their ancient victims to an eternal empire of happiness and Glory [my translation].

1 *Thy sun is near meridian height*: it is nearly noon; Chitham suggests an echo of Shelley's *Prometheus Unbound*, II, iv: 'as light from the meridian sun'; the phrase was quoted in an article on Shelley published in *Fraser's* (June 1838), a magazine Brontë might have got from Elizabeth Patchett, the headmistress at Law Hill, where she went as a teacher in September 1838 (*LEB*, pp. 112, 135, 261).

12 *creation's*: no apostrophe in the ms.; Hatfield reads the word as a plural, not a possessive; it may also be a plural possessive.

53 *Lethean*: oblivious.

60 *Elderno's shores*: Elderno is a lake in Gondal; Fernando is recalling his love affair with A. G. A., who has now imprisoned him.

71-6: Fernando here contradicts his earlier faith in the impossibility of eternal damnation, as he remembers his own willingness to accept eternal punishment as the price of A. G. A.'s love. He takes some comfort in imagining that if there is a God, A. G. A. will suffer a similar 'hell'.

113. First published in 1902, this poem is in the Honresfeld ms., where it is dated March 1840. The loneliness evident in the first stanza may be related to Emily's loss of both Anne and Charlotte; they left Haworth in March to assume their posts as governesses. The identity of the 'shade' and 'corpse' addressed as 'Deserted one' has puzzled readers. 'It seems impossible to prove that this was Shelley, but if not, then who was it?' For Chitham, the foreign place of burial, the 'blighted name', and the assignment of the death to the past all suggest Shelley (*LEB*, p. 134).

9 *blighted name*: a Byronism; among the five works in which this phrase appears are *The Giaour*, l. 1227; *Marino Faliero*, V, 503; and *Sardanapalus*, IV, 394.

18 *Gomorrah's howling plain*: the scene of divine destruction; the word 'deluge' in the previous line recalls the Flood.

33 *have*] written above 'do', cancelled.

114. First published in 1902, this poem is in the Honresfeld ms. and dated April 1840. Written only a month after the poem above, it follows no. 75 in the notebook and shares its theme; both poems are concerned with the decay of light or loss of 'golden visions'. According to Homans, Brontë 'internalizes this visionary faculty

only as it diminishes because, like Dorothy Wordsworth, she cannot believe that any poetic power could be at once internal and powerful' (p. 111). But compare Wordsworth's 'Immortality Ode', which makes a similar point.

3 *For every joy that lit my brow*: compare no. 75: 'Long years have past away/ Since last, from off thine angel brow/ I saw the light decay' (ll. 2–4).
4 *after-storm*: no hyphen in the ms.

115. See note to no. xix above.

116. First published in 1902, this poem is in the Honresfeld ms., where it is dated 18 May 1840. It was given the title 'The Appeal' in 1923. The poem describes its speaker's longing for imaginative release, and addresses imagination as an 'angel', 'idol', and 'Beloved'.

13: Hatfield adds '[thee]' at the end of the line; the ms. gives no warrant for this addition, and the sense of the line does not require it.

117. First printed in 1910, this poem is in the NYPL and is dated 19 May 1840. It offers an idealized image of a sleeping or dead woman who has become almost a part of the natural scene as she lies lit by the midnight moon and sheltered by the trees.

4 *Breathes sweet thoughts everywhere*: Hatfield reads 'Breathes sweetly everywhere'.

118. This poem was first printed in 1850, between poems nos. 122 and 123, with the following commentary by Charlotte Brontë:

> Here again is the same mind in converse with a like abstraction. The Night-Wind, breathing through an open window, has visited an ear which discerned language in its whispers.

Charlotte Brontë probably altered 'church-yard' (l. 34) to 'church-aisle' because her sister was buried beneath the church-aisle (H, p. 147).

The Honresfeld ms. provides a composition date of 11 September 1840. The title 'The Night-Wind' has been added to the ms.; according to Chitham, it was added by Emily Brontë, presumably when she considered publishing the poem in 1846. 'The Shelleyan influence would appear to predominate, although this refers to the thought rather than the form or language of the poem' (*SBP*, p. 247). According to Homans, the poem is about the night wind's efforts to seduce the speaker. 'His seductions are all invitations to death . . .' (p. 124). Brontë herself does not use the masculine pronoun 'his' to refer to the night wind, though she describes the wind's voice as 'wooing'. Barbara Hardy compares Brontë's night wind to Keats's nightingale: 'It can outlast the individual . . . but what this sweetness sings is less a solace than a threat' (Smith, p. 106).

2 *A cloudless moon shone through*: on the night of 11 September 1840, the moon was full and the wind was blowing; the moon would have shone through the Brontës' parlour window (*BFBP*, p. 66).
16 *Instinct with spirit*: compare Shelley, 'instinct with infinite life' (*Daemon*, II, 246); and Wordsworth, 'But each instinct with/Spirit' (*The Excursion*, 7, 509).
21–4: this stanza opposes animate and inanimate worlds.

25 *leave*: Charlotte Brontë has written 'heed' above this word.

119. First published in 1910, without the last four stanzas, this poem was printed in its entirety in *BST* 9:3:48 (1938). The poem is dated 17 September 1840 on the ms. in the PML. Below the date, Brontë has written her own initials (E. J. B.) and the name of a Gondal character, R. Gleneden, the poem's speaker. R. Gleneden is also the speaker of no. 81, which mourns a brother Arthur, left behind in Gondal when the others returned to Gaaldine. M. Douglas addresses an E. R. Gleneden, identified by Ratchford as R. Gleneden, in the ms. version of the poem Brontë called 'Honour's Martyr' in 1846 (*GQ*, p. 113), but see the note to no. 81 above.

The text agrees with the ms. except that a dash has been added in line 29, where a space in the ms. suggests a break or pause.

25 *Edmund's*: the name does not occur elsewhere in the poems.
35 *Zedora's strand*: Zedora is identified as a large province in Gaaldine in Anne's notes (rpt. *GQ*, p. 18).
36 *Ula's Eden sky*: Ula is a kingdom in Gaaldine; see also no. 93 ('Ula's hall') and no. 142 ('Ula's bowers').
37 *Mary and Flora*: the name 'Flora' appears together with those of four other Gondal characters on the bottom of the ms. leaf that contains nos. 99, 135, and 136.

120. First published in 1910, incorporating no. 177, but the poems are in separate mss., and Hatfield finds nothing to connect them (H, p. 162). This poem is in the NYPL; its composition date is 27 February 1841. The date in the upper right-hand corner, and the name Anne at the bottom, are written in the same cursive hand. On the back of the ms. leaf, there are eight lines of Latin, also in cursive.

A. C. Benson titled the poem 'The Caged Bird' in 1915. The bird is probably a hawk; it is held by a chain, not a cage, and it soars among the 'breezy hills'. In 1841, Brontë had a hawk called 'Hero', which had been rescued from an abandoned nest on the moors (*SP*, p. 31). Compare Anne's poem about a caged bird, 'The Captive Dove', composed on 31 October 1843.

5 *equal*: adequate or fit.

121. See note to no. xxi above.

122. First published in 1850, this poem is in the Honresfeld ms., where it is dated 16 May 1841. Charlotte Brontë made no changes in the text of the poem before publication and provided this note:

> The following little piece has no title; but in it the Genius of a solitary region seems to address his wandering and wayward votary, and to recall within his influence the proud mind which rebelled at times against what it most loved.

According to Barker, the poem shows Brontë's pantheism 'in its most extreme form, partly because there is no comment from the "fond idolater" herself' (*SP*, p. 132). Homans asserts that the wind (of no. 118) has so successfully pre-empted the poet's voice as to become the only speaker (p. 127), but the speaker of the poem is not a masculine wind but a feminine Earth.

4 *bow*: to cause to bend (archaic or dialect), or figuratively, to incline or influence the mind, usually with a direct object (obsolete) (*OED*); 'thee' is the implied object here; compare ll. 15–16, which suggest bowing in submission to a divine influence.

21–4: compare Catherine Earnshaw's dream of being in heaven and breaking 'my heart with weeping to come back to earth' (*WH*, I, 9).

123. First published in 1850, this poem is in the Honresfeld ms., where it is dated 6 July 1841. Charlotte Brontë revised eight of the poem's lines, added five lines at its end, and attached this note:

> In these stanzas a louder gale has roused the sleeper on her pillow: the wakened soul struggles to blend with the story by which it is swayed.

Gérin cites Shelley's 'Ode to the West Wind' (*EB*, p. 154). According to Homans, 'both wind and mind are spirit; both pour their presence into all; the mind has joined the wind in becoming a universal principle' (p. 123). Compare no. viii, especially lines 37–52.

3 *flash*: gleam, perhaps with the additional sense of light emitted intermittently.
12 *foam-bells*: the bubbles formed by the tide; *OED* cites Hogg, *Queen's Wake* (1813): 'Light as the foam-bells floating on the brine'.
17 *A universal influence*: all-embracing, or overpowering all others; the word 'influence' appears frequently in Wordsworth; in *The Excursion*, influences are 'sweet', 'gladsome', 'soft', 'kindly', 'blended', 'sacred', and 'salutary'.
18 *From Thine own influence free*: presumably, 'Thine' refers to the influence of the 'thou' to whom the poem is addressed, now a 'spirit', a 'presence', an 'essence', and a 'universal influence' outside the control of the 'thou' imagined as possessing a will of her own.
20 *Lost to mortality*: Homans notes the ambiguity of 'mortality', which she suggests means both 'life' and 'death' (p. 124), but the sense seems to be that a 'principle of life' has been lost to mortal nature or existence. Compare the 'Immortality Ode'.
21 *truly*: as in 'The Prisoner (A Fragment)', the visionary experience warrants the release from a confining mortality through death.

124. First published in 1902, this poem is in the Honresfeld ms. and is dated 17 July 1841. Barker notes the view of tombstones from the Parsonage window as well as the poem's 'startlingly unorthodox ideas', especially 'the rejection of the Christian heaven' (*SP*, p. 133). The speaker is not indoors but outside, however, and walking through a graveyard over the buried dead. According to Homans, the poem sets up the same categories as no. x and Brontë's devoir, *Le Papillon* – a 'dark and fatal earth' versus an 'eternally happy heaven' – while blocking the path from one to the other (p. 147). But the poem also merits comparison with Catherine's dream of heaven as an inhospitable place and her longing to be home again on earth (*WH*, I, 9). Heaven is rejected in this poem because its inhabitants are in no way 'akin' to the speaker; her 'children fair' do not seem to be the offspring of the same mother Earth.

1 *tombstones grey*] or 'piteous tombstones grey', but 'piteous' may be cancelled; the phrase 'tombstones grey' appears in *The Lay of the Last Minstrel*, II, 24.
4 *low and lone*: compare no. 120, written just five months earlier: 'And like myself lone wholly lone'.

8 *hoards*: preserves, but also cherishes.

15 *Sweet land of light*: heaven.

18 *each mortal cell*: cavities in the structure of any tissue, especially the imagined compartments of the brain, as in Cowper's reference to 'all the cells/Where Mem'ry slept' (*The Task*, 1784).

21 *ecstasy*: an exalted state of feeling or transport; used here, with great originality, to emphasize the exclusion of strong feeling.

27 *careless*: Chitham reads 'curseless' (*SBP*, p. 136).

34 *unutterable*: a stock word often applied to strong emotions like grief.

125. First published in 1902, this poem is in the *Gondal Poems* notebook, where it is dated 17 August 1841. Between composing it and composing the poem that precedes it (no. 124), Emily and Anne wrote diary papers on the occasion of Emily's twenty-third birthday on 30 July. All the Brontë siblings except Emily were at this time gone from Haworth. In her note, Emily mentions the 'scheme . . . at present in agitation for setting us up in a school of our own' and notes that the 'Gondalians (+ + +) are at present in a threatening state but there is no open rupture as yet' (quoted in *LEB*, pp. 136-7).

The last stanza of the poem appears to have been added to the ms. after the succeeding poem, no. 62, composed almost exactly three years earlier, had been transcribed into the *Gondal Poems* notebook (H, p. 169). In the ms., the name of the poem's central figure, Geraldine, appears at the poem's head; I follow Hatfield in treating it as the poem's title. Julius Brenzaida addresses a Geraldine S. in no. 66. On Geraldine's identity, see my Introduction: This Edition, Gondal; the note to no. 66; and the note to no. iv. The poem following this one in the *Gondal Poems* notebook is headed by the initials A. G. A.

9: Gaaldine, which is the setting for this poem, has a tropical climate, hence the palm trees and cedars.

16 *witching*: bewitching, enchanting.

22 *Zedora*: a large province in Gaaldine.

32: Geraldine identifies the child here as the offspring of Julius Brenzaida, thereby confirming the narrative relation of this poem to no. 66. According to Paden and Ratchford, Julius is Geraldine's husband, and to Ratchford, her 'one true and lasting passion' and the father of her daughter Alexandria (*GQ*, pp. 41, 43). According to Paden, Julius and Geraldine have one child, a son H. A. or Henry Angora (p. 49).

126. First published in 1902, this poem is in the *Gondal Poems* notebook, where it is dated 1 September 1841. In the ms., the name of the poem's central figure, Rosina, appears at the head of the poem after the initial E. for Emily. On the identities of Julius and Rosina, see the note to no. iv. Regardless of whether Rosina is or is not A. G. A./Geraldine, this poem, which describes Rosina's immediate response to the news of Julius Brenzaida's death, supports the identification of Rosina as the R. Alcona who laments that death fifteen years later in no. iv. In this poem, Julius is referred to as King Julius, Almedore (a kingdom in Gaaldine), and Brenzaida. Compare no. 33, in which Julius Angora proclaims or anticipates a victory in battle.

13 *Angora's hills*: Angora is a kingdom in Gondal.

14 *crimson flag*: Julius Brenzaida's standard.

15 *Elderno's waves*: Lake Elderno is in Gondal; according to Ratchford, Gondal's capital, Regina, is located on Lake Elderno (*BWC*, p. 65).

27 *fled*: Hatfield reads 'bled', but gives 'fled' as an alternative.

59 *Exina's arms*: the reference is to the ruler of Exina, one of the kingdoms of Gondal (*GQ*, p. 45).

65 *this*: Hatfield suggests 'his' may have been intended.

127. Charlotte Brontë titled this poem 'Encouragement' for publication in 1850 and revised it only slightly, substituting 'sister' for 'Gerald' in line 14. The poem is in the *Gondal Poems* notebook, where it is dated 19 December 1841. According to Ratchford, the initials A. S. refer to Angelica, daughter of Lord Alfred S. of Aspin Castle and stepdaughter of A. G. A. (H, p. 19; *GQ*, p. 44); the Gerald mentioned in this poem is identified as her brother or half-brother.

24 *earthly woe*: compare 'a world of woe' (*Paradise Lost*, VIII, 333) and 'the world and all our woe' (*Paradise Lost*, I, 3).

128. First published in 1902, this poem is in the *Gondal Poems* notebook. Its composition date of 17 May 1842 makes it the first poem written in Brussels (where Emily and Charlotte had been since mid-February) and the only poem completed there. A. S. has been identified as Angelica (see the note to no. 127 above) by Ratchford (*GQ*, p. 76) and as Alexandria by Paden (p. 50). H. A. has been identified as Henry of Angora by Paden (p. 50) and as Amedeus by Ratchford, who notes that 'information interpreting the initials H. A. is lacking' (*GQ*, p. 76). There is no evidence to support Ratchford's identification of the poem's speaker as Lord Eldred (*GQ*, p. 76).

The subject of this poem, like that of the two poems preceding it and 'Remembrance', is the survivor's response to death. Like *Wuthering Heights*, this poem considers the possibility that the pain of those who have been left behind can recall the dead to life. The image of the two children, one dark, one light, looks ahead to the dark and fair pairs in *Wuthering Heights*, Hareton and Catherine Linton and (with the colouring reversed) Edgar Linton and Cathy Earnshaw. Charlotte Brontë has written some verses in the margins of the ms. and made some revisions, probably, as Hatfield suggests, when she was considering poems for publication in 1850.

13: the speaker turns from the memory of an earlier couple (a light-haired *he*, a dark-haired *she*) to a dream (or dreams) of the couple at the time of the boy's death.

26 *The grass grown grave*: the lover who is left alive continues to mourn her dead mate long after his death.

27-8: the tomb is probably located in Gaaldine.

31-2: compare no. 124, ll. 9-10: 'For Time and Death and Mortal pain/ Give wounds that will not heal again'.

36 *When she had ceased to mourn*: compare no. iv.

129. First published in 1902, this poem is in the *Gondal Poems* notebook. Dates at the top of the ms. page indicate that the poem was begun in Brussels on 20 August 1842 and completed in Haworth on 6 February 1843. In August of 1842, Brontë wrote three French essays, *L'Amour Filial*, *Lettre d'un Frère à un Frère*, and *Le Papillon*. Aspin Castle is the seat of Lord Alfred S. Ratchford suggests that

in this poem, a dead Lord Alfred's spirit returns to Aspin Castle to grieve (*GQ*, p. 89).

8 *Rockden's*: the name does not appear elsewhere in the poems.

25: although Hatfield prints ll. 21–9 as a single stanza, a space in the ms. divides l. 25 from l. 26; three cancelled lines follow l. 25.

26 *evening's pensive hour*: compare no. i, l. 5.

52: although Hatfield prints ll. 52–8 as a single stanza, a space in the ms. separates l. 55 from l. 56.

62: although Hatfield prints ll. 59–66 as a single stanza, a space in the ms. separates l. 62 from l. 63.

67 *Daughter divine*: Ratchford identifies Lord Alfred's daughter as the blonde, blue-eyed Angelica (*GQ*, p. 91). The name Angelica appears only once in the poems. In no. 148, Angelica speaks of A.G.A., now her enemy, as once her 'childhood's mate' and 'girlhood's guide'.

76 *Sidonia's deity*: Sidon is a Phoenician city. Brontë may be remembering *Paradise Lost*, I, 338–42:

> . . . With these in troop
> Came *Astoreth*, whom the *Phoenicians* call'd
> *Astarte*, Queen of Heav'n, with crescent Horns;
> To whose bright Image nightly by the Moon
> *Sidonian* Virgins paid their Vows and Songs . . .

Ratchford plausibly takes 'Sidonia's deity' to refer to A.G.A. (*GQ*, p. 69), Lord Alfred's 'idol queen' and his daughter's victorious rival.

79 *enthusiast's*: an enthusiast is, literally, inspired by a god; someone who is zealous for a person or cause, or someone who is self-deluded; the pejorative sense is dominant here and in no. 168, l. 31.

95 *Nature's face divine*: compare Milton's 'human face divine' (*Paradise Lost*, III, 44) and Blake's 'human form divine' ('The Divine Image', l. 11).

96 *wold*: a piece of open country; a plain (*OED*).

96 *fell*: chiefly in the north of England or Scotland, a 'wild elevated stretch of waste or pasture land; a moorland ridge, down' (*OED*).

130. See the note to no. xv above.

131. First published in 1902, this poem is in the *Gondal Poems* notebook, where it is dated 24 February 1843. The initials E.J. appear at the head of the ms. Zalona is the name of a kingdom, and perhaps a city, in Gaaldine; in Anne's list of place names, it is spelled 'Zelona'. Hatfield follows Ratchford in identifying Gerald Exina as the King of Zalona (H, p. 181). Whether the speaker of this poem is or is not Gerald Exina, the battle's outcome is described from the point of view of Zalona, and the victorious forces are those of Julius Brenzaida, who bears a crimson flag. Compare no. 33, in which Brenzaida exults in his victory over an unidentified city that flies a 'sea-green Standard'. See also no. 126.

32: I follow Hatfield in adding quotation marks at the end of this line.

37–40: compare Pope's *Iliad*, ll. 5–6: 'Whose Limbs unbury'd on the naked shore/ Devouring Dogs and hungry Vultures tore'.

40 *forbear*: perhaps bear up against or control (this sense was obsolete in the nineteenth century); but the more gruesome sense is that the masters are hungry enough to envy the dogs their feast.

55 *tears*: the pronunciation is uncertain; the rhyme with 'prayers' also appears in no. 148, l. 85 and no. 169, l. 10; Brontë more frequently rhymes 'tears' with 'years', but 'tears' rhymes with 'cares' in no. 18 and with 'airs' in no. 78, and 'prayer' rhymes with 'hear' in no. 165. See the note to no. 78, l. 8.

79 *We dare not shrink from slavery's chain*: the sense is obscure.

132. See note to no. xii above.

133. First published in 1902, this poem is in the *Gondal Poems* notebook, where it is dated 1 May 1843. Emily was at home without her sisters and brother; Charlotte had returned to Brussels, and Anne had returned to Thorp Green, taking Branwell with her as tutor to the Robinsons' son. Nicholls made a transcript of this poem and titled it 'Grave in the Ocean'. Ratchford is unable to connect the events recorded in this poem to others in the Gondal narrative (H, p. 19).

Title the initials A.S. refer to Lord Alfred of Aspin Castle or to his daughter.

5: the allusion amalgamates Job 3:17 ('there the weary be at rest') and Matthew 8:20 ('but the son of man hath not where to lay his head'); the title of Branwell's unfinished novel, *And the Weary Are at Rest* (1840), also alludes to the phrase in Job.

12 *Eternal midnight there*: compare Blake's 'Holy Thursday' (*Songs of Experience*): 'It is eternal winter there' (l. 12).

16 *undergloom*: a deeper gloom, or gloom beneath the gloom; *OED* cites 1897 as the first use of this word; Wordsworth is fond of compounds using 'under', e.g., 'underboughs' in *The Excursion*, 5, 148.

134. First published in 1902, this poem is in the *Gondal Poems* notebook and is dated 4 May 1843. Under the heading to this poem in the ms., Charlotte has written 'A Serenade', the poem's title in 1923; above 'honour's' in line 11, she has written 'true love's'; and above 'Gleneden's' in line 23, she has written 'honour's'. She probably considered this poem for publication in 1850.

Title E.G. is E. Gleneden and M.R. is Mary R.; a Mary is mentioned in no. 119.

5 *careering*: moving swiftly over an expanse.

14 *Entailed*: necessitated as a consequence.

135. First published in 1902, this poem is in the BPML and is dated 26 July 1843. The last digit is indistinct, and Hatfield reads it as '3', while suggesting that it may be meant for '2'. If this poem was composed in 1842, then it and poems 136 and 137, which are thematically closely related, were written while Brontë was in Brussels; if it is dated 1843, then all three poems were written the following summer, while Brontë was alone in Haworth. It follows that in one of these summers she wrote no poems, or none that have survived. It seems more likely that she would have stopped writing poems while she was in Brussels, especially since she was busy writing essays in June, July, and August of 1842. The poem is probably incomplete. Paden's suggestion that this poem and no. 99 form a single poem can be discarded (see the note to no. 99).

136. The poem as a whole was first published in 1938, although an earlier version of the first six stanzas was published in 1934, and the seventh and eighth stanzas were also published in 1934 as a separate poem. It is in the *Gondal Poems* notebook, and is undated, but variant drafts of portions of it, also undated but probably composed at widely spaced intervals, survive on separate leaves in the ms. in the BPML. One of these variant drafts corresponds to lines 27–34 in the fair-copy version of the poem, and appears just below no. 135 on the same ms. leaf and in the same handwriting. I have conjecturally placed this poem in the compositional sequence on the basis of no. 135. The other variant draft corresponds to the first six stanzas of the poem in the *Gondal Poems* notebook but includes an additional six lines. It is written in a different handwriting, and appears on a separate ms. leaf, together with no. 93, dated 19 July 1839, on the reverse. This variant includes an additional stanza after line 9:

> The murmur of their boughs and streams
> Speaks pride as well as bliss
> And that blue heaven expanding seems
> The circling hills to kiss

Two lines follow line 26:

> I dreamt one dark and stormy night
> When winter winds were wild

Hatfield suggests that the rest of this poem may have been on another leaf, which has not survived. Hatfield published as Emily's a poem by Charlotte Brontë which begins, 'I've been wandering in the greenwoods' and is dated 14 December 1829. He did not see the ms. of the poem, which is signed by Charlotte Brontë, but relied on Shorter's transcription and the attribution of the poem to Emily Brontë in 1910.

The competing lovers in no. 136, as different from each other as night and day, figure again in *Wuthering Heights*, where Catherine Earnshaw refuses to acknowledge that 'only one/ Can light my future sky'.

Title for A. G. A., see the note to no. 10 above.
1 *Thou standest in the greenwood*] I'm standing in the forest.
1 *greenwood*: a wood or forest in leaf; typically a setting for outlaws.
3 *fresh*] green.
11 *O question not with me*] No whisper not to me.
12 *Lady*] dreamer.
18 *whate'er betide*] and you deride.
19 *faithful*] changeless.
21 *rolling*] ocean's.
22 *sorrow*] trouble.
28 *ardent*] radiant.
29 *Then*] And.

137. First published in 1902, this poem is in the BPML, where it is undated. It appears on the other side of the leaf on which nos. 99, 135, and the early draft of two stanzas of 136 appear. It is written in the same handwriting as no. 135 and the two draft stanzas of 136 and has conjecturally been placed in the compositional sequence accordingly. Moreover, it is thematically related to nos. 135 and 136 above.

Gondal sleuths have agreed that this poem represents A.G.A.'s farewell to a
wronged husband but have disagreed about his identity; Ratchford (*GQ*, p. 85)
and Barker (*SP*, p. 134) identify him as Lord Alfred S., whom A.G.A. betrays
for Julius Brenzaida, while Paden identifies him as Alexander of Elbë, whom
A.G.A. betrays for Lord Alfred S. (pp. 37–40). Lines 21–4 closely echo the
opening stanza of no. 145, 'A.G.A. to A.S.', and suggest that Lord Alfred may be
addressed in no. 137 also.

8 [*longed*]: this word is illegible; 'longed' is Hatfield's reading.
19 [*grieve*]: an uncertain reading.
21 [*herald*]: Hatfield reads 'wild', but suggests 'herald' as an alternative.

138. First published in 1902, this poem is in the *Gondal Poems* notebook, where it
has two composition dates, 6 May 1840 and 28 July 1843. The later date brings it
into close relation to nos. 135, 136, and 137. If A.G.A. speaks to Lord Alfred S.
in no. 137 as well as in this poem, then either this poem records an earlier time in
the relation, when A.G.A. was deeply in love and unable to imagine the 'woe'
ahead, or the poems explore alternative directions for the Gondal plot. If the latter
is the case, then A.G.A. may banish Lord Alfred in no. 137 and cleave to him in
no. 138. In a poem written much earlier, no. 48, A.G.A. watches over A.S.'s
death. Nicholls transcribed no. 138 and titled it 'Love's Contentment'.

Title for A.G.A., see no. 10 above. Lord Alfred is mentioned in no. 129, where
he is described as having golden hair and 'spirit-eyes of dreamy blue' (l. 33). Two
other poems, nos. 48 and 145, have the title 'A.G.A. to A.S.'
29 *twilight's shade forlorn*: the position of the adjective is Miltonic; compare 'wild
Woods forlorn' (*Paradise Lost*, IX, 910) and 'Stygian cave forlorn' ('L'Allegro', 3);
Brontë may also be recalling Milton's 'Nativity Ode', l. 188: 'The Nymphs in
twilight shade of tangled thickets mourn'.

139. First published in 1850, this poem is in the *Gondal Poems* notebook and is
dated 6 September 1843. Charlotte Brontë gave it the title 'Warning and Reply'
and slightly altered the poem's text when she printed it (see the note to line 23
below). The poem seems closely related to no. 137. Both refer to a 'resting place'
and involve farewells. The speaker of the second and fourth stanzas may be the
lover who is banished in no. 137. If he is Lord Alfred S., his 'sunny' hair is the
right colour (see the note to no. 138 above). In no. 129, Lord Alfred is said to
haunt Aspin Castle, his ancestral home, although he is buried in distant England.
The poem's second voice, which warns him he is destined for oblivion, may also
belong to him.

23 *One heart broke, only, there*: the reference of both 'there' and 'only' is
ambiguous. Charlotte Brontë altered the line to read 'One heart breaks only –
here', connecting 'only' to 'one' and suggesting that the heart that breaks belongs
to the lover who will soon be dead and buried. In the line as written, 'only' looks
in two directions, and 'there' refers to the place where the lover used to live, and
where he sometimes believes his 'sworn friends' still 'prize my memory'. The
warning voice tells him that only one lover was faithful to him, probably not
A.G.A.

140. First published in 1902, this poem is in the *Gondal Poems* notebook and is

dated 18 December 1843. Charlotte Brontë may have considered this poem for publication in 1850; in the ms., she has written the name 'Rodric' below the title and 'war-worn comrades' above 'monarch's legions' in line 20.

Title Rodric Lesley does not appear elsewhere; the date suggests a Gondal chronology.

141. See the note to no. ix above.

142. First published in 1902, the poem is in the *Gondal Poems* notebook and is dated 19 December 1843. Nicholls transcribed this poem and titled it 'North and South', a title retained in 1923. The poem contrasts the northern world of Gondal with the southern world of Gaaldine. The speaker seems to be reassuring himself or herself about the will of her comrades to return from Gaaldine to Gondal.

Title M. G. has not been identified; U. S. stands for the Unique Society. In her diary paper of 31 July 1845, Anne writes that the Unique Society 'above half a year ago, were wrecked on a desert island as they were returning from Gaul. They are still there, but we have not played at them much yet.' Shorter received the diary papers for 1841 and 1845 from Arthur Bell Nicholls and published his transcription of them in *Charlotte Brontë and Her Circle* (1896); Ratchford suggests that Shorter may have mistranscribed 'Gaaldine' as 'Gaul', though this seems unlikely (*GQ*, p. 194). Chitham also quotes this portion of Anne's diary paper for 1845, but omits the phrase 'as they were returning from Gaul' (*LEB*, p. 180).
9 *Ula's bowers*: Ula is a kingdom in Gaaldine.
14 *her Eden isle*: compare 'Ula's Eden sky' in no. 119.
16: perhaps a reference to the stranded members of the Unique Society.

143. First published in 1910, this poem is in the NYPL and is dated 2 February 1844. It was in this month that Brontë began to transcribe her poems into two notebooks, one untitled, the other titled *Gondal Poems*. The situation to which this poem refers cannot be established, but Ratchford connects it to no. 148, and suggests that Amedeus, who has been designated to assassinate Julius, addresses Angelica here (*GQ*, p. 101).

Title 'At Castle Wood' in all editions prior to 1941; H reads the 'At' as the initials 'A. S.'; this is the only occurrence of 'Castle Wood' in the poems.
3 [*h*]*as*: the ms. has 'as'; I follow Hatfield in adding the 'h'.
4 *hearts*] written above 'beams', cancelled; Hatfield reads 'beams'.
5–6: compare no. iv, ll. 17–18.
6 *morn*: Hatfield reads 'moon'; compare no. 89, l. 35: 'How bright the morn will shine'.
8 *ways*] written above 'joys', cancelled.
9 *Life*['*s*]: my emendation; there is no 's' in the ms., and Hatfield reads 'Life', which makes no sense.
11 *without its*] cancelled.
13 [*living*]: barely legible.
16 *hire*] written above 'pang', cancelled.
19 *the mate of care*: Brown (p. 376) cites Byron, *The Prisoner of Chillon*: 'I was the mate of misery' (l. 258).

20 *The foster child of [sore] distress*: compare Keats, 'Ode on a Grecian Urn': 'Thou foster child of silence and slow time'.
21: there is no comma in the ms., but a large space between 'me' and 'no' suggests a heavy pause.
24 *Unwept for let the body go*] 'Unmourned, the body well may go', cancelled.

144. See the note to no. xx above.

145. First published in 1902, this poem is in the *Gondal Poems* notebook and is dated 2 March 1844. The poem has been substantially revised in the notebook, and the last stanza has been written above four cancelled lines. Hatfield notes that the first stanza is a variation of the last stanza of no. 137. In this poem, A.G.A. says farewell to Lord Alfred S. But compare no. 48, written almost six years earlier and also titled 'A.G.A. to A.S.', where A.G.A. mourns a dying Lord Alfred S., and no. 138, also titled 'A.G.A. to A.S.'.

Title for A.G.A., see the note to no. 10 above; for A.S., see the note to no. 138 above.

146. See the note to no. x above.

147. First published in 1850, this poem is in the *Gondal Poems* notebook and is dated 11 March 1844. Beneath the title, Charlotte Brontë has written 'On a life perverted'. For the 1850 edition, she titled the poem 'The Wanderer from the Fold'. Clement Shorter thought the poem referred to Branwell Brontë's history, an idea rejected by both Hatfield and Barker. But despite the Gondal framework and Branwell's still being alive and apparently settled in his job at Thorp Green in 1844, Brontë may have had his history in mind when she wrote this poem, and Charlotte Brontë probably had it in mind when she selected it for publication after his death. C. Day Lewis notes the poem's 'Cowperish thought and tone' (p. 86), and Brontë may be recalling Goldsmith and Gray as well (see below).

Title E.W. has been identified as Lord Eldred W., A.G.A.'s friend, on the basis of the role Lord Eldred plays in no. 148. Ratchford assigns Lord Eldred a substantial part in the Gondal saga, identifying him as the Captain of the Queen's Guard (in no. 148), an astrologer and soothsayer (in no. 1), and the speaker of several other poems.
1: this line echoes l. 429 of Goldsmith's *The Traveller*, marked by Johnson as one of his contributions to the poem: 'How small, of all that human hearts endure'.
23–4: Brontë may be remembering Gray's 'The Bard,' ll. 73–4: 'In gallant trim the gilded Vessel goes;/ Youth on the prow, and Pleasure at the helm'.
36 *save*: an absolute construction, with the direct object omitted; see also the note to no. 11, l. 50, above.

148. First published in 1902, this poem is in the *Gondal Poems* notebook, where it has two widely spaced dates of composition, January 1841 and May 1844. It is Brontë's longest poem, and according to Ratchford, the 'key to the theme and plot of the A.G.A.–Julius poems' (*GQ*, p. 24). It tells the story of the assassination of A.G.A. by the outlaw Douglas, following the commands of Angelica, whom Ratchford identifies as Lord Alfred's daughter. See no. 129, where Lord Alfred's spirit haunts his ancestral home, lamenting his preference for a woman called

'Sidonia's deity', and identified by Ratchford as A.G.A. (see also no. 148, line 330 below), over his golden-haired daughter. In this poem, Angelica identifies A.G.A. as once her 'childhood's mate' and 'girlhood's guide', now her 'mortal foe', and accuses A.G.A. of having driven her and another, perhaps Lord Alfred, into exile.

The ellipses after lines 138, 198, and 261 mark changes of scene; lapses of time; the omission from the narrative of an action, the stabbing of A.G.A.'s friends, Fair Surry and Lord Lesley (after line 138); and the introduction of a new character, Lord Eldred (after line 261).

Title in the ms., the title of the poem is 'A.G.A. the Death of'.

9 *One was a woman*: identified (l. 29) as Angelica.

14 *cruel*: a trochee.

25 *And he was noble too*: identified (l. 93) as Douglas.

89 *My dearer self*: probably a reference to Lord Alfred.

100 *A wildering dream of frenzied crime*: compare Scott, *The Lay of the Last Minstrel*, Introduction: 'And scenes, long past, of joy and pain,/ Came wildering o'er his aged brain'.

110 *Amedeus*: this is the only occurrence of this name in the poems; according to Ratchford, Amedeus is Angelica's foster brother and her accomplice in assassinating Julius (*GQ*, p. 44).

115 *lea*: open ground.

117 *braes*: slopes or hillsides; the word also appears in no. 76 and no. x; see the note to no. x above.

129 *our hunted band*: both Angelica and Douglas are outlaws.

141 *their dying bed*: Fair Surry's and Lord Lesley's.

166 *fill*: weep.

171 *fondly*: foolishly; affectionately.

218 *Elmor Hill*: Elmor, or Elnor, is a lake in Gondal.

240 *the Murderer's gaze*: his knife as well; see ll. 242–3.

249 *False friend*: Angelica, who has presumably watched the struggle between Douglas and A.G.A.; she is also the 'False Love' addressed in l. 255.

280 *he*: Lord Eldred, whose name is given in l. 290.

286 *treason*: A.G.A. is Gondal's queen.

290 *Lord Eldred*: A.G.A.'s faithful friend; he laments her death in no. 147.

302 *moorcock*: the male of the red grouse; one of the feathers Cathy Linton pulls from her pillow during her illness is the moorcock's (*WH*, I, 12).

331 *unweeting*: unwitting.

339 *calmer wave*: Milton, *Paradise Lost*, II, 1042.

340 *save*: see the note to no. 11, l. 50.

149. See the note to no. vi above.

150. See the note to no. xi above.

151. First published in *Gondal Poems* (1938), this poem is in the *Gondal Poems* notebook and is dated 2 October 1844. On the same day, Charlotte Brontë wrote to Ellen Nussey to thank her for her efforts to attract pupils to a boarding school to be established at the Parsonage. 'I, Emily and Anne are truly obliged to you for the efforts you have made on our behalf, and if you have not been successful, you are only like ourselves' (*EB*, p. 162). In her diary paper for 31 July 1845, Anne writes about a conflict between Republicans and Royalists that may be reflected in this poem.

Title D.G.C. is unidentified and does not appear elsewhere in the poems; J.A. may designate Julius Brenzaida, also called Julius Angora.

7: Hatfield makes this line part of the previous one, but the ms. clearly indicates a separation.

9 *so we shall be*: Hatfield reads 'so shall we be'.

152. See the note to no. xiv above.

153. See the note to no. i above.

154. The poem is in the *Gondal Poems* notebook, and is dated 11 November 1844. Lines 1–28 were first published in 1850 as 'The Elder's Rebuke'; lines 39–60 were first published in 1934 as 'Love's Rebuke'; the poem as a whole was first published in 1938.

The initials E.J.B. appear on one side of the ms.; on the other are the initials J.B. and the Gondal date September 1825. J.B. is Julius Brenzaida, who is addressed in lines 1–34 and who addresses Rosina in lines 35–60. He accuses her of responsibility for his imprisonment, and the crime for which he is being punished may be his unfaithfulness to her. Under the title in the ms., Charlotte Brontë has written 'T[he] Old Man's lecture'. When she printed lines 1–28 in 1850, she added eight lines of her own.

Title according to Ratchford, Southern College was in Gaaldine (*GQ*, p. 53), but Julius speaks of being kept from 'Those wondrous southern isles' in l. 46.

39: Rosina is Rosina Alcona, here identified as Julius Brenzaida's 'queen'; on her role in the poems, see the Introduction: This Edition, Gondal, and the note to no. iv above.

155. See the note to no. xviii above.

156. See the note to no. v above.

157. See the note to no. iii above.

158. See the note to no. iv above.

159. See the note to no. xvi above.

160. See the note to no. ii above.

161. First published in 1902, this poem is in the *Gondal Poems* notebook and is dated 22 April 1845. Nicholls titled this poem 'Despair' when he transcribed it, a title retained in 1923.

10: the violet and wood-rose are medicinal plants; the violet was used to induce sleep, and the wood-rose was thought to be effective against the bite of a rabid dog.

30 *hope*] 'life' is written over 'hope' in the ms., or vice versa.

34 *Life's conscious Death*: despair; the phrase is the antecedent for 'it' in this and the following line.

162. First published in 1850, with the title 'The Two Children', this poem is in the *Gondal Poems* notebook, and is dated 28 May 1845. In the ms., the line 'Child of Delight! with sunbright hair' begins the second half of this poem; lines 37–60 have been moved three or four characters to the left of the lines that precede them, so that the second part of the poem is centred under the first part. Hatfield follows 1910 and 1923 in printing this poem as two poems, but it was printed as one poem in 1850 and 1934. Blake's *Songs of Innocence and Experience* would have provided a model for the paired poems, and Brontë's diction and prosody, especially in the second part, are reminiscent of Blake's. C. Day Lewis argues, however, that Brontë's 'occasional resemblances to Blake' evidence 'a certain mental affinity, a shared quality of innocence, child-like and visionary', and cannot be attributed to 'literary influence' (p. 90). The melancholy figure described in the first part of the poem anticipates Heathcliff, bereft of Guardian Angel or 'kindred kindness', destined to a 'grim Fate', and unblessed by heaven or earth.

Above the title of this poem in the ms., Charlotte Brontë has written her title, 'The Two Children'. She added a stanza of four lines after line 56:

> Watch in love by a fevered pillow,
> Cooling the fever with pity's balm;
> Safe as the petrel on tossing billow,
> Safe in mine own soul's golden calm!

Title the initials A.E. usually stand for Alexander of Elbë, but R.C. does not appear elsewhere in the poems.
41 *shouldest*: the metre suggests a one-syllable word.
52 *beamy*: radiant.
60: compare Charlotte Brontë's 1850 revision: 'And *my* love is truer than angel-care'.

163. See the note to no. vii above.

164. First published in 1902, this poem is in the *Gondal Poems* notebook and is dated August 1845. Branwell had returned to Haworth in disgrace in July, having been dismissed from his post as tutor at Thorp Green; neither Emily's nor Anne's diary paper (written on 30 July and 31 July) mentions this event, although both review the changes that have occurred for the family, including Anne's return from Thorp Green in June. Anne writes that Branwell has had 'much tribulation and ill health'; both Emily and Anne hope that he will 'be better and do better . . .'.

Emily's diary paper also mentions an excursion she and Anne took to York during which they 'were Ronald Macalgin, Henry Angora, Juliet Augusteena, Rosabella Esmalden, Ella and Julian Egremont, Catharine Navarre, and Cordelia Fitzaphnold, escaping from the palaces of instruction to join the Royalists who are hard driven at present by the victorious Republicans'. The initials M.A. at the head of the ms. and at its end identify the speaker, but these initials do not occur elsewhere. Nicholls transcribed this poem and titled it 'The Captive's Lament'.

Title N.C. stands for 'North College'; see the note on the title of no. v above.
1: the ms. has 'is' twice.
31 *morning*: spelt 'mourning' in the ms.

165. This poem was first published as a whole in 1938. It is in the *Gondal Poems*

notebook and is dated 9 October 1845. 'One day, in the autumn of 1845,' Charlotte Brontë discovered her sister's poems, a discovery that led to the publication of *Poems by Currer, Ellis, and Acton Bell*. It has been suggested that Emily was at this time copying poem no. 165 into her *Gondal Poems* notebook, and that this may be the poem Charlotte Brontë first read. Lines 13-44 and 65-92 were printed in 1846 with four lines added by Emily Brontë as 'The Prisoner (A Fragment)'. For a discussion of the portions of the poem published in 1846, see the note to no. viii above.

Lines 1-12 were published in 1850, with eight lines added by Charlotte Brontë, as 'The Visionary'. Charlotte Brontë has written 'The Signal Light' under the title in the ms. 1850 substitutes a 'visitant of air', probably the imagination, for the 'Wanderer', and makes the speaker of the poem a woman awaiting inspiration.

1846 omits the frame, which narrates the events that follow those recorded in 'The Prisoner (A Fragment)': the release of the prisoner, A. G. Rochelle, from the 'dungeon crypts' by Lord Julian; her recovery, under his watchful care, from a dangerous illness lasting thirteen weeks; his secret devotion to her, which involves giving up his pursuit of fame in battle; and her secret, nightly visits to him, or, less likely, his nightly visits to her (lines 1-12). Although Julian is clearly the speaker of lines 13-152, some readers have identified A. G. Rochelle as the speaker of lines 1-12. If A. G. Rochelle is the speaker of lines 1-12, then Julian is the 'Wanderer', an unlikely notion. Brontë refers to wanderers in four other poems; in two of them (no. 71 and no. 118, 'The Night-Wind'), the wanderer is the wind, in two of them (nos. 97 and 148), the wanderer is a solitary human being, and in one of these two poems (no. 97), the wanderer is in close communion with nature. Brontë may have Wordsworth's Wanderer (*The Excursion*, Book I especially) in mind, but wanderers are a staple feature of Romantic poems. An early version of Branwell's 'Sir Henry Tunstall' is titled 'The Wanderer' and dated 31 July 1838. T. J. Wise attributed it to Emily, apparently because he mistook the handwriting for hers, but Branwell submitted 'Sir Henry Tunstall' to *Blackwood's* in 1842.

Title Julian M. and A. G. Rochelle do not appear elsewhere in the poems.
2 *snow-wreaths*: banks or drifts of snow, chiefly Scottish.
9-12: Ratchford (*GQ*, p. 168) notes the parallel in a poem Anne Brontë wrote a few days earlier, 'Parting Address from Z. Z. to A. E.':

> A mother's sad reproachful eye,
>   A father's scowling brow –
> But he may frown, and she may sigh;
>   I will not break my vow!

63 *headsman's*: executioner's.
95 *As I had knelt in scorn*: a reference to his earlier contempt for the dungeon inmates.
113-16: the only epic simile in the poems.

166. See note to no. viii above.

167. First published in 1850, this poem is in the Honresfeld ms. and is dated 2 January 1846. Charlotte Brontë was mistaken in thinking these the last lines Emily Brontë wrote, though not in recognizing the poem as an ultimatum. It is probably the first poem Emily Brontë wrote after Charlotte discovered her poems. It has been much commented upon.

The poem's diction is scientific and philosophical. In a note on Brontë and Epictetus, Maison suggests that Brontë may have read Epictetus, in whose works there are references to 'atoms, inward essences, chained and chainless souls, and all the Stoic attitudes to love, liberty, duty, fame, riches, poverty, pain and death that feature so finely in her poetry' (p. 230). The last chapter of the third book of *The Discourses of Epictetus* concerns the fear of death. The following is Elizabeth Carter's popular translation of its final paragraph (1758):

> Why, do you not know, then, that the origin of all human evils and of the mean-spiritedness and cowardice is not death, but rather the fear of death? Fortify yourself, therefore, against this. Hither let all your discourses, readings, exercises tend. And then you will know that thus alone are all men made free. (199)

Maison identifies a source for the phrase 'coward soul' in an 'irregular ode' by Hester Chapone, which was printed in Carter:

> No more repine, my coward Soul!
>   The Sorrows of Mankind to share,
> Which He, who could the world controul
>   Did not disdain to bear!

Chapone, a friend of Carter's, was an opponent of Stoicism and 'quite vociferously anti-Epictetus'. Maison cites her *Letters on the Improvement of the Mind* (1773) as a possible link between Brontë and Epictetus. Miss Wooler prized it enough to give it as a prize to her pupils at Roe Head; Ellen Nussey was one of those who received it. Maison reads Brontë's poem as an answer to Chapone's ode (pp. 230–31).

3–4: Barbara Hardy marks these lines as the only assertion in Brontë's poems of a 'perfect equivalence' between internal and external light (Smith, p. 116).

4–9: Homans suggests that although the symmetry of 'in me ... in Thee' suggests mutual dependence, the lines formulate a hierarchical rather than an equal relation. 'All the sources of poetry seem to be external, and the poetic self invariably loses any competition with a divine figure external to the poem' (p. 132).

8 *thee*: both Charlotte Brontë and Hatfield capitalize the first letter, but it is clearly lower-case in the ms.

12: compare no. 123, in which the memory of the world is 'dashed ... from thy mind/Like foam-bells from the tide –' (ll. 11–12).

15–16: Gérin cites a source in the words of Ephraim Macbriar in Scott's *Old Mortality*: 'but I trust my soul is anchored firmly on the rock of ages' (*EB*, p. 214).

17–20: this stanza suggests Brontë's familiarity with Coleridge's *Biographia Literaria* (1817); compare his well-known description of the secondary imagination in Ch. 13:

> It dissolves, diffuses, dissipates, in order to recreate; or where this process is rendered impossible, yet still, at all events, it struggles to idealize and to unify. It is essentially *vital*, even as all objects (*as* objects) are essentially fixed and dead.

19 *broods*: hovers, with some reference to the action of a brooding bird (*OED*);

compare Milton, *Paradise Lost*, I, 21–2: 'brooding on the vast Abyss,/ And mad'st it pregnant'.

21–4: several readers have connected this stanza to Cathy's famous words about Heathcliff:

> I cannot express it; but surely you and every body have a notion that there is, or should be, an existence of yours beyond you. What were the use of my creation if I were entirely contained here? My great miseries in this world have been Heathcliff's miseries, and I watched and felt each from the beginning; my great thought in living is himself. If all else perished, and *he* remained, I should still continue to be; and, if all else remained, and he were annihilated, the Universe would turn to a mighty stranger. I should not seem a part of it. (*WH*, 1, 9)

26–7: Barbara Hardy notes that Brontë 'can only imagine spirit through nature. "Atom" and "Breath" are physiological terms being made into absolutes' (Smith, p. 115). Compare the different absolutism of Charlotte Brontë's introduction of emphatic capital letters and punctuation in ll. 27–8:

> Thou – THOU – art Being and Breath,
> And what THOU art may never be destroyed.

168. Thirty-nine lines were printed in 1915, but the poem was first published as a whole in 1938. It is dated 14 September 1846. It and the revised version composed many months later are the last entries in the *Gondal Poems* notebook, and Brontë's last surviving poems. These poems are evidence 'that so far from growing out of Gondal during the composition of *Wuthering Heights*, she returned to it to write some of her most impressive verse' (Jonathan Wordsworth, p. 85). On 14 September 1846, Emily, Anne, and Branwell were at home. Charlotte was in Manchester with her father, who was recovering from cataract surgery. Anne also wrote a Gondal poem on 14 September, 'Z—'s Dream'. Although Emily's and Anne's poems tell different stories, the stories have a family resemblance: both involve remorseless acts and a failure to repent, and both may owe something to the spectacle presented by Branwell. In a letter written the previous spring, Charlotte tells Ellen Nussey that Branwell is 'stupefied', and that Emily calls him 'a hopeless being' (3 March 1846). Emily's words are more ambiguous than the apocalyptic account of lost opportunities and despair provided by her poem.

In the ms., the poem is heavily revised and very difficult to read after line 156. From this point on, Brontë is no longer transcribing a poem but using the notebook for a first draft. Two large sections of the poem are cancelled with a cross in the ms.; their omission would not disrupt the poem's narrative line. The cancelled sections are lines 149–56 and lines 172–89. Brackets in the text indicate doubtful readings.

31 *Enthusiast*: a self-deluding zealot; see the note to no. 129, l. 79, above.

73 *cairns*: pyramids of rough stones raised as a monument, often for the dead.

79 *ken*: range of vision or sight, usually with a preposition; compare Milton, 'within ken' (*Paradise Lost*, III, 622) and 'in clearest ken' (*Paradise Lost*, II, 379).

85 *kill*: an absolute construction.

87 *harshly*] above 'fiend-like', cancelled, with 'coldly' written below 'fiend-like'.

131 *Through this long night*] Brontë originally wrote 'Night following night' and under it, 'Through this long night'; neither reading is cancelled.

138 *west wind*: here the breeze renews the speaker's spirits, but only to freshen his contempt and inspire his theft of his captive's jewellery.

149–56: these lines are cancelled with a single cross; from this point on, the ms. is rougher and more rapidly or carelessly written.

158 *harsh*] written above 'cold', not cancelled.

194 *wailed*] the first 'wailed' is written above 'prayed', cancelled.

223 *come*] written above 'tomorrow', cancelled.

224 *stranglers*: the sense is obscure; perhaps a mistake for 'stragglers' (H, p. 252).

244: the line is cancelled, and the three previous lines are written in the margin of the ms.

248 *My treasure*: a reminder of the spoil taken from the captive.

249–50] two alternative lines also appear in the ms., not cancelled:

> And I would freely, gladly then,
> Have given his saviour life again

257: this line does not appear in Hatfield; it is almost illegible, and is omitted from *Gondal Poems*, although a note indicates that there are two partly legible lines, which the editors read as follows:

> And mercy's God
> The last look of that glazing eye.

I take the first line to be an incomplete revision of l. 257 and include my reading of the second.

169. First published in 1915, this is the last poem in the *Gondal Poems* notebook and is dated 13 May 1848. Written in the last year of Brontë's life, after the publication of *Wuthering Heights*, this poem is a reworking of the preceding one and is probably incomplete. It intensifies the apocalyptic feeling of no. 168.

15 *That August's*: Hatfield reads 'The August'.

Notes to Undated Poems

170. First published in 1910, this poem is one of fourteen poems and poetical fragments the mss. of which were unavailable to Hatfield when he prepared his 1941 edition. The ms. in the PUL is a single leaf, torn at the bottom, with no date of composition. Hatfield does not explain his conjecture that the poem was written between March and May 1837, but he may have been influenced by similar dates on the other poems now in the PUL collection. The poem is probably an early effort. It was printed as undated in 1923.

Barker (*SP*, p. 136) shares Ratchford's view that this is a Gondal poem, but there is no evidence to support this. The poem is a prayer, and the temptation to heed both 'passion's call' and her 'own wild will' can easily be ascribed to Brontë.

12 *summer's sky*: Shorter transcribed 'summer sky'.

171. First published in 1910 as the last two stanzas of no. 25 above. Hatfield printed it as a separate poem without having the ms. of no. 25 available to him; this ms. supports his judgement that the two poems are not connected. The ms. of this poem is in the NYPL, and there is no date of composition. Hatfield prints the poem immediately after no. 25, which is dated 14 October 1837, and does not explain his dating of the poem. The poem is written in pencil, and the pencil has smudged. The words in brackets are illegible.

5 [*morn*]: 1910 prints 'moor'.
7 [*borne*]: 1910 prints 'lour'.

172. First published in 1910, this poem is in the NYPL. The poem is undated, and Hatfield does not explain his conjectured date of composition, between 17 September 1840 and January 1841. It was printed as Anne's in 1920, but the ms. is in Emily's handwriting and the tone is hers, not Anne's.

Emily Brontë would have encountered the bleeding branch in *The Faerie Queene*, I, ii, where Redcrosse 'pluckt a bough; out of whose rift there came/ Small drops of gory bloud, that trickled downe the same'. Spenser draws on Virgil's story of Polidorus (*Aeneid* 3, 20f.), but uncanny trees have a rich folklore history. In *The Brontë Country*, Stuart records a story of Emily and a tree, 'which has never yet seen the light of day'. On the anniversary of the Restoration (29 May 1830), the Brontë siblings celebrated by representing King Charles in the oak. Emily crawled out of the bedroom window into the branches of a fruit tree, breaking one of its boughs. None of the children would tell their father how the bough came to be broken, but Emily confessed the offence 'on her death bed' (quoted in *LEB*, pp. 59–60).

Broken branches occupied a distinct place in Brontë's imagination. A drawing by her of a pine tree with a split trunk and a broken branch lying behind is reproduced on the cover of the present edition. In no. xvi, the speaker implores Death to 'Strike again, Time's withered branch dividing/ From the fresh root of Eternity!' (ll. 3–4) Lockwood dreams of a fir-tree branch that metamorphoses into a child's bleeding limb (*WH*, 1, 3).

Ratchford connects this poem to other Gondal poems 'of memory and remorse' (H, p. 19); its concentration on suffering and atonement makes a Gondal context plausible, though not requisite.

173. First published in 1910, this poem is in the NYPL and is clearly dated 27 March 1832. The date has been questioned because it is four years earlier than the date of any other surviving poem. 1910 accepts the date of 1832, but Hatfield suggests 1842 in 1923 and 1839 in 1941. The initials A. G. A. appear at the head of the ms.

174. First published in 1910, together with no. 176, as a single poem. The ms. is in the NYPL, and according to Hatfield, it and the ms. on which no. 176 appears, now in the UT, were originally a single leaf (H, p. 65). The poem is undated, and Hatfield does not explain his conjectured date of composition, between February and March 1838. The poem is incomplete, and the questions in line 5 suggest that the poet is uncertain of its direction. Compare the use of a question, together with a turn, in no. 8.

4: the words in brackets are illegible; 'weir and' is a possible alternative reading, as is 'never the'.
5 *Never again*: these two words appear under the illegible words above and may suggest a revised line: 'Through rain and never again the wailing wind'.

175. First published in 1941, although Mansell incorrectly cites 1910; this poem is in the NYPL. It is cancelled in the ms. and undated. Hatfield does not explain his conjectured date of composition, between February and March 1838. The poem is a fragment.

1 *Iernë*: in the ms., the letters 'er' are cancelled and illegible; in l. 6, the name is spelled 'Irenë', but in no. i [153], 'Faith and Despondency', the name appears as 'Iernë', and I have altered its spelling here to accord with the spelling Brontë chose in 1846.
4: this line revises one above, illegible except for its last word, 'stream'.

176. First published in 1910 as a continuation of no. 174 (see note above), this poem is in the UT and is undated. Hatfield does not explain his conjectured date of composition, between February and March 1838. The poem is incomplete. Hatfield prints a last line consisting of a single letter, 'B'; the letter is legible on the ms., but it is surrounded by calligraphic doodles and may figure as a shape rather than as the start of a word.

4 *forsaken*: an absolute construction.

177. First published in 1910 as part of no. 120. Hatfield notes that this poem is in a separate ms. and that there is no apparent connection between it and no. 120. The ms. is in the NYPL, and is undated. Hatfield does not explain his conjectured date of composition, between 27 February and 1 March 1841. The initials M.A.A. appear at the poem's head, identifying a Gondal speaker, but these initials do not appear elsewhere in the poems. The Gondal surname 'Almeda' appears upside down in the margin of the ms. leaf, and the words '2nd October 30th' appear upside down at the bottom.

1 *awhile*: strictly two words, but regularly written as one; *OED* cites Scott, *The Lady of the Lake*, I, 20: 'Awhile she paused, no answer came'.

178. First published in 1910, with the last word omitted, this poem is in the NYPL and is undated. Hatfield does not explain his conjectured date of composition, between 14 and 19 December 1839. The poem is incomplete.

7 *them*: the reference of the pronoun is obscure.

179. First published in 1910, with lines 4 and 8 of each stanza indented and the name 'Harold' substituted for 'Gerald'. In 1923, the poem was titled 'Harold'. The poem is in the NYPL and is undated. Hatfield does not explain his conjectured date of composition, between 23 and 28 November 1839. The poem was originally separated into two parts, lines 1–16 and lines 17–24, which were pasted on separate leaves of an album; the close echo of lines 1–4 in lines 17–24 is unusual for Brontë and may suggest revision rather than conclusion. There are two cancelled lines after line 2 and one cancelled line after line 10. The words in brackets are uncertain.
  Gerald, named in line 17, is one of the rulers of Gondal. He is mentioned in no. 127, where his sister comforts him on the death of their mother, and in no. 42, where his kinsman, Julius Brenzaida, falsely pledges concord or peace. Since Gerald and his people are captive in this poem, its action logically follows Julius's breaking of his pledge.

1 *His*: Gerald's (see l. 17).

180. First published in 1910, this poem is in the NYPL and is undated. Hatfield does not explain his conjectured date, between 18 June and 12 July 1839.

1 *She dried her tears and they did smile*] 'I've dried my tears and then did smile,' cancelled.
3 *How little dreaming*] these words are cancelled in the ms., but the words that have been written above them are illegible; Hatfield reads 'Nor did discern how all the while'; Chitham reads 'A fond delusion all the while' (*BFBP*, p. 35).

181. First published in 1850, this poem is in the Honresfeld ms. and is undated. Hatfield conjectures a date between 29 October and 14 November 1839, probably on the basis of the poem's place between dated poems in the transcript volume. Charlotte Brontë titled the poem 'Love and Friendship' and altered only its punctuation when she printed it in 1850. Hatfield notes that it was incorrectly attributed to her when it was set to music and published by W. Marriott and Sons in 1879 (H, p. 131).

182. See the note to no. xiii above.

Poems of Doubtful Authorship

'Often rebuked, yet always back returning'

First published in 1850, this is the only poem in the 1850 volume for which no manuscript has ever been known and the only one of the seventeen printed there not taken from one of Brontë's two transcript notebooks. Hatfield printed it in an appendix in 1941, believing that it sounded more like Charlotte and seemed to express her feelings about her sister rather than Emily Brontë's own thoughts (H, p. 255). In fact, Charlotte expresses similar feelings in a letter to W.S. Williams, her main correspondent at Smith, Elder, the previous year: 'No matter – whether known or unknown – misjudged or the contrary – I am resolved not to write otherwise. I shall bend as my powers tend' (21 September 1849).

Chitham argues for Emily's authorship on the grounds that the 'general content of the poem is quite characteristic of Emily in certain ways' and that 'some of its language resembles that of other poems written by her' (*BST* 20 [1983]). Neufeldt agrees that the 'language and content are characteristically Emily's, especially the last two stanzas. Undoubtedly Charlotte "edited" the poem, as she did others, in preparation for the 1850 edition . . .' (*PCB*, p. 374). Anne has also been suggested as the poem's author (Flora Katherine Willett, 'Which Brontë Was "Often Rebuked"? A Note Favouring Anne', *BST* 19 [1982]).

The strongest argument in favour of Emily's having written the poem is the obvious one that Charlotte would not have represented her work as her sister's. But this argument is vitiated by her extensive revisions of the other poems in the 1850 volume, and undermined by her deep conviction that it was her duty to act as her sister's 'interpreter' (see her 'Biographical Notice' for the 1850 edition). On balance, the resemblances between this poem and others by Emily Brontë are not striking, and may be the product of Charlotte's not incompetent attempt to write a poem that her sister might have written. Emily Brontë composed only six poems

NOTES TO P. 199

in iambic pentameter, while a significant proportion of Charlotte Brontë's poetic output is in this metre.

'To the Horse Black Eagle which I Rode at the Battle of Zamorna'

This poem appears on an undated, unsigned ms. leaf in the NYPL. First published as Emily's in 1910, it has since been attributed to both Branwell and Charlotte. The main argument for Emily Brontë's authorship is that the poem is in her handwriting (*BFBP*, p. 17). The main argument against her authorship is that Zamorna is an Angrian character, and Emily is not known to have written about Angria. Neufeldt prints the poem along with other 'Items of Disputed Authorship' in *PCB*, but indicates that the 'content and language would seem to be Branwell's rather than Charlotte's' (p. 375). Winnifrith doesn't include the poem in *PPBB*, but cites it in a 'Preliminary List of Other Poems by Branwell Brontë, Not Published in This Edition': 'Published as Charlotte's, though the handwriting is Emily's, and the poem may be by Emily, in *The Complete Poems of Charlotte Brontë* (1923)' (*PPBB*, p. 333).

Index of Titles

Index of First Lines

PENGUIN CLASSICS

JANE EYRE

CHARLOTTE BRONTË

'The more solitary, the more friendless, the more unsustained I am, the more I will respect myself'

Jane Eyre endures loneliness and cruelty in the home of her heartless aunt and the cold charity of Lowood School. This troubled childhood strengthens Jane's natural independence and spirit – which proves necessary when she takes a position as governess at Thornfield Hall. But when she finds love with her sardonic employer, Rochester, the discovery of a shameful secret forces her to make a terrible choice. A novel of intense emotional power, heightened atmosphere and fierce intelligence, *Jane Eyre* (1847) dazzled and shocked readers with its passionate depiction of a woman's search for equality and freedom on her own terms.

'The masterwork of a great genius' William Makepeace Thackeray

Edited with an Introduction by STEVIE DAVIES

PENGUIN CLASSICS

WUTHERING HEIGHTS

EMILY BRONTË

*'May you not rest, as long as I am living. You said I killed you – haunt me,
then'*

Caught in a snowstorm, Lockwood, the new tenant of Thrushcross Grange
on the bleak Yorkshire moors, is forced to seek shelter at Wuthering Heights.
There he discovers the history of the tempestuous events that took place years
before: the intense passion between the foundling Heathcliff and Catherine
Earnshaw, her betrayal of him and the bitter vengeance he now wreaks on
the innocent heirs of the past. Emily Brontë's novel of impossible desires,
violence and transgression is a masterpiece of intense, unsettling power.

Edited with an Introduction a by PAULINE NESTOR

Preface by LUCASTA MILLER

PENGUIN CLASSICS

THE PROFESSOR

CHARLOTTE BRONTË

'She was not handsome, she was not rich, she was not even accomplished, yet she was my life's treasure; I must then be a man of peculiar discernment'

Working as a professor in M. Pelet's establishment in Brussels, William Crimsworth meets the fascinating Directrice of the neighbouring school, Mlle Zoraïde Reuter, and, recognizing her as an intellectual equal, becomes powerfully attracted to her. Despite her betrothal to M. Pelet, Mlle Reuter will not release her hold over William, and she tries to stand in the way of his finding love elsewhere. But new possibilities open up to him and he is not to be so easily deterred. Published two years after the author's death, *The Professor* draws on Charlotte Brontë's own professional and personal experiences as a teacher in Brussels. Like *Jane Eyre* and *Villette*, this is an intimate first-person account of a life that brings extremes of despair and joy.

Edited with an Introduction by HEATHER GLEN

PENGUIN CLASSICS

SHIRLEY

CHARLOTTE BRONTË

'Half a century of existence may lie before me. How am I to occupy it?'

Struggling manufacturer Robert Moore has introduced labour saving machinery to his Yorkshire mill, arousing a ferment of unemployment and discontent among his workers. Robert considers marriage to the wealthy and independent Shirley Keeldar to solve his financial woes, yet his heart lies with his cousin Caroline, who, bored and desperate, lives as a dependent in her uncle's home with no prospect of a career. Shirley, meanwhile, is in love with Robert's brother, an impoverished tutor – a match opposed by her family. As industrial unrest builds to a potentially fatal pitch, can the four be reconciled? Set during the Napoleonic wars at a time of national economic struggles, *Shirley* (1849) is an unsentimental yet passionate depiction of conflict between classes, sexes and generations.

Edited by JESSICA COX

With an Introduction by LUCASTA MILLER